I0154081

God's Heart As It Relates To Sovereignty – Free Will

Written by Bob Warren

Much thanks to the following saints who devoted countless hours to the production of this work:

Trey Alley
Brent Armstrong
Dan Carter
Myra Cleaver
Jhonda Johnston
Rick Underhill

www.lifeonthehill.org

ISBN: 978-1-62727-030-4

All Scripture, unless otherwise noted, is from the New American Standard Bible.

Table of Contents

Chapter Seven (Cont.)

The Hill

CHAPTER ONE

INTRODUCTION

I AM NOT ARMINIAN. Nor am I a follower of Calvinism (or Reformed Theology), as I have previously demonstrated in *God's Heart as it Relates to Foreknowledge/Predestination*. Having reviewed a variety of resources generated by both systems of thought, I conclude that each is severely flawed. As I lay out my findings, realize that I harbor no intentions of being vindictive or malicious. In fact, I apologize should my passion outweigh my sensitivity.

Today's general teaching regarding the sovereignty of God and the free will of man greatly concerns me. How can we possibly know what is true when such a variety of conclusions are drawn from the same subject matter? Our only answer is to take everything we hear, regardless of who says or writes it, through every word, of every phrase, of every verse, of every chapter, of every book in God's inerrant Word. I encourage you to take my findings through the same scrutiny.

A debate that has raged for centuries lingers today. Must God cause all things to retain His position as the sole Ruler of the universe? Or, within the realm of His sovereignty, does He grant man the right of choice, even the freedom to choose to repent and believe while depraved? We must comprehend the disparity that exists over this issue. Thus, I will cite quotes from Arminians and Calvinists. I will also submit what I deem to be the "full counsel," Scriptural view. More quotes are listed from Calvinists than from Arminians because of Calvinism's extreme view of God's sovereignty. Keep in mind that many Calvinists refer to themselves as Reformed theologians—a subject covered more thoroughly later (Diagram 11 in the Reference Section might be a profitable resource to consult at this time).

Our goal is to view sovereignty and free will from God's frame of reference.

Our goal is to view sovereignty and free will from God's frame of reference. Allowing the Scriptures to speak for themselves will be an enlightening journey.

Arminians Jerry L. Walls and Joseph R. Dongell, in their book, *Why I am not a Calvinist*, page 47, write:

> Calvinists believe that Arminians can cling to their theology only by diminishing or denying the sovereignty of God in order to accommodate certain understandings of human freedom. Such distortion at the very foundation of Christian theology, Calvinists warn, must not only twist every other Christian doctrine but also threaten to strip the very "godness" from God, since a god who is not sovereign *of all* fails to be god *at all*. (Dongell, 2004)[1]

Note other quotes from the same work:

> Calvinists commonly charge that the sweeping transformation of American Protestant Christianity from being mostly Calvinist during the founding stages of our nation's history to being mostly Arminian during the present era has been caused by a turning away from the hard, clear teaching of Scripture toward the smooth and easy heresy of humanism....
>
> According to the Calvinist analysis, Arminianized Christianity has pushed God to the edge of the stage and has shoved the human being to the center. In this revolution, human beings have now assumed the role of judging truth by their own reason, conscience or personal taste. Humans have assumed the power of determining their own destinies by making autonomous choices, and they have thereby assumed the right of overriding God's will by rejecting God's salvation plan. The marginalized God can now only hope for the best resolution to the drama of redemption; he occasionally negotiates or intervenes in the play but is unable to overcome the foundational principle of all reality—human autonomy. (p.44)[2]
> This Calvinist understanding of divine sovereignty necessarily generates a set of doctrinal conclusions denying human free will (in the sense of the power of contrary choice), asserting God's grace as perfectly triumphant and restricting God's saving intentions to a subset of humanity. We believe these conclusions create such turbulence in reading the Bible that one should be driven to reexamine the Calvinist understanding of divine sovereignty. (p.50)[3]

In contrast, RC Sproul, a Reformed theologian (Reformed Theology is extreme and hyper-Calvinism—see Diagrams 10 and 11 in the Reference Section), in his book, *Chosen by God*, pages 23-24 records:

> ...we must ...observe the crucial importance of the sovereignty of God. Though God is not a creature, he is personal, with supreme dignity and supreme freedom. We are aware of the ticklish problems surrounding the relationship between God's sovereignty and human freedom. We must also be aware of the close relationship between God's sovereignty and God's freedom. The freedom of a sovereign is always greater than the freedom of his subjects.[4]

On page 27 of that same work, Sproul writes:

> ...Without sovereignty God cannot be God. If we reject divine sovereignty then we must embrace atheism....[5]

Regarding God's sovereignty, John MacArthur, a Reformed theologian, remarks:

> Reformed theology has historically been the branch of evangelicalism most strongly committed to the sovereignty of God.... (*The Love of God* p.17)[6]

James White, also a Reformed theologian, comments:

> I am Reformed because of one thing: Consistently, honestly, and thoroughly read, God's Word, the Bible, teaches that God is sovereign over all things, that man is a fallen creature, and that God saves perfectly in Jesus Christ.... (*Debating Calvinism,* p.14).[7]

God's sovereignty, not His love, is at the forefront of the Reformed position (made up of extreme and hyper-Calvinists, for lack of better terms—consult Diagrams 10 and 11.) One of the major differences between extreme and hyper-Calvinism (in their minds at least) is that the hyper-Calvinist views God as having predestined both the elect and the non-elect—the elect to salvation and the non-elect to damnation. The extreme Calvinist, on the other hand, views God as having predestined the elect to salvation while having left the non-elect to the consequence of their sin. We will soon discover that, bottom line, no difference exists between these two systems of thought.

White (a Reformed theologian) writes:

> ...God is the Creator, and therefore He is King over all that He has made. The King rules over His creation. This is the divine truth of God's sovereignty: His right to rule over what He has made. Those who love their king and are subject to Him find His sovereignty a great comfort and delight. Those who are in rebellion against Him fight and chafe against this divine truth. Much can be determined concerning our true subjection to God by asking if, in fact, we love God as He has revealed Himself to be, the divine ruler over all things, or whether we seek to "edit" Him down to a more "manageable" and "manlike" deity. (*Debating Calvinism*, p.36)[8]

White's assessment of God's sovereignty leaves no room for the free will of man. From his frame of reference, God would be edited "down to a more 'manageable' and 'manlike deity'" should man possess the freedom of choice (especially should man be allowed to determine where he will spend eternity). Consequently, White writes in *The Potter's Freedom*, page 45, that God decrees everything that comes to pass. In fact, he states emphatically that the Bible is clear on this matter. Is it? Later, we will confirm that the Bible teaches just the opposite.

Again, I am not a Calvinist, nor am I Arminian. I do believe, however, in the free will of man and, therefore, that the depraved can exercise personal repentance and faith—as do the Arminians. Even some Calvinists (moderate Calvinists) perceive man as capable of choosing Christ while depraved—a topic addressed in depth later in this study. Neither extreme nor hyper-Calvinists (Reformed theologians) could tolerate accepting this view of depravity, yet they disagree on other foundational issues. (Consult Diagrams 10 and 11 in the Reference Section for additional input.)

God, Jehovah God, the God of the universe, is unmatched in power and might. Because His strength is without equal, nothing can thwart His authority or frustrate His supremacy. Paul, in 1Timothy 6:15-16, verifies this truth (be mindful that words and phrases are underlined in passages for emphasis):

> *He who is the blessed and only Sovereign, the King of kings and Lord of lords; who alone possesses immortality and dwells in unapproachable light; whom no man has seen or can see. To Him be honor and eternal dominion! Amen.* (1Timothy 6:15-16)

The New King James renders this verse:

> *He who is the blessed and only Potentate, the King of kings and Lord of lords, who alone has immortality, dwelling in unapproachable light, whom no man has seen or can see, to whom be honor and everlasting power. Amen.* (1Timothy 6:15-16)

"Sovereign," or *"Potentate,"* is from the Greek *dunastes* (doo-nas'-tace), meaning "a ruler or officer, one of great authority, mighty." Merriam Webster's *Dictionary* defines "sovereign" as: "One that exercises supreme authority within a limited sphere; an autonomous state." Of course, believers understand that God's sovereign rule is exercised over more than "a limited sphere," as confirmed by Psalm 103:19—making Him autonomous in every way.

> *The LORD has established His throne in the heavens; And His sovereignty rules over all.* (Psalm 103:19)

Merriam Webster defines "sovereignty" as: "Supreme power, especially over a body public; freedom from external control." None of creation tells God what to do. God can choose as He pleases. However, He (as the Source of truth) will never defy His character by violating His truth. This fact makes His letter to man the most intriguing document imaginable—that is, when interpreted in context and according to all the verses rather than a select few.

The Calvinists view their interpretation of the Scriptures as superior, often mentioning the term "sola scriptura," which is defined below:

> ***Sola scriptura*** (Latin ablative, "by scripture alone") is the doctrine that the Bible is the only infallible or inerrant authority for Christian faith, and that it contains all knowledge necessary for salvation and holiness. Consequently, *Sola Scriptura* demands that no doctrine is to be admitted or confessed that is not found directly or logically within Scripture. However, Sola Scriptura is not a denial of other authorities governing Christian life and devotion. Rather, it simply demands that all other authorities are subordinate to, and are to be corrected by, the written word of God. *Sola scriptura* was a foundational doctrinal principle of the Protestant Reformation held by the Reformers and is a formal principle of Protestantism today. (*Wikipedia*)[9]

Edwin Palmer (a Calvinist), in the forward of his book, *The Five Points of Calvinism*, alludes to *Sola Scriptura*:

> ...John Calvin's goal in his preaching, teaching, and writing was to expound all the Word of God—and the Word of God alone. *Scriptura tota*: *Scriptura sola.* Calvinism is an attempt to express all the Bible and only the Bible....[10]

We will hold the Calvinists accountable to their perception of *sola scriptura* by taking their theology through the full counsel of God's Word. After all, Paul stated:

> *For I have not shunned to declare unto you all the counsel of God.* (Acts 20:27 KJV)

Paul's theology was based on the full counsel of God's Word—not on a few verses (taken out of context) combined with the logic of man. Can the same be said of Calvinism's ideology? We will allow Scripture alone to provide the answer.

James White, a Reformed theologian, comments below regarding his view of the Scriptures. Note: Words are inserted in brackets [ ] for clarification, as is the case throughout this study.

> ...To truly practice *sola scriptura* we must test our traditions by the ultimate authority of God's Word, even if they are beliefs we have held for many years and have had pounded into our heads in sermon after sermon....
>
> ...I do not believe the doctrines of grace [Calvinism, or Reformed theology] because of Augustine or Calvin or Jonathan Edwards or Charles Spurgeon or Benjamin Warfield or RC Sproul. I rejoice in their company and am thankful for the testimony of men of God down through history. But first and foremost, I believe in the doctrines of grace because of the exegesis [interpretation] of the text of the God-breathed Scriptures, the Holy Bible. This is the firm foundation of Reformed theology, and it is what must be dealt with by anyone who would seek to truthfully convince men that the doctrines of grace are not divine truth.
>
> ...I have chosen to present the positive case for the doctrines of grace based upon the test of Scripture. The reader is encouraged to hold both sides to the same standards [the other side being those who hold to the non-Reformed view]. Who presents consistent arguments? Who presents a biblically

> based position that provides a consistent and *sound* exegetical basis for the assertions made? Does one side simply state basic assumptions over and over again, while refusing to respond to a critique of those presuppositions? *(Debating Calvinism*, pp.14-15*)*[11]

White contradicts himself in other writings, as will be verified later in this study.

RC Sproul, also a Reformed theologian, has the following to say concerning his view of the Scriptures:

> ...the term *antinomy* is "against law." What law do you suppose is in view here? The law of contradiction. The original meaning of the term was "that which violates the law of contradiction." Hence, originally and in normal philosophical discussion, the word *antinomy* is an exact equivalent of the word *contradiction*.
>
> ...if we are to avoid confusion we must have a clear idea in our minds of the crucial difference between a real contradiction and a seeming contradiction. It is the difference between rationality and irrationality, between truth and absurdity.
>
> ...If the Bible contained antinomies in the sense of real contradictions, that would be the end to inerrancy.
>
> ...if God's truth is contradictory truth it is no truth at all. Indeed the very word *truth* would be emptied of meaning. If contradictions can be true we would have no possible way of discerning the difference between truth and a lie.... (*Chosen by God*, pp.45-46)[12]

In his book, *Almighty over All* (page 132), R. C. Sproul Jr., also a Reformed theologian, states:

> ...If he [God] were not bound by the law of noncontradiction or by the necessity of telling the truth, we could not believe anything he [God] says. Without the law of noncontradiction, whenever the Bible affirms, "Believe on the Lord Jesus Christ, and you will be saved..." (Acts 16:31), it could at the same time be affirming, "Believe on the Lord Jesus Christ and you will be damned...."[13]

I agree. God's Word has no antinomies (contradictions). I also believe that the conclusions drawn from the Scriptures, if they are to be void of contradiction, must be based on the context of all the verses recorded in God's letter to man. Thus, as we proceed, we will allow the full counsel of God's Word to be the final say rather than any man-made traditions. It should be much fun, so enjoy the journey as we allow the Scriptures to reveal what we are to believe regarding God's heart. Many verses will be addressed, examined, and dissected; so have your Bible open and ready for use.

"God is love" (1John 4:8, 16). In other words, when all of His attributes are combined, one term best describes His essence: *"love,"* unconditional *agape* love. God demonstrated His love as well as His sovereignty on the cross. His love was revealed by His dying—a sinless God-man for sinful, undeserving mankind. The timing of Jesus' crucifixion, exactly when the Old Testament prophets predicted, demonstrated God's sovereignty. However, ask a thousand people what first comes to mind when they think of the cross—God's love or His sovereignty—and the majority will probably say, "God's love." As we read the Scriptures, we must never allow His sovereignty to take precedence over His love (1John 4:8, 16). *"God is love"* (1John 4:8, 16), meaning that He loves even when His love is not reciprocated.

When all of God's attributes are combined, one term best describes His essence: "love."

We must make certain that our conclusions regarding God's sovereignty in no way undermine His love. God is love, no matter where we start or finish. In fact, the whole of what is written (and known) about Him rests upon this truth. As He rules and reigns, He is love—which causes everything else relating to His flawless character to function, not only void of contradiction, but in perfect, uninterrupted accord. Yes, His sovereignty is breathtaking, awesome, spectacular, magnificent, amazing, wonderful, and so much more. His love, however, is never at the mercy of His sovereignty. In fact, without His love His brand of sovereignty could not exist. Therefore, in environments void of unconditional, agape love, leadership is totally misguided:

> *Man in his pomp, yet without understanding, is like the beasts that perish.* (Psalm 49:20)

Power in the hands of an unloving ruler results in abuse and ultimate ruin. Only the God of love possesses the stability and wisdom to rule as the righteous, just, and upright Sovereign of the universe. We must remain mindful of this fact as we examine His heart through the pages of His flawless letter. Nothing takes precedence over His love. Hence, man walks in error when one of His other attributes is allowed to displace or lessen love's significance. God's love serves as the greatest motivator in one's pilgrimage of faith—not His sovereignty:

For in Christ Jesus neither circumcision nor uncircumcision means anything, but faith working through love. (Galatians 5:6)

For the love of Christ controls us.... (2Corinthians 5:14-15)

Much debate exists as to the degree of freedom granted to man by this supreme Ruler. Is man free to choose as he pleases, or has God ordained man's every action by means of eternal decrees? Your reply is dependent on how you answer this next question. Because God knows all past, present, and future events, must He cause all things to know all things? Some people would say that His sovereignty is compromised if He does not ordain and, thus, cause all things. These individuals conclude that if man could make choices outside of God's will, man would rule rather than God, dethroning Him in the process. Other people would say that man is free to make choices without reducing His sovereignty in the least. Are solutions available that reconcile this dilemma? With all of my heart, I believe they are.

"Omniscience," in theological terms, points to God's ability to know all. He, being God, not only knows what has transpired in the past, but understands well what will occur in the future. But, if God's knowledge of all events, including the events which are yet to come, is contingent upon His causing them, His omniscience is compromised. For instance, which would be the greater God?: (1) The God who is required to cause all things to know all things, thus eliminating man's free will in the process (2) The God Who knows all things simply because He sees all things (all past, present, and future events) at once (constantly), having ordained that man possess the freedom of choice. Would He not be more sovereign by knowing the future without causing it?

What if, within the realm of His sovereignty, and without anyone holding Him at gunpoint, God chose to grant mankind a free will—not just in some areas, but in every area of life? This gift of free will would in no way diminish His right to rule sovereignly, for operating totally within the realm of His authority (and autonomy) He would create man a free moral agent. Hence, should He force a being to love Him whom He had granted the freedom of choice would prove Him unworthy to reign.

God did not diminish His sovereignty by granting man a free will.

Scripture validates that God has set limits upon Himself in other areas; so why not in the area of free will? For example, He promised to never again flood the earth with water (Genesis 9:15). Does this mean that He lacks the power to do so? Or, does it mean that He has set limits on what He will do? Obviously, He has set limits upon Himself without a loss of power (and sovereignty), for these limits were self-generated. Should man's decision prevent God from again flooding the earth, then man would be sovereign with God his servant.

God limited Himself by granting man a free will, but that decision in no way diminished His sovereignty. His ultimate plan for man will be fulfilled even with man possessing the freedom of choice—making Him a much greater God in the process. What He cannot do, however, is force a free moral agent to act against his (the free moral agent's) will—even believe. Our prisons are filled with individuals who have violated the free will of man. These violations are classified by our judicial system as crimes, crimes against not only innocent people, but against the laws which govern our land. Consequently, should God violate man's free will, having granted him the right of choice, He would violate Himself and, thus, commit sin. God acting in this manner would be totally unjust, unrighteous, and unloving. Forced love is rape and carries with it a penalty equal to the crime. God forbid that He respond as such to beings created to love Him should they choose.

We will continue to expose the error in Reformed Theology's view of sovereignty by discussing the subject of "man's strongest inclination." Quotes from leading Reformed theologians will be followed by a Scriptural rebuttal.

The Hill

CHAPTER TWO

REFORMED THEOLOGY'S VIEW OF "MAN'S STRONGEST INCLINATION"

R.C. SPROUL JR., A REFORMED THEOLOGIAN (review Diagrams 10 and 11 in the Reference Section for more input regarding Reformed Theology), addresses God's sovereignty in *Almighty over All.* Beginning with page 52, he discusses the fall of Adam and Eve:

> ...He is God; he can do whatever he wishes. There is no power greater than him which could somewhat stop him from changing Eve's inclination. We know also that it not only is possible for God to change a person's inclination, we know that in fact it is his habit to do so. He does it all the time....[14]

Sproul's perception of the phrase, "a person's inclination," is based on erroneous logic rather than Biblical truth. In fact, his view of this phrase was molded by the mistaken logic of Jonathan Edwards. Follow what Sproul writes regarding Edwards:

> ...Did Eve have it in her power to create sin? To answer that question we need to learn a lesson from the greatest analytical mind ever to grace the American scene–Jonathan Edwards.... Supreme Court jurist Oliver Wendell Holmes, not one to carry a brief for orthodox Christianity, said of Edwards that his was the greatest mind of the last two hundred years. *(Almighty over All,* p.46*)*[15]

Sproul's goal is to elevate God's sovereignty above His other glorious attributes (including His love) by attempting to prove that God created sin. Sproul realizes that should Eve have partaken of the forbidden fruit without God's assistance, Reformed Theology's perception of God's sovereignty would be shattered and their movement destroyed. This problem is why sovereignty is emphasized so heavily among Reformed theologians (as demonstrated by John MacArthur's earlier quote). Sproul continues:

> ...Edwards wrote that all men everywhere always act according to their strongest inclination at a given time.
> Stop to consider whether there was ever a time when you acted against your strongest inclination....
> ...Edwards was right; we always choose according to our strongest inclination given our choices. *(Almighty over All*, pp. 46-47*)*[16]

Are these assumptions Biblical? We will find out shortly, but let's follow Sproul's line of thinking a while longer. After a very long, "logical," but in essence illogical explanation, Sproul concludes that neither Eve nor Satan changed her good inclination to evil. According to Sproul, God caused Eve to sin by changing her inclination Himself. The following quote illustrates that Sproul's ultimate goal is to elevate God's sovereignty by making Him the reason for Eve's sin. After all, should Eve be responsible for her own disobedience, Sproul's "logical" (yet illogical) conclusion is that God would be dethroned due to His compromised sovereignty. Consider Sproul's words:

> ...God would have a motive for Eve's fall into sin. We know that, because it came to pass. Every Bible-believing Christian must conclude at least that God in some sense desired that man would fall into sin. The only other option is to say that this event became reality against God's wishes, that God sat upon his throne wringing his hands in frustration as Eve took a bite. Such a notion is repugnant, for it means that someone or something is more powerful than God himself.
> God wills all things which come to pass....
> ...I am suggesting that he created sin. *(Almighty over All,* pp.53-54*)*[17]

Sproul adopted Jonathan Edwards' faulty logic, believing that man <u>always</u> responds according to his strongest inclination. This view finds its origin in a distorted perception of God's sovereignty, one which makes Him the cause of all things. According to Sproul, should Eve have chosen (by herself) to eat of the forbidden fruit, a decision would have been made independent of God's sovereignty—thus dethroning Him in the process. This scenario is inconsistent with God's character, yet Sproul attempts to defend his beliefs:

> Somehow, though, it just doesn't seem fair of God to bring evil into the world and then turn around and express his wrath against it. One could just hear this complaint from people who want to defend God against the charge that he created evil.... And the underlying assumption would be that fairness and justice would keep God from changing Eve's inclination and then turning around and punishing her for acting on that inclination. Such an action would be an evil action by God, and therefore could not have happened. Treating Eve this way would be inconsistent with his character. (*Almighty over All*, pp.54-55)[18]

After presenting this argument against what he believes, Sproul then offers a lengthy explanation as to how God's hardening of Pharaoh's heart (according to the Reformed definition of "hardening"—giving Pharaoh no opportunity to believe) confirms that He can respond according to the Reformed mindset yet remain both sovereign and just (as well as a God of truth). (We will take a long look at the hardening of Pharaoh's heart later in this series and draw different conclusions.) Sproul then writes a troubling statement regarding the fall of Adam and Eve:

> It was his desire to make his wrath known. He needed, then, something on which to be wrathful. He needed to have sinful creatures. He wanted to make his mercy known. He needed, then, something that deserved wrath on which he could show mercy instead. All of this serves his eternal and ultimate desire, to glorify himself. (*Almighty over All*, p.57)[19]

Sproul's view depicts God as having caused Eve to sin: (1) So He might have "something on which to be wrathful"—the non-elect (2) So He could have something which deserved His wrath but received His mercy—the elect.

Does this thinking line up with the full counsel of God's Word? If God should be the cause of all things (as Sproul advocates), and yet desires that none perish (1Timothy 2:4; 2Peter 3:9), why did He not display His mercy on all mankind (Adam and Eve included) by eliminating sin and suffering in the first place? R.C. Sproul, in his book, *Chosen by God*, page 37, attempts to answer this question:

> The only answer I can give to this question is that I don't know. I have no idea why God saves some but not all. I don't

> doubt for a moment that God has the power to save all, but I know that he does not choose to save all. I don't know why.[20]

And why is a straightforward answer unavailable to Sproul? Reformed Theology (extreme and hyper-Calvinism) is built on a foundation that prevents a reply. Consider the following from R.C. Sproul Jr.'s *Almighty over All,* page 52:

> ...After the fall, the Bible teaches, our strongest inclination at any given moment is always to sin. The only way this process can be arrested, such that anyone could come to faith, is if God sovereignly changes our inclination first....[21]

In other words, Sproul and his fellow Reformed theologians view man (in his depraved state) as incapable of making a choice to repent and accept Christ. This mindset forces Reformed Theology to view God as follows:

1. God must first spiritually regenerate man for the purpose of changing man's inclination (a topic discussed in much depth later in the study).
2. After changing man's inclination, God must give man repentance and the faith to believe (another topic addressed in more depth later).
3. After God spiritually regenerates man and gives him repentance and the faith to believe, man then repents, believes, and is saved.

This thinking finds its origin in an improper view of God's sovereignty: (1) If God must cause all things to remain sovereign, He must have caused Adam and Eve to sin (2) If He caused Adam and Eve to sin, He must cause all of the elect to repent and believe.

The problem with these faulty assumptions is that the Scriptures communicate just the opposite—that repentance and faith precede spiritual regeneration (read Acts 16:31, Romans 10:9-10, and 2Corinthians 3:16 for starters). God's Word never suggests that spiritual regeneration precedes repentance and faith.

However, RC Sproul, in *Chosen by God* (pages 72-73), writes:

> A cardinal point of Reformed theology is the maxim: "Regeneration precedes faith." Our nature is so corrupt, the power of sin is so great, that unless God does a supernatural work in our souls we will never choose Christ. We do not believe in order to be born again; we are born again in order that we may believe.[22]

Dave Hunt writes of this weakness within the Reformed view:

> ...If the problem of sin is all God's doing, then He could undo it as well—but not if He has foreordained it! (*What Love is This?*, p.188)[23]

Considering all of the preceding arguments, we must ask ourselves a pertinent question. Can a proper answer exist as to why God only saves some while desiring to save all? We will pursue this answer, not through the use of logic or tradition, but through the Scriptures alone—protecting God's name and reputation in the process. My hope is that the answer might encourage every man, woman, and child to view Him appropriately—according to the full counsel of His Word. Are you ready? One of the greatest truths I have been privileged to glean from the Scriptures is recorded next—a truth relating to the subject of "man's strongest inclination." My prayer is that it will be meaningful to you as well.

The Hill

CHAPTER THREE

THE SCRIPTURAL VIEW OF "MAN'S STRONGEST INCLINATION"

THE GENES OF ALL MANKIND WERE IN ADAM when he sinned (Romans 5:17-18). As a result, man is born with a sinful nature, the same nature that Adam possessed after he sinned—a nature that is dead to (separated from) God (Ephesians 2:3, 5). (Scripture refers to this nature in different ways—Adamic nature, sinful nature, old self, old man, or dead spirit—all being synonymous.) In fact, to have introduced me properly during the twenty-seven-year span that I was without Christ, you would have needed to say, "This is Bob Warren, the sinful nature," or "This is Bob Warren, the Adamic nature," etc. Before I became a believer, in fact, I woke up enjoying sin and went to bed enjoying sin. I was on the throne of my life like you were on the throne of yours when you were without Christ. We were good sinners weren't we? Consequently, our absolute "strongest inclination" was to wallow in sin.

When a person makes a choice to receive Christ (John 1:12; Acts 16:31; Acts 26:18; Romans 10:9-10; etc.), God kills (eradicates) that person (Romans 6:6; 7:4; Galatians 2:20; etc.):

> *knowing this, that our old self was crucified with Him, that our body of sin might be done away with, that we should no longer be slaves to sin;* (Romans 6:6)
>
> *Therefore, my brethren, you also were made to die to the Law through the body of Christ, that you might be joined to another, to Him who was raised from the dead, that we might bear fruit for God.* (Romans 7:4)
>
> *"I have been crucified with Christ; and it is no longer I who live, but Christ lives in me; and the life which I now live in the flesh I*

> *live by faith in the Son of God, who loved me, and delivered Himself up for me.* (Galatians 2:20)

As a result of the eradication (crucifixion) of the sinful nature, the individual who loved sin no longer exists (2Corinthians 5:17):

> *Therefore if any man is in Christ, he is a new creature; the old things passed away; behold, new things have come.* (2Corinthians 5:17)

This transformation means that God, after killing (eradicating) the person who originally lived in my body (the sinful nature, or old self, etc.), created a totally new person to live inside my same body (2Corinthians 5:17). The person who inhabited it originally was Bob Warren, the sinful nature. The person who inhabits it now is Bob Warren, the new man.

Do you see what the Scriptures are communicating? If you are a believer, the person you used to be is gone, never to be dealt with again. That person was crucified with Christ on His cross in 30 AD (Romans 6:6; 7:4; Galatians 2:20). How could this change occur? Once you repented and believed (while depraved), God took who you were (the sinful nature), placed that nature into Christ through the avenue of the Holy Spirit (1Corinthians 12:13), *"crucified"* that nature (Romans 6:6; 7:4; Galatians 2:20), *"buried"* that nature (Romans 6:4; Colossians 2:12), and made you into a *"new"* creation (2Corinthians 5:17). You were then the new man, or the new self—both synonymous.

If you are a believer, the person you used to be is gone...having been crucified with Christ on His cross.

Having received Christ's kind of life (Colossians 3:4), this new man (new creation) is an eternal being—with no beginning and no end. If the new creation (the New Testament believer) has no beginning and no end, he was in Christ when Christ was crucified, buried, and raised. For this reason Paul could say, *"I have been crucified with Christ"* (Galatians 2:20)—because the old man (old self, sinful nature) was placed in Christ and eradicated. Paul could also teach that the New Testament believer has been *"buried"* (Romans 6:4; Colossians 2:12) and *"raised"* with Christ (Ephesians 2:6; Colossians 2:12).

With the above input in mind, we can conclude that in your unredeemed state, you were (fill in your name), _______ the sinful nature (which is sometimes called the old man, old self, Adamic nature, or dead spirit—all synonymous). Today you are (fill in your name) ________, the new man (which is sometimes called the new self or new creation—all synonymous). God did more than just wound who you were. He eradicated who you were as an unbeliever. How could He possibly allow the old man (sinful nature) to live inside your body alongside the new man? Should the old man and new man cohabit your body, you would be part evil and part good, making you nothing more than a lowly sinner saved by grace.

The Scriptures teach that you became anything but a saved, lowly sinner when you accepted Christ. In fact, you were made into a righteous (2Corinthians 5:21), *"holy"* (Ephesians 1:4), *"perfect"* (Hebrews 10:14), *"complete"* (Colossians 2:10), *"forgiven"* (Ephesians 4:32; Colossians 2:13; 1John 2:12), *"glorified"* (Romans 8:30), *"justified"* (Romans 5:1), never to be condemned (Romans 8:1), *"saint"* (1Corinthians 1:2), who sometimes sins. The most natural thing you do, therefore, is walk in righteousness—proving that the most unnatural thing you do is walk in sin. Yes, you disobey at times; but disobedience is unnatural, and very troubling to your soul.

Should the old man (sinful nature) be alive in you, though wounded, living alongside the holy, blameless, and glorified new man (as some have taught and continue to teach), to desire to sin would remain somewhat natural. However, with the old man eradicated, your "strongest inclination" is to walk as righteously as possible. Stated differently, your "strongest inclination," the moment you accepted Christ, was (and continues to be) to abandon sin. The following explains why.

All New Testament believers are ushered into the presence of God the moment their earthly bodies cease operating (2Corinthians 5:8). Consequently, when my body dies, I (my soul and spirit) will eject out of the body and enter heaven. The same truth applies to you if you are a believer. Once in heaven, we will walk in sinless perfection for the first time in our existence (1John 3:2), never once disobeying the Master. Why? We will no longer dwell in an unredeemed body (1Corinthians 15:50-55), a body which houses Satan's agent, the power of sin (Romans 7:23)—the means through which Satan tempts the New Testament believer during his stay on earth:

> *but I see a different law in the members of my body, waging war against the law of my mind, and making me a prisoner of the law of sin which is in my members.* (Romans 7:23)

We can conclude, therefore, that the only reason we sin is due to the power of sin's presence in our unredeemed bodies (Romans 7:23), a power which regularly tempts us to sin. When we sin, we hate our sin, because our strongest inclination is to avoid sin.

> *Believer, your strongest inclination is to abandon sin.*

Because our souls and spirits were perfected (made holy, righteous, and complete) the moment we accepted Christ, the holiness, righteousness, and completeness of our souls and spirits will not be enhanced when we are taken to heaven. No doubt, our behavior becomes increasingly holy as we mature in the faith while on earth (and will be made completely holy once we are in heaven), but our souls and spirits (who we really are) will never be more holy and blameless than at the point of the new birth. (This truth is addressed in much greater detail in the *Romans 1-8* course distributed by this ministry.)

Conclusion: The moment I accepted Christ and was made new, my "strongest inclination" was to walk in holiness. In fact, my "strongest inclination" remains the same today. I never want to sin again, but at times I find myself sinning due to believing the enemy's lie. However, when I sin, I hate my sin because my "strongest inclination" is to not sin. How do I know that this is my "strongest inclination?" Let my heart stop beating and I will never sin again. In heaven, the new man (Bob Warren) will cease being tempted and will respond according to his "strongest inclination" one hundred percent of the time. Consequently, my "strongest inclination" from the moment I became a child of God has been to avoid sin. Not sinning was Paul's desire as well after becoming a believer, but the Scriptures confirm that he, the great apostle, disobeyed at times:

> *For that which I am doing, I do not understand; for I am not practicing what I would like to do, but I am doing the very thing I hate.* (Romans 7:15)

Paul also wrote:

> *...for the wishing is present in me, but the doing of the good is not.* (Romans 7:18)

He followed by writing:

> *For the good that I wish, I do not do; but I practice the very evil that I do not wish.* (Romans 7:19)

As a believer, Paul's "strongest inclination" was to walk in unwavering obedience. These verses verify, however, that in certain situations he made choices against (or contrary to) his "strongest inclination." Consequently, Jonathan Edwards' logic is in error, along with R.C. Sproul's. Note how Sproul's words contradict the truth of Paul's message:

> ...The hard truth is that at the moment of our sin we desire the sin more strongly than we desire to obey Christ. If we

> always desired to obey Christ more than we desired to sin, we would never sin. (*Chosen by God*, p.58)[24]

Sproul is incorrect in his assumptions. Paul's bottom line in Romans 7 is this: Even when he sinned as a believer, he was not doing what he (the new man) truly desired. So how does Sproul respond to Paul's words of Romans 7:19? I will repeat Sproul's previous quote along with his subsequent thoughts:

> ...The hard truth is that at the moment of our sin we desire the sin more strongly than we desire to obey Christ. If we always desired to obey Christ more than we desired to sin, we would never sin.[25]
>
> Does not the Apostle Paul teach otherwise? Does he not recount for us a situation in which he acts against his desires? He says in Romans, "The good that I would, I do not, and that which I would not, that I do" (Rom. 7:19, KJV). Here it sounds as if, under the inspiration of God the Holy Spirit, Paul is teaching clearly that there are times in which he acts against his strongest inclination. (Sproul, *Chosen by God*, p.58)[26]

Based on Sproul's use of "as if," he is insinuating that Paul is not teaching that the believer can act against (contrary to) his "strongest inclination." Yet, Paul is communicating precisely that the believer can act against (contrary to) his "strongest inclination." Sproul's problem is that Paul has proven Jonathan Edwards' "logic" illogical, refuting his (Sproul's) logic in the process. Consider Sproul's response:

> It is extremely unlikely that the apostle is here giving us a revelation about the technical operation of the will. Rather, he is stating plainly what every one of us has experienced. We all have a desire to flee from sin. The "all things being equal" syndrome is in view here. All things being equal, I would like to be perfect. I would like to be rid of sin, just as I would like to be rid of my excess weight. But my desires do not remain constant. They fluctuate.[27]

Sproul contradicts Paul's words of Romans 7:19, proving his (Sproul's) logic to be in error. Paul stated empathically in Romans 7:19 that his desires never fluctuated. In his heart, he always wanted to do *"good."* In committing sin, however, he found himself practicing what he did not wish. Paul confirms the same truth in Romans 7:15 and Romans 7:18:

> *For that which I am doing, I do not understand; for I am not practicing what I would like to do, but I am doing the very thing I hate.* (Romans 7:15)

> *For I know that nothing good dwells in me, that is, in my flesh; for the wishing is present in me, but the doing of the good is not.* (Romans 7:18)

Should Sproul and Jonathan Edwards' reasoning be correct, they, along with all who follow their teaching, can view the depraved as incapable of choosing to repent and believe. After all, if man always responds according to his "strongest inclination" (the Reformed view), it would naturally follow that the depraved (spiritually unregenerated) could never choose Christ. In Romans 7:15 and Romans 7:18-19, Paul refutes this argument by stating that as a believer he made choices against his strongest inclination, and that those choices produced sin. Yes, when the holy, perfect, and righteous new man makes choices opposite his strongest inclination, he commits acts of sin.

Paul states that as a believer, he made choices against his strongest inclination.

But the Reformed view (extreme and hyper-Calvinism) allows God to remain sovereign under one condition only—that He be the cause of all things. According to their system of thought, only by being the cause of all things can He be the sole reason the elect are saved and the non-elect damned. Hence, by their estimation, God was required to predestine the elect to salvation and reject the non-elect—neither the elect nor the non-elect ultimately having a choice as to where they will spend eternity. God would then possess the ability to draw only the elect to Himself, through His irresistible grace, and thus retain His sovereign right to rule. This arrangement may sound logical to some individuals, but it certainly isn't Scriptural for the following reasons.

Man possesses a free will to repent and exercise faith while depraved (John 1:12; Acts 16:31; Acts 26:18; Romans 10:9-10; etc.). Consequently, predestination has to do with future blessings promised to New Testament believers once they are placed in Christ—subsequent to their repenting and believing while depraved (a topic covered extensively in *God's Heart as it Relates to Foreknowledge/Predestination*, the first book of this four book series.) Election points to the special office (or position) a New Testament believer receives once placed in Christ—after repenting and believing while depraved. (Election is addressed in depth in the fourth book of this series, *God's Heart as it Relates to Election/Atonement/Grace/Perseverance*.) This arrangement in regard to predestination and election allows all contradictions to vanish. God remains sovereign, having granted man a free will by means of His sovereignty, no one holding Him at gunpoint while doing so.

Don't misunderstand. God draws all the lost (all the depraved) to Himself through the power of the Holy Spirit (a subject discussed in detail later). Along with His drawing, however, the depraved must choose to repent and believe before spiritual regeneration becomes a reality.

With the above input in mind, consider J. Denham Smith's quote included in Arthur Pink's, *The Sovereignty of God*, page 104 (Pink being a Calvinist). See if you can detect the error:

> ...I believe in free will; but then it is a *will only free to act according to its nature.*[28]

Pink again quotes Smith in the same work:

> ...The sinner in his sinful nature could never have a will according to God. For this he must be born again.[29]

Our having confirmed that man can respond against (contrary to) his strongest inclination totally refutes these inconsistencies. Dave Hunt, in *What Love is This?*, quotes Philip F. Congdon on page 159:

> Classical Calvinists may talk about man having a "free will," but it is a very limited freedom! That is, a person may choose to reject Christ–all people do–but only those who have been elected may choose to accept Him. This is no "free will"! Are the open invitations to trust Christ in the Bible actually a cruel hoax? I don't think so. Are all people free to put their trust in the Lord Jesus Christ as personal Savior for their sin? Yes. That is why the call to missions is so urgent.[30]

With our present discoveries, we should be free to walk in the confidence of the Scriptures (all of the Scriptures—in proper context) the rest of our days. To God be the glory!

The Hill

CHAPTER FOUR

AN EXAMPLE OF IMPROPER EXEGISIS

WE WILL EXAMINE MANY "IDEAS" as we address the topic of God's sovereignty and the free will of man, but the Scriptures will remain the final say as to what we accept or reject. The importance of a proper view of these subjects is enormous, in fact, beyond words. If we miss the mark here, it sets off a domino effect that not only generates insurmountable theological inconsistencies, but even more damaging, shames God's name beyond repair. For this reason, James White's ideology from *The Potter's Freedom* must be addressed.

While addressing the subject of God's sovereignty, White mentions God's involvement in the affairs of the Assyrians in the Old Testament Scriptures. I agree that God is sovereign, but the Old Testament (like the New Testament) must be addressed in context for proper interpretation. White does not apply this principle of exegesis (interpretation) and totally misconstrues the account of the Assyrian invasion of Israel addressed in Isaiah 10:5-19. Accordingly, in an attempt to exalt God's sovereignty above all His impeccable attributes (including His love), he states that God used the Assyrians to punish Israel—yet followed by punishing the Assyrians for doing so. White is forced to draw these improper conclusions. Being a Reformed theologian, he must believe that God causes all things, regardless of the result. (We desired to quote White word-for-word from his work, *The Potter's Freedom*, but permission was denied. Therefore, we contextually summarized his conclusions.)

White totally misses the point here. Assyria received God's judgment, not because she overthrew the northern kingdom of Israel, as God desired, but because she overstepped her boundaries and came against the southern kingdom of Judah. Thus, were all of Assyria's desires (and actions) in this matter the fulfillment of God's plan (or will), as White supposes? Absolutely not! To make my point, I have recorded quotes from the *Isaiah* commentary distributed by this ministry. (I taught the book of Isaiah over a span of five semesters—every verse of every chapter). My quotes relate to Isaiah 10:5-7:

> *Is. 10:5 Woe to Assyria, the rod of My anger And the staff in whose hands is My indignation,*
>
> Even though the Gentile Empire of Assyria served as both a *"rod of"* God's *"anger"* and *"staff of indignation,"* in verses 5-34 God judged the Assyrians for overstepping their boundaries. Even though God commissioned Assyria to punish the Jews, Assyria was more severe in its punishment than God desired. God would, therefore, judge Assyria. God later judged the Babylonians for the same reason (Jeremiah 50:11-18)—after they took the southern kingdom into captivity (2Kings 25:1-21; Jeremiah 52:1-30). Consider too what happened to Nazi Germany during WWII after attempting to exterminate every Jew. Zechariah 1:15 says it well:
>
> *But I am very angry with the nations who are at ease; for while I was only a little angry, they furthered the disaster.* (Zechariah 1:15)
>
> No matter what era in history, one principle remains consistent. God promises to *"bless those"* Gentile nations who *"bless"* the Jews, yet *"curse"* those Gentile nations who *"curse"* the Jews (Genesis 12:3). Listen up America!! In fact, listen up world!!
>
> Isaiah 10:5 confirms that Assyria was a *"rod"* and a *"staff"* in God's hand. In fact, He chose Assyria as the means through which He would punish the Hebrew people. God did choose Assyria to come against the Jews, but he gave every person in that empire a free will. Consequently, every leader in Assyria made decisions void of programming from God. God also, due to His foreknowledge, understands how every person will respond in every situation of life. He can, therefore, without removing their right of choice, place individuals in leadership roles who will accomplish His purpose (Romans 13:1). What an amazing God we serve!
>
> *Is. 10:6 I send it against a godless nation and commission it against the people of My fury To capture booty and to seize plunder, And to trample them down like mud in the streets.*

> God commissioned Assyria to go *"against"* His *"people,...a godless nation"* (the northern kingdom of Israel). The Assyrians realized this fact. However, in their attempt to overthrow Judah (the southern kingdom—after they had conquered and ransacked the northern kingdom), Rabshakeh, an Assyrian, stated that the *"Lord...approved"* of their coming *"against"* Jerusalem, located in the southern kingdom (2Kings 18:25). He was grossly mistaken. God sent Assyria against the northern kingdom, Israel. He did not commission Assyria to come against the southern kingdom, Judah.
>
> Everything that God says must be interpreted in its context. Also, before perceiving as reliable the things written or taught by man concerning God's words, they must agree with <u>all</u> of the Scriptures—never a few Scriptures interpreted out of context. Rabshakeh was dead wrong, for he had misstated God's purpose for political advantage. The Assyrians paid a huge price for overstepping God's boundaries and intentions.
>
> *Is. 10:7 Yet it does not so intend Nor does it plan so in its heart, But rather it is its purpose to destroy, And to cut off many nations.*
>
> Assyria exceeded what God desired in that, after overthrowing the northern kingdom, it not only came against the southern kingdom, but against a variety of Gentile *"nations"* as well (confirmed in verses 9-11).
>
> Assyria failed to carry out God's perfect will in this matter. She overstepped her boundaries, proving that nations (as well as individuals within nations) can reject God's will by making decisions based on their own desires (read Matthew 23:37). This fact confirms that man is not a programmed being incapable of choosing his own destiny.

My reason for including the previous input is: The Assyrians were judged because they chose to overstep God's boundaries by responding outside His will. Had they conquered the northern kingdom (Israel) only, God's original plan, no *"Woe"* would have been pronounced against the empire (Isaiah 10:5). Instead, after overthrowing the northern kingdom, they came south to Judah. This additional aggression is what initiated God's judgment—not the fact that Assyria had previously overthrown Israel (the northern kingdom), an event sanctioned by God. Consequently, White's remarks in *The Potter's Freedom*, which stem from improper context, are incorrect. He was clearly mistaken by writing that Assyria responded as it desired yet fulfilled God's decree.

Assyria's assault against Judah (the southern kingdom) was in disagreement with God's decree. White's radical view of God's sovereignty (that God must cause all things to retain His sovereignty) resulted in his misinterpretation of these events. He uses this same inconsistent argument regarding Isaiah 10 in *Debating Calvinism*: *Five Points, Two Views*, page 44:

> In one passage we have God's holy intention of judging His people through the means of Assyria–yet God holds Assyria accountable for her sinful attitudes in being so used! God judges them on the basis of their *intentions*, and since they come against Israel with a haughty attitude that does not recognize God's power and authority, they too are judged.... God uses the sinful actions of the Assyrians for the good purpose of judging His people, and yet He judges the Assyrians for their sinful intentions. God's action in His sovereignty is perfectly compatible with the responsibility, and culpable, actions of sinful men.[31]

God did not punish the Assyrians for what He had commissioned them to perform. Such an action on God's part would have proven Him unjust. The punishment must always match the crime or God stands condemned. However, because the Assyrians chose to hate Israel on their own, could God not have used such hatred for His own purposes? Of course He could have—as He has done time and time again throughout history. Assyria did not receive God's judgment due to warring against the northern kingdom with "sinful intentions"—as White supposes. God judged Assyria for continuing south to war against Judah—something He most definitely opposed. This event verifies that man can violate God's will.

The error associated with elevating God's sovereignty above His other glorious attributes reaps abundant contradictions. The answer to the dilemma is free will, where all persons are held accountable for their choices. Free will, therefore, allows God to remain sovereign and, at the same time, just. Hence, free will plays a major role as we seek to view God properly.

More than illogical logic and tradition are necessary to correctly view the Scriptures. Nevertheless, John Calvin writes:

> ...Now, since the arrangement of all things is in the hand of God, since to him belongs the disposal of life and death, he arranges all things by his sovereign counsel, in such a way that individuals are born, who are doomed from the womb to certain

> death, and are to glorify him by their destruction. (Institutes: Book 3; Chapter 23, Section 6)[32]

> ...it is clear that all events take place by his sovereign appointment. (*Institutes*: Book 3; Chapter 23, Section 6)[33]

> ...For we do not with the Stoics imagine a necessity consisting of a perpetual chain of causes, and a kind of involved series contained in nature, but we hold that God is the disposer and ruler of all things, that from the remotest eternity, according to his own wisdom, he decreed what he was to do, and now by his power executes what he decreed. Hence we maintain, that by his providence, not heaven and earth and inanimate creatures only, but also the counsels and wills of men are so governed as to move exactly in the course which he has destined. (*Institutes*: Book 1; Chapter 16, Section 8)[34]

> Augustine everywhere teaches, that if anything is left to fortune, the world moves at random. And although he elsewhere declares, (Quaestionum, lib. 83) that all things are carried on, partly by the free will of man, and partly by the Providence of God, he shortly after shows clearly enough that his meaning was, that men also are ruled by Providence, when he assumes it as a principle, that there cannot be a greater absurdity than to hold that anything is done without the ordination of God; because it would happen at random. For which reason, he also excludes the contingency which depends on human will, maintaining a little further on, in clearer terms, that no cause must be sought for but the will of God. (*Institutes*: Book 1; Chapter 16, Section 8)[35]

God's sovereignty, not His love, was clearly at the forefront of Calvin's mind as he addressed God's dealings with man.

Edwin H. Palmer, another Calvinist, is quoted next (*The Five Points of Calvinism*, pages 98-99). Observe the degree of logic (reason) rather than Scriptural substance employed in his argument. No wonder he yields to "mystery" as the answer to the contradictory dilemma presented by his faulty theology:

> Yet he [Augustine] realized that simply to say God permits sin is contrary to God's sovereignty and would make Him a bystander in the bleachers, watching to see how the events on history's playing field turn out. So Augustine said that the

> permission is efficacious....God permits sin; thus man is to blame and not God. But God *efficaciously* permits sin: Sin is not only foreknown by God, it is also foreordained by God. In fact, because God foreordained it, He foreknew it.
>
> Calvin is very clear on this point. "Man wills with an evil will what God wills with a good will." Evil, "which is in itself contrary to the will of God, is not done without the will of God, because without God's will it could not have been done at all." "To turn all those passages of Scripture...into a mere permission on the part of God is a frivolous subterfuge, and a vain attempt at escape from a mighty truth.
>
> Calvin approvingly quotes Augustine: "In a wonderful and ineffable way, that is not done without His will which is even done contrary to His will, because it could not have been done had He not permitted it to be done; and yet, He did not permit it without His will, but according to His will."
>
> To say it another way, God willingly permits sin. To be sure, God hates sin and does not desire it. Furthermore, He sincerely desires the salvation of all. He does not want "anyone to perish, but everyone to come to repentance" (II Peter 3:9). In this sense God unwillingly permits sin. It is against His holy nature and His revealed will. On the other hand, God willingly permits sin in that it is in accordance with His decree and not outside of His sovereign will.
>
> To speak of God efficaciously permitting sin may not appreciably help our understanding. It is a feeble attempt to describe what the Bible says. In the final analysis, we cannot really understand. When it comes to these deepest of divine mysteries, we stumble and stutter. All we can do is to parrot the Bible.[36]

Palmer concludes that we can only "parrot the Bible" due to our inability to comprehend the "mysteries" that so inundate God's Word. Palmer is in error, for *"mystery"* (in Scripture) points to truth that God is in the process of revealing (read Ephesians 3:3 and Colossians 1:27 for starters). However, Calvinism's "mysteries," generated by unsound doctrine, can never be reconciled. Here is yet another example of Calvinism, and the contradictions generated by its unhealthy view of sovereignty, leaving its followers at the mercy of "mystery"— at the mercy of their inability to generate concrete solutions to their illogical reasoning. Surely, a "better way" exists as to how to view the Scriptures! We will address this "better way" as we continue.

The Hill

CHAPTER FIVE

WHAT ABOUT GOD'S LOVE?

LET'S ASSUME FOR A MOMENT that Calvin, MacArthur, Palmer, Pink, Piper, Sproul, and all who follow their schools of thought ("schools" is implemented because they are not in agreement on all theological matters) are correct in regard to their very similar views of God's sovereignty. Where does this thinking leave the Calvinist while attempting to describe God's love? John MacArthur Jr. approached the subject in his work, *The Love of God,* page 16:

> At this point, however, an important distinction must be made: God loves believers with a particular love. It is a family love, the ultimate love of an eternal Father for His children. It is the consummate love of a Bridegroom for His bride. It is an eternal love that guarantees their salvation from sin and its ghastly penalty. This special love is reserved for believers alone. Limiting this saving, everlasting love to His chosen ones does not render God's compassion, mercy, goodness, and love for the rest of mankind insincere or meaningless. When God invites sinners to repent and receive forgiveness (Isa. 1:18; Matt. 11:28-30) His pleading is from a sincere heart of genuine love....Clearly God *does* love even those who spurn His tender mercy, but it is a different quality of love, and different in degree from His love for His own.[37]

MacArthur has no right to speak of God's love for the non-elect, even a "different quality of love" for the non-elect. Why? God, according to MacArthur's theology, restricts their ability to believe and be saved. Remember, Reformed Theology (extreme and hyper-Calvinism) teaches that God elected the elect to salvation from eternity past, never giving the non-elect an opportunity to be saved. If God has the power to save all, which the Calvinists believe, how can He love (in any shape, form, or fashion) those whom He dooms to eternal punishment while preventing them from believing? With no success at all, MacArthur writes an entire book attempting to explain this irreconcilable inconsistency. On page 17 of that work, *The Love of God*, he writes:

> God's love for the elect is an infinite, eternal, saving love. We know from Scripture that this great love was the very cause of our election (Eph. 2:4). Such love clearly is not directed toward all of mankind indiscriminately, but is bestowed uniquely and individually on those whom God chose in eternity past.
>
> But from that, it does not follow that God's attitude toward those He did not elect must be unmitigated hatred. Surely His pleading with the lost, His offers of mercy to the reprobate, and the call of the gospel to all who hear are all sincere expressions of the heart of a loving God....[38]

MacArthur can't be serious! How could God's love for the non-elect be "sincere" should He plead with those whom He has purposely rejected? Such an arrangement would be equivalent to God pleading with mankind to jump over the moon after creating man with the capability of jumping only a few feet high. Would He not appear foolish by offering such a request? He would appear more than foolish! In fact, we would classify Him as insane, totally unworthy of His rightful position as the Sovereign Ruler of the universe. Consequently, MacArthur's unhealthy view of sovereignty (that God's choice, not man's, determines every person's destiny) actually robs God of His right to rule. Yes, contradictory theology makes a mockery of God's flawless attributes.

Dave Hunt, in *What Love is This?*, page 192, quotes John Piper (a Reformed theologian) for the purpose of revealing the error inundating Piper's theological mindset:

> We do not deny that all men are the intended beneficiaries of the cross *in some sense*.... What we deny is that all men are intended as the beneficiaries of the death of Christ *in the same way*. All of God's mercy toward unbelievers–from the rising sun (Matthew 5:45) to the worldwide preaching of the gospel (John 3:16)–is made possible because of the cross.... Every time the gospel is preached to unbelievers it is the mercy of God that gives this opportunity for salvation.[39]

Piper (according to his view of the Scriptures) is incorrect in saying that God's mercy is shown every time the gospel is preached to unbelievers. How can God's mercy be displayed toward the non-elect who hear the gospel when, according to

Reformed Theology, the non-elect are incapable of repenting and believing due to a choice God made from eternity past? Yet, note Piper's words regarding God's love in *The Pleasures of God*, pages 338-339:

> Therefore, I affirm with John 3:16 and 1Timothy 2:4 that God loves the world with a deep compassion that desires the salvation of all men. Yet I also affirm that God has chosen from before the foundation of the world whom he will save from sin. Since not all people are saved, we must decide whether we believe that God's will to save all people is restrained by his commitment to human self-determination or whether we believe that God's will to save all people is restrained by his commitment to the glorification of his sovereign grace (Ephesians 1:6, 12, 14; Romans 9:22-23).
>
> This decision should not be made on the basis of metaphysical assumptions about what we think human accountability requires. It should be made on the basis of what the Scriptures teach. I do not find in the Bible that human beings have the ultimate power of self-determination. As far as I can tell, ultimate human self-determination is a philosophical inference based on metaphysical presuppositions. On the other hand, this book aims to show that the freedom and sovereignty of God's grace in salvation is taught in Scripture. It is not merely inferred with the help of metaphysical assumptions. It is explicitly set forth in many biblical passages. [40]

Wow! Do you see the inconsistencies that inundate Piper's thinking?

These additional quotes display the Calvinists' improper view of God's love that they "claim" is addressed in the Scriptures. How could it possibly be a portrayal of God's mercy and love for Him to offer salvation to those whom He declined to offer an opportunity to believe? This contradiction not only insults God's character but His mental stability as well. Yet Piper states:

> ...I rejoice to affirm that God does not delight in the perishing of the impenitent and that he has compassion on all people. (*The Pleasures of God*, p.315)[41]

John MacArthur Jr. heartily agrees with Piper:

> God's love for the reprobate is not the love of value; it is the love of pity for that which *could* have had value and has none. It is a love of compassion. It is a love of sorrow. It is a love of

> pathos. It is the same deep sense of compassion and pity we have when we see a scab-ridden derelict lying in the gutter. It is not a love that is incompatible with revulsion, but it is a genuine, well-meant, compassionate, sympathetic love nonetheless. (*The Love of God*, p.120)[42]

Again, surely they can't be serious!

As was mentioned earlier, Calvinists are in disagreement over the extent that God loves the non-elect. Interestingly, MacArthur quotes Arthur W. Pink on page 13 of his work, *The Love of God*:

> ...The fact is, that the love of God, is a truth for the saints only, and to present it to the enemies of God is to take the children's bread and cast it to the dogs....[43]

MacArthur responds to Pink's words in the following manner:

> Unfortunately, Pink took the corollary too far. The fact that some sinners are not elected to salvation is no proof that God's attitude toward them is utterly devoid of sincere love.... (*The Love of God*, p.14)[44]

One can safely say that the Calvinists are in disagreement over this issue, yet each view violates the full council of Scripture. All of the abovementioned contradictions are easily reconciled if one believes that God, in His sovereignty, allows the depraved the freedom to exercise repentance and faith—thus, taking nothing away from His sovereignty. Each person can then choose (while depraved) where he/she will spend eternity, God all along loving even those who reject Him (John 3:16). What an amazingly loving God we serve!

The Hill

CHAPTER SIX

MUST GOD POSSESS TWO WILLS?

ONE OF THE MAJOR DOGMAS, or tenets, of extreme Calvinism is the "idea" that God possesses two wills. This misconception is introduced within extreme Calvinism in an attempt to: (1) Protect their incorrect perception of sovereignty (2) Reconcile the following dilemma their theology generates. The dilemma is: If God is *"not wishing for any to perish but for all to come to repentance"* (2Peter 3:9), *"desires all men to be saved and to come to the knowledge of the truth"* (1Timothy 2:4), and does not take *"pleasure in the death of the wicked,"* desiring that man *"turn from his ways and live"* (Ezekiel 18:23), how could He (God) have predestined and unconditionally elected so few people to salvation according to Calvinism's view of the Scriptures while rejecting the hoard of individuals who remain? In other words, if God has the power to save all, desires that all be saved, but has predestined and elected so few people to salvation (Calvinism's view), how can He remain a God of love? This dilemma has plagued all forms of Calvinism since its inception; therefore, many of its followers have attempted to present a solution. We will examine some of these attempts to see if any are void of error, and thus plausible.

In *The Pleasures of God*, John Piper writes:

> Affirming the will of God to save *all*, while also affirming the unconditional election of *some*, implies that there are at least "two wills" in God, or, better, two ways of willing. It implies that God decrees one state of affairs while also willing and teaching that a different state of affairs should come to pass.... (p.315)[45]
>
> My aim...has simply been to show that God's will for all people to be saved is not at odds with the sovereignty of God's grace in election. There are "two wills in God" when it comes to salvation. They do not contradict. They are ordered according

> to God's infinite wisdom and one holds sway over the other when it is fitting in God's unfathomable mind.... (p.339)[46]

Piper is forced to say that only "God's unfathomable mind" can comprehend His ability to possess two wills as He deals with the affairs of man. In other words, Piper perceives the finite mind of man as incapable of understanding this proposed duality. At least this message seems to be what he is communicating. If so, his position is remarkably dangerous. Why? When contradictory ideas are classified as mystery yet presented as fact, the student is left at the mercy of the teacher rather than the Scriptures. We discovered at the outset of this series that when a system of thought rests on a contradictory foundation, additional contradictions abound as the structure races toward completion. Is the "idea" that God possesses two wills yet another contradiction that forces extreme Calvinists to yield to mystery? I view it to be. (Reference Diagrams 10-11 for more input regarding Reformed Theology.)

After Piper addresses some of the criticisms that the two-will concept attracts, he pens the following in *The Pleasures of God*, page 316:

> But in spite of these criticisms, the distinction stands, not because of a logical or theological deduction, but because it is inescapable in the Scriptures....[47]

Is the concept of "two wills" found in the Scriptures, and, therefore, "inescapable"—or is it an invention of man? I believe that man's mind devised the two-will concept due to an illogical view of God's heart. Consider Piper's words from *The Pleasures of God*, page 314:

> It is possible that careful exegesis of 1Timothy 2:4 would lead us to believe that God's willing "all men to be saved" does not refer to every individual person in the world, but rather to all *sorts* of persons, since the "all men" in verse 1 may well mean groups like "kings and all who are in authority" (v.2) [1Timothy 2:2]. It is also possible that the "you" in 2Peter 3:9 (the Lord "is patient toward *you*, not wishing for any to perish") refers not to every person in the world but to "you" professing Christians.... [48]

This is just one example of what must be done with the Scriptures for Reformed Theology to attempt to carry on. Piper perceives the phrase, *"all men,"* in 1Timothy 2:4, as pointing to "all sorts of persons" rather than to *"all men"* in general. He also views the pronoun, *"you,"* in 2Peter 3:9, as referencing believers only. For his definition of sovereignty to stand (in his mind at least), such unreasonable conclusions must be drawn. Why? Should God be the cause of all things (Reformed Theology's view), 1Timothy 2:4 cannot teach that He desires for all mankind be saved with so few believing. Neither can 2Peter 3:9 teach (within Reformed Theology) that God is not *"wishing"* for any man or woman to perish, but must communicate that God does not wish that any "believer" perish. Such interpretations do not fit the context (a topic addressed in detail later in this series), yet they must be accepted for the two-will logic of Piper to survive. No wonder Piper mentions that the doctrine of "two wills" has been criticized.

John MacArthur, another Reformed theologian, also views God as possessing "two wills." Consider his commentary on 1Timothy 2:4 in *The MacArthur Study Bible*:

> **2:4 desires all men to be saved.** The Gr. Word for "desires" is not that which normally expresses God's will of decree (His eternal purpose), but God's will of desire. There is a distinction between God's desire and His eternal saving purpose, which must transcend His desires. God does not want men to sin. He hates sin with all His being (Ps. 5:4; 45:7); thus, He hates its consequences—eternal wickedness in hell. God does not want people to remain wicked forever in eternal remorse and hatred of Himself. Yet, God, for His own glory, and to manifest that glory in wrath, chose to endure "vessels...prepared for destruction" for the supreme fulfillment of His will (Ro 9:22). In His eternal purpose, He chose only the elect out of the world (John 17:6) and passed over the rest, leaving them to the consequences of their sin, unbelief, and rejection of Christ (cf. Rom. 1:18-32). Ultimately, God's choices are determined by His sovereign, eternal purpose, not His desires.[49]

According to MacArthur, God possesses "two wills": (1) His "will of decree" (2) His "will of desire." Should MacArthur be correct, God could decree what He does not desire. Thus, He could desire what is contrary to "His sovereign, eternal purpose," making Him double minded in the process. That James warns against this state of mind (James 1:8; 4:8) is no accident.

Based on Ephesians 1:11, God has one will, not two:

> *...who works all things after the counsel of His will* (Ephesians 1:11)

If God possesses two wills, why doesn't Ephesians 1:11 say, "who works all things after the counsel of His [wills]"? Again we find Calvinism's arguments in violation of the full counsel of Scripture. Ephesians 1:11 is used heavily by Reformed theologians when attempting to prove that God wills all things that come to pass. We will study this passage, along with Romans 9:22 and John 17:6, more intensely later. MacArthur's interpretation (in the previous quote) will be found unjustifiable.

Are you seeing the need to hold all individuals, no matter who they are, accountable to what they teach concerning the God we serve? Can you now understand why John Piper would write the following regarding the previous subject matter?

> ...My aim...is to show from Scripture that the simultaneous existence of God's will for "all men to be saved" (1Timothy 2:4) and his will to elect unconditionally those who will actually be saved is not a sign of divine schizophrenia or exegetical confusion. A corresponding aim is to show that unconditional election therefore does not contradict biblical expressions of God's compassion for all people and does not nullify sincere offers of salvation to everyone who is lost among all the peoples of the world. (*The Pleasures of God,* p.313)[50]

After reading this quote, and more, I find it impossible to view Piper's words regarding 1Timothy 2:4 and 2Peter 3:9 as something other than "a sign of ...exegetical confusion" (to quote Piper). I also conclude that God would be engaging in "divine schizophrenia" (Piper's words) should He respond as Piper describes. Again, we observe the fallout when the first button is placed in an improper buttonhole, a subject addressed in *God's Heart as it Relates to Foreknowledge/Predestination* (the first book of this series). God's reputation suffers greatly in the wake of such illogical reasoning.

MacArthur and Piper (both extreme Calvinists) teach that God possesses two wills, evidently to distance themselves from the hyper-Calvinists—who believe that God, from eternity past, not only predestined the elect to salvation but also predestined the non-elect to damnation. Extreme Calvinists view God as having predestined the elect to salvation from eternity past but having left the non-elect to the consequence of their sin—which, in essence, is no different from hyper-Calvinism when taken to the bottom button. Make use of Diagrams 10 and 11 in the Reference Section should you need assistance. As was stated earlier, we will examine 1Timothy 2:4 and 2Peter 3:9 in greater depth later in this series.

CHAPTER SEVEN

KEY VERSES USED BY CALVINISTS IN THEIR ATTEMPT TO ELEVATE SOVEREIGNTY AND NEGATE FREE WILL

WE ARE NOW EQUIPPED TO TACKLE additional verses that address sovereignty and free will. The subject matter we have covered thus far will be invaluable as we proceed.

Exodus 34:24

> *For I will drive out nations before you and enlarge your borders, and no man shall covet your land when you go up three times a year to appear before the LORD your God.*

Many Calvinists use this verse in an attempt to prove that God's sovereignty allowed Him to decree all things that come to pass, thus removing man's freedom of choice. They view Israel's enemies in this passage as no longer coveting the land due to a choice God makes—never a choice their enemies make.

Rebuttal:

Those who agree with the previously mentioned view fail to consider that God takes *"no pleasure in the death of the wicked"*:

> *I take no pleasure in the death of the wicked, but rather that the wicked turn from his way and live.* (Ezekiel 33:11)

God desires that the *"wicked"* man *"turn from his way and live"*—choose to walk in obedience. How, then, could Jehovah instruct Joshua and Israel to attack (and kill) wicked nations in Canaan and not violate what is taught in Ezekiel 33:11? This question is easily answered. God, by means of His foreknowledge, realized that these wicked nations would never repent. Yes, Joshua's wise choices (recorded in the book of Joshua) were used of God to bring about the destruction of these enemies. However, their habitual commitment to evil was the foremost reason they were destroyed. Once Israel was in the land, Joshua instructed the Hebrew people to choose whom they would serve (Joshua 24:15), again displaying man's freedom of choice.

God promised (in Exodus 34:24) that Israel's enemies would no longer *"covet"* the land once driven from the land, a promise contingent upon Israel's obedience—again confirming the free will of man. Reformed theologians conclude that this promise could be fulfilled only through God removing the enemies' internal desire to return—an argument easily defused through realizing that Israel's obedience would have resulted in such an overwhelming manifestation of God's power that her adversaries would gladly choose to live elsewhere. Deuteronomy 11:25 verifies this fact:

> *There shall no man be able to stand before you; the LORD your God shall lay the dread of you and the fear of you on all the land on which you set foot, as He has spoken to you.* (Deuteronomy 11:25)

God's capability of fulfilling His promises associated with Exodus 34:24 and Deuteronomy 11:25 was made evident even prior to Israel warring against her enemies in Canaan. Note Rahab's words in Joshua 2:9-11:

> ... *"I know that the Lord has given you the land, and that the terror of you has fallen on us, and that all the inhabitants of the land have melted away before you. "For we have heard how the Lord dried up the water of the Red Sea before you when you came out of Egypt, and what you did to the two kings of the Amorites who were beyond the Jordan, to Sihon and Og, whom you utterly destroyed. "And when we heard it, our hearts melted and no courage remained in any man any longer because of you; for the Lord your God, He is God in heaven above and on the earth beneath.* (Joshua 2:9-11)

This *"dread"* (Deuteronomy 11:25) would have continued had Israel walked in uninterrupted submission to Jehovah. Consequently, Exodus 34:24 says nothing about God removing the free will of Israel's enemies. Free will is emphasized throughout this passage when taken through the full counsel of God's Word.

Oh, had Israel only obeyed! She chose rebellion instead and was eventually driven from the land by enemies lacking fear of the very people who, through obedience (and God's power), would have otherwise destroyed them. In the future, and shortly before the Second Coming of Christ, the Jewish nation (all Jews living on the earth at that time) will repent and accept Jesus as Savior. The Millennium is then established, the one-thousand-year reign of Christ, and Israel will control (for the first time) the entirety of the land promised to the nation in Genesis 15:18. None of her enemies will covet the land for the first time in the nation's history, fulfilling God's original promise of Exodus 34:24.

Lamentations 3:37-38

> *Who is there who speaks and it comes to pass, Unless the Lord has commanded it? Is it not from the mouth of the Most High That both good and ill go forth?*

Some Calvinists use these verses in an attempt to prove that God causes all things (that He wills all things that come to pass). Note John Piper's words from, *The Pleasures of God,* page 328:

> There are passages that ascribe to God the final control over all calamities and disasters wrought by nature or by man.... Noteworthy...is that the calamities in view involve human hostilities and cruelties that God would disapprove of even as he wills that they be.[51]

Piper takes passages such as Lamentations 3:37-38 and attempts to prove that God sometimes wills what does not meet His approval. Piper can support this belief only by perceiving God as possessing two wills, a will of decree and a will of desire, an idea proven invalid earlier.

Rebuttal:

Lamentations 3:37-38 addresses something other than what Piper supposes. In fact, these passages supply information regarding God's prophets, who spoke of incidents that God would bring to fruition. Yes, Jehovah commanded what the prophets should speak, but the *"good and ill"* they spoke, on many occasions, contained a warning against disobedience. Obedience would bring *"good"*;

disobedience would bring *"ill."* The ill will that the prophets addressed did not result from God, within the realm of His sovereignty, causing the people to disobey. Deuteronomy chapters 27-28, along with a stockpile of additional verses, confirm this same truth. God promised blessings for obedience, calamity for disobedience. Israel could choose the route she would follow.

Many Calvinists use Lamentations 3:37-38 in an attempt to prove that God's sovereignty allowed Him to decree all things that come to pass, thus removing man's freedom of choice. Lamentations 3:37-38, by no stretch of the imagination, teaches that God causes all events, including those which are evil. Consider as well that even God's prophets could choose to remain silent rather than speak God's words, as confirmed by the early stages of Jonah's prophetic ministry. Yes, God can remain sovereign without decreeing all things, granting man the freedom of choice in all matters of life.

Genesis 20:6

> *Then God said to him in the dream, "Yes, I know that in the integrity of your heart you have done this, and I also kept you from sinning against Me; therefore I did not let you touch her.*

(You might want to read Genesis 20:1-6 to understand the context of verse 6 in regard to Abimelech and Sarah.)

Many Calvinists argue that God, in His sovereignty, kept Abimelech from sinning against Sarah. They "logically" (yet illogically) conclude that if God could prevent Abimelech from sinning in this instance He could do so in other instances as well. They follow by taking yet another illogical leap and argue that God could do the same with all mankind by both preventing and causing sin. Thus, they conclude that God is the cause of all things, even man's disobedience, in an attempt to justify their unhealthy view of sovereignty.

Rebuttal:

This verse proves nothing in regard to God causing man to refrain from sin. Note that Abimelech was innocent, having chosen not to touch Sarah due to *"the integrity of"* his *"heart."* The entire account, Genesis 20:1-18, proves that Abimelech was totally blameless in the matter. Yes, God warned him through a dream (verse 3) that Sarah was Abraham's wife, but that warning in no way forced Abimelech to protect her. In fact, as soon as he understood the situation, he chose to immediately return Sarah to her husband.

Proverbs 21:1

> *The king's heart is like channels of water in the hand of the LORD;*
> *He turns it wherever He wishes.*

Calvinists generally view this verse as teaching that a king (or leader) has no choice in any matter of life—that God determines (and causes) the king's (or leader's) every move.

Rebuttal:

Solomon, the king of Israel, wrote this proverb during the latter stages of his reign. Having realized the futility of self-centered living, he expressed his personal submission to the Lord—a submission that had resulted in a change of desire. As in Psalm 37:4, *"delight yourself in the Lord; And He will give you the desires of your heart,"* our desires will increasingly mesh with God's desires as we mature in the faith. Thus, through pursuing God, Solomon found himself pursuing what God desired for the nation. Only in this sense did God turn His heart—no coercion or force was involved at any stage. Paul agrees with this mindset, for he wrote in New Testament Scripture:

> *For all who are being led by the Spirit of God, these are sons of God.* (Romans 8:14)

We most definitely can be *"led by the Spirit of God"* without being forced to respond in a particular manner. We can also *"grieve the Holy Spirit of God"* (Ephesians 4:30) by refusing His promptings and choosing disobedience. For God to cause what brings grief to Himself would be nonsensical—again negating the two-will theory addressed earlier.

Job 42:2

> *"I know that Thou canst do all things, And that no purpose of Thine can be thwarted.*

The argument from the side of Reformed Theology (extreme and hyper-Calvinism) is that God must cause all things if His purposes are to be fulfilled.

Rebuttal:

The truth is quite the contrary. God's purposes are fulfilled with man possessing a free will, making Him even more sovereign than a god who must cause all things to retain his sovereignty.

Isaiah 45:6-7

> *That men may know from the rising to the setting of the sun That there is no one besides Me. I am the Lord, and there is no other, The One forming light and creating darkness, Causing well-being and creating calamity; I am the Lord who does all these.*

John Piper was thinking of passages such as these while writing the following in *The Pleasures of God*, page 328—a quote referenced earlier:

> There are passages that ascribe to God the final control over all calamities and disasters wrought by nature or by man.... Noteworthy...is that the calamities in view involve human hostilities and cruelties that God would disapprove of even as he wills that they be.[52]

Piper (a follower of Reformed Theology) views these verses in this manner due to believing that God's sovereignty is forfeited should He not cause (or decree) all things. Piper, therefore, along with his fellow Reformed theologians, views God as knowing all things only because He causes (decrees) all things.

Rebuttal:

God can retain His sovereignty without causing all things, a fact established earlier. Much of the following is taken from my commentary on the book of Isaiah:

> *Isaiah 45:6 That men may know from the rising to the setting of the sun That there is no one besides Me. I am the Lord, and there is no other,*
>
> Isaiah 45:1-5 reveals that Jehovah had granted power to Cyrus (head of the Medo-Persian Empire) so all mankind (nations) might *"know"* that He is the only true God. However, the events that transpired subsequent to Cyrus' rise to power show that the nations

> continued to reject the God of the Jews. How then is this apparent contradiction reconciled? Through the deeds of Cyrus, the Jews were allowed to return to their land. As a result, the Messiah would later be born, crucified, resurrected, taken up to the Father, and return at the Second Coming. In conjunction with the Tribulation and Second Coming all nations (on the earth at that time) will accept Jehovah as the only true God, fulfilling precisely the prophecy of Isaiah 45:6. Apparent contradiction resolved!
>
> *Is. 45:7 The One forming light and creating darkness, Causing well-being and creating calamity; I am the Lord who does all these.*
>
> The phrases, *"The One forming light and creating darkness, Causing well-being and creating calamity"* are interesting indeed. The Persian religion in Cyrus' day was Zoroastrianism. One school of thought within Zoroastrianism promoted a cosmic dualism which divided the one nature of the deity into two independent powers, forces, or gods....
>
> With this background in mind, note the last phrase of verse 7—*"I am the Lord who does all these."* This phrase confirms that the God of the Jews is superior in that He need not be divided into two separate deities—for He, being totally sovereign and omnipotent, rules over all, even the powers of "darkness." This ability is why He (Jehovah), who brings *"light"* and *"well-being"* upon the obedient, can, at the same time, bring *"darkness"* and *"calamity"* upon the disobedient—a principle witnessed throughout the Scriptures. That God can bring all of this about with man possessing a free will to choose as he pleases is truly amazing.

Individuals who believe that God causes all things (that He decrees all things that come to pass) use Isaiah 45:7 in an attempt to prove that God, in order to retain His sovereignty, must be the author of evil. A great difference exists, however, between bringing *"calamity"* upon the disobedient by means of the free will of the powers of darkness (which He does) versus being the author and source of evil. Even Romans 5:12 teaches that *"sin"* (a power controlled by Satan) entered into man (Romans 5:12) through Adam's choice to disobey, for Adam's decision was blatant disobedience—not a result of being deceived (1Timothy 2:14).

If man does not possess a free will, then God is the author of evil (Adam would have been programmed to sin, God being the cause of his disobedience). But, if man possesses a free will, evil can be generated without God being responsible. How? Adam's choice to rebel against God, freely (and intentionally) choosing to partake of the forbidden fruit (1Timothy 2:14), was the means through which evil entered into *man* (Romans 5:12). Interestingly, even Satan, who tempted Adam in the first place, chose to rebel against God long before Adam came on the scene (read Isaiah 14:12-14 and Ezekiel 28:14-15). Thus, evil first came into existence through Satan's decision to rebel, but sin (and its accompanying evil) entered into man as a result of Adam's decision to rebel. Can we, therefore, afford to believe anything other than free will? If we can, then God is the author of evil, tarnishing His name and everything else associated with His impeccable character.

Isaiah 46:9-10

> *...I am God, and there is no other; I am God, and there is no one like Me, Declaring the end from the beginning And from ancient times things which have not been done, Saying, 'My purpose will be established, And I will accomplish all My good pleasure';*

In his work, *The Attributes of God* (page 40), Arthur Pink, a Calvinist, writes:

> The sovereignty of God may be defined as the *exercise* of his supremacy.... Being infinitely elevated above the highest creature, He is the Most High, Lord of heaven and earth. Subject to none, influenced by none, absolutely independent; God does as he pleases, only as he pleases, always as he pleases. None can thwart him, none can hinder him....[53]

No doubt, God is the supreme Ruler of all things at all times. But Pink's view of sovereignty depicts God as ordaining all events of life. On page 41 of *The Attributes of God*, he quotes Charles Spurgeon (a fellow Calvinist) in an attempt to make his point:

> There is no attribute more comforting to His children than that of God's Sovereignty. Under the most adverse circumstances, in the most severe trials, they believe that Sovereignty has ordained their afflictions, that Sovereignty overrules them, and that Sovereignty will sanctify them all. There is nothing for which the children ought more earnestly to contend than the doctrine of their Master over all creation–the Kingship of God over all the works of His own hands–the Throne of God and His right to sit upon that Throne. On the other hand, there is no

> doctrine more hated by worldings, no truth of which they have made such a football, as the great, stupendous, but yet most certain doctrine of the Sovereignty of the infinite Jehovah. Men will allow God to be everywhere except on His throne. They will allow Him to be in His workshop to fashion worlds and make stars. They will allow Him to be in His almonry to dispense His alms and bestow His bounties. They will allow Him to sustain the earth and bear up the pillars thereof, or light the lamps of heaven, or rule the waves of the ever-moving ocean; but when God ascends His throne, His creatures then gnash their teeth. And we proclaim an *enthroned* God, and His right to do as He wills with His own, to dispose of His creatures as *He* thinks well, without consulting them in the matter; then it is that we are hissed and execrated, and then it is that men turn a deaf ear to us, for God on His throne is not the God they love. But it is God upon the throne that we love to preach. It is God upon His throne whom we trust.[54]

Intriguingly, Spurgeon, an evangelist, still believed that the gospel was to be preached to all men (and not exclusively to the "elect"). His acceptance of this view caused him to assume that many of his Calvinist contemporaries would classify him as Arminian. Note his strong stand on the universal preaching of the gospel:

> If I am to preach faith in Christ to a man who is regenerated, then the man, being regenerated, is saved already, and it is an unnecessary and ridiculous thing for me to preach Christ to him, and bid him to believe in order to be saved when he is saved already, being regenerate. Am I only to preach faith to those who have it? Absurd, indeed! Is not this waiting till the man is cured and then bringing him the medicine? This is preaching Christ to the righteous and not to sinners. ["The Warrant of Faith" (Pasadena Tx: Pilgrims Publications; 1978), 3, One-sermon booklet from 63-volume set—taken from Dave Hunt's book, *What Love is This?*, p.126[55]

Spurgeon (a follower of Calvinism) strongly disagreed with the idea that man has no choice as to where he will spend eternity, so he defined certain types of Calvinists as follows:

> "a class of strong-minded hard-headed men who magnify sovereignty at the expense of [human] responsibility" (a quote

> taken from "God's Will and Man's Will," No. 442–Newington, Metropolitan Tabernacle; sermon delivered Sunday morning, March 30, 1862).[56]

Note how this quote from Spurgeon, taken from Dave Hunt's work, *What Love is This?*, page 158, contradicts his (Spurgeon's) previous quote from Pink's, *The Attributes of God,* page 41. The following from his January 16, 1880 sermon, "Salvation by Knowing the Truth," [www.apibs.org/chs/1516.htm], also taken from Hunt's, *What Love is This?*, page 254, does the same:

> As it is my wish that it should be so, as it is your wish that it might be so, so it is God's wish that all men should be saved; for assuredly, he is not less benevolent than we are.[57]

Spurgeon, in the same sermon, also states the following regarding God's love ("benevolence") and how it relates to His omnipotence (power and sovereignty):

> Then comes the question, "But if he wishes it to be so, why does he not make it so...[God] has an infinite benevolence which, nevertheless, is not in all points worked out by his infinite omnipotence; and if anybody asked me why it is not, I cannot tell. I have never set out to be an explainer of all difficulties, and I have no desire to do so." (A quote taken from Dave Hunt's, *What Love is This?*, p.254)[58]

Spurgeon had no answers to the contradictions spawned by Calvinism, requiring him to say—"and if anybody asked me why it is not, I cannot tell. I have never set out to be an explainer of all difficulties, and I have no desire to do so." This approach is another way of saying that he was forced to yield to "mystery." All Calvinists must yield to mystery if they are honest with themselves. Why? They can't explain (without contradiction) how a God of love, Who according to their view has the power to save all, has chosen to elect and predestine only some to salvation (according to their view) when He could have (according to their view) elected and predestined all.

Rebuttal:

My rebuttal is simple. People who adhere to the Reformed view of sovereignty (even men such as Spurgeon) must yield to "mystery" in their attempt to justify their beliefs. Free will, on the other hand, where man (while depraved) chooses his own destiny through personal repentance and faith, faith not being a work (Romans 4:5; 9:32; Galatians 3:5), is a non-contradictory fact taught throughout the Scriptures. After all, free will, where God grants man, within the realm of His sovereignty, the ability to accept or reject Christ (while depraved), lines up with every word, of every phrase, of every verse taught from Genesis through Revelation.

Let's take a long, hard look at the last phrase of Isaiah 46:10, which states, *"And I will accomplish all My good pleasure."* If MacArthur, Piper, and other Calvinists are correct in assuming that God possesses two wills (and causes all things), and that He sometimes decrees what He does not desire, how can He *"accomplish all"* His *"good pleasure"* (note the all-inclusive *"all"*) if some of the things He accomplishes are not His desire? This scenario would have Him taking pleasure in fulfilling what He does not desire. Do you see the contradiction in such thinking? Is this the God that the Scriptures portray as the omniscient, omnipotent, wise, and sovereign Ruler of the universe? I think not!

Some individuals who accept the two-will theory might argue that Isaiah 46:10 references only what God accomplishes that brings Him pleasure. If so, does this negate the two-will theory by proving that He never wills what does not bring Him pleasure? The "two-will" theory brings consistent contradiction into play.

Daniel 4:35

> *"And all the inhabitants of the earth are accounted as nothing, But He does according to His will in the host of heaven And among the inhabitants of earth; And no one can ward off His hand Or say to Him, 'What hast Thou done?'*

Reformed theologians (extreme and hyper-Calvinists), due to their exaggerated view of sovereignty, perceive this verse as teaching that God is the cause of all things. Their goal is to portray God as determining, within the realm of His sovereignty, the destiny of man.

Rebuttal:

We have already seen that God cannot decree man's every move (both good and bad) and condemn him for his disobedience. This scenario would make Him extremely unjust. We also know that should God be the cause of all things, He is also the cause of evil. This fact does not prevent the Calvinist from accepting such contradiction, as confirmed by Edwin H. Palmer in, *The Five Points of Calvinism*, page 97:

> Although sin and unbelief are contrary to what God commands (His perceptive will), God has included them in His sovereign decree (ordained them to certainly come to pass).[59]

On page 97, Palmer adds:

> All things that happen in all the world at any time and in all history—whether with inorganic matter, vegetation, animals, man, or angels (both the good and evil ones)—come to pass because God ordained them. Even sin—the fall of the devil from heaven, the fall of Adam, and every evil thought, word, and deed in all of history, including the worst sin of all, Judas' betrayal of Christ—is included in the eternal decree of our holy God.[60]

Why would Palmer, a Calvinist, perceive God in this manner? He answers this question on page 116 of *The Five Points of Calvinism*:

> ...If God has ordained only the good and pleasant things in life, then it is obvious that the unbelief of reprobation has not been foreordained. On the other hand, if all things are ordained by God—including sin and unbelief—then God has ordained who will be unbelievers. So, for the teaching of reprobation it is essential to establish the Biblical data on the foreordination of sin.[61]

Do you see how Palmer's unhealthy view of sovereignty affects his thinking? His conclusions are:

1. "If God has ordained only the good and pleasant things in life," He has not foreordained the destiny of the reprobate (the lost).

2. "If all things are ordained by God—including sin and unbelief," He must have foreordained the destiny of the reprobate (the lost).

The flaw is apparent. Should God be the author of sin, sin being rebellion against God, then God authored that which opposes Himself. Impossible! Such thinking can be traced to the false idea that a truly sovereign God must cause all things to know all things. The error results from failing to differentiate between what God decrees and what God allows.

The answer is free will. If man can choose his destiny (choose heaven or hell while depraved), then man is responsible for his sin (not God)—allowing God to be innocent in the matter. But how can man possess a free will without diminishing God's sovereignty? The answer is simple. God, within the realm of His sovereignty, and without anyone holding Him at gunpoint, granted man the freedom of choice—a topic discussed earlier in this study.

Psalm 115:3

But our God is in the heavens; He does whatever He pleases.

Reformed Theology uses this verse in an attempt to prove that God causes all things, every action of man included. They perceive this passage in this manner due to believing that God's sovereignty is destroyed should man possess a free will (especially in the area of the depraved exercising personal repentance and faith).

Rebuttal:

Unquestionably, God's sovereignty allows Him to do *"whatever He pleases."* It would never please Him, however, to do anything in violation of His character or His truth. Consequently, He cannot create man void of a free will and judge him for failing to believe. Such an arrangement would make Him totally unjust. The same conclusions can be drawn from verses such as Psalm 135:6:

Whatever the LORD pleases, He does, In heaven and in earth, in the seas and in all deeps.

Proverbs 16:33

The lot is cast into the lap, But its every decision is from the LORD.

Reformed theologians perceive this verse as communicating that the Lord determines all of man's actions—that man is void of a free will.

Rebuttal:

The lot was sometimes used during Old Testament times to "assist" in decision making (Joshua 7:18; 1Samuel 14:37-42; Proverbs 18:18), but it, by no stretch of the imagination, forced a person to obey its instruction. This verse, therefore, does not teach that man is void of a free will—that God is the cause of all things.

Proverbs 16:9

The mind of man plans his way, But the LORD directs his steps.

Proverbs 19:21 states basically the same truth:

Many are the plans in a man's heart, But the counsel of the LORD, it will stand.

Several Calvinists, due to overemphasizing God's sovereignty, use such verses in an attempt to prove that the Lord ordains all things, leaving man void of the right of choice.

Rebuttal:

These verses actually confirm free will. Man can plan (make choices), but regardless of the choices man makes, God's ultimate *"counsel...will stand"* (Proverbs 19:21). In other words, the free will of man cannot, by any stretch of the imagination, thwart God's purposes. This truth verifies how prophecy can be fulfilled, just as God has stated, even with man possessing the freedom of choice. Consider as well that *"The mind of man plans his way, But the LORD directs his steps"* (Proverbs 16:9). Man most definitely makes choices, but God can direct man's steps through the variables he faces throughout life. If Balaam's plans and decisions (while possessing a free will) could be affected by God opening the mouth of a donkey (read Numbers 22), God can direct our steps without removing our freedom of choice. What an amazingly, sovereign God we serve!

Proverbs 20:24

> *Man's steps are ordained by the LORD, How then can man understand his way?*

Reformed theologians interpret such verses as teaching that God, not man, directs the actions of all mankind—leaving man void of a free will. These assumptions are made for the purpose of elevating God's sovereignty above all of His other wonderful attributes, including His love.

Rebuttal:

The context of the term, *"Man's,"* is interesting, normally pointing to man in general but in this case a valiant man or warrior. Note the following quote from *Jamieson, Fausset, and Brown Commentary*, Electronic Database. Copyright (c) 1997 by Biblesoft:

> Man's (Hebrew, gaaber (OT:1397): a mighty man's) goings (are) of the Lord. Whatever success attends mighty warriors, as Julius Caesar, Alexander, Napoleon, etc., is entirely due to the Lord.[62]

God is free to direct the affairs of man through placing mighty leaders in positions of authority (since all authority is ordained of the Lord—Romans 13:1), knowing (without causing) the choices they will make while functioning in these positions of leadership. For instance, David (2Samuel 23:1) was *"ordained by the Lord"* (Proverbs 20:24) to lead in a particular area of influence (as king of Israel). This facet of God's sovereignty is also played out in Isaiah 44:8 and 45:1, where He prophesied through Isaiah that Cyrus (a future leader of the Medo-Persian Empire) would be raised up for the purpose of overthrowing the Babylonian Empire—knowing full well (by means of His foreknowledge) how Cyrus would respond once in office. Consequently, God was not surprised when Cyrus (who did *"not know"* Him—Isaiah 45:4) chose to allow the Jews to return to Canaan once he (Cyrus) defeated the Babylonians (read Ezra 1:1-4). Had God caused Cyrus' every move, certainly He would have had him be saved and become part of his family (1Timothy 2:4; 2Peter 3:9).

God strengthens leaders so they can carry out their own decisions (and desires), and in this manner ordains (Proverbs 20:24) their ways. In other words, God's sovereignty does not require that He decree their choices beforehand. They are free moral agents, but agents used of God, within the realm of His sovereignty, to fulfill His plans for man. Because God is sovereign enough to act in this manner, we cannot comprehend all that He is accomplishing through the choices of those He places in strategic positions of leadership. Hence, we, on many occasions, fail to realize how these leaders' decisions will affect our lives circumstantially.

Jonah struggled with this issue when called to go to Nineveh to preach truth to the Assyrians. God's directive made no sense to the prophet; for Assyria, whose capitol was Nineveh, would eventually overthrow the northern kingdom of Israel, Jonah's homeland (a fact Jonah understood well). As a result, he initially rebelled against God's mandate instead of fulfilling his commission as God's prophet.

Every believer struggles periodically while attempting to see and understand God's hand in the midst of trying circumstances. Could God actually lead a person to do something that, on the surface, seems unreasonable in the realm of the physical? He did so with Abraham (the father and leader of the Jewish nation), as verified by the following.

Romans 8:14 states, *"for all who are being led by the Spirit of God, these are the sons of God."* Undoubtedly, the Spirit of God can lead a believer (without making the choice for him) in a way that confuses the believer's understanding:

> *By faith Abraham, when he was called, obeyed by going out to a place which he was to receive for an inheritance; and he went out, <u>not knowing where he was going</u>.* (Hebrews 11:8)

This verse refers to the events of Genesis 11:26–12:9, where God encouraged Abraham to leave his homeland and travel to Canaan. Abraham exhibited great faith by moving to a foreign land, *"not knowing where he was going."* Without understanding his *"way"* (Proverbs 20:24), Abraham, led by God's Spirit, made a choice to obey—which resulted in immeasurable blessings.

Faith in the truth, power, love, grace, and sovereignty of God is the key to victory, especially when struggling to understand God's ways in the midst of the trials of daily living.

Jeremiah 10:23

> *I know, O LORD, that a man's way is not in himself; Nor is it in a man who walks to direct his steps.*

Reformed Theology uses this verse in an attempt to prove that God (in His sovereignty) causes all things—that man is void of a free will. John Piper, a Reformed theologian, records in *The Pleasures of God*, pages 327, 329-330:

> Behind this complex relationship of two wills in God [we addressed earlier what Piper means by God's "two wills"] is the foundational biblical premise that God is indeed sovereign in a way that makes him ruler of all actions....
>
> This sense of living in the hands of God, right down to the details of life, was not new for the early Christians. They knew it already from the whole history of Israel, but especially from their wisdom literature.[63]

After quoting Proverbs 16:1, 9, 33; 19:21 and Jeremiah 10:23, Piper adds:

> Jesus had no quarrel with this sense of living in the hand of God. If anything, he intensified the idea with words like those in Matthew 10:20, "Are not two sparrows sold for a cent? And yet not one of them will fall to the ground apart from your Father."
>
> This confidence that the details of life were in the control of God every day was rooted in numerous prophetic expressions of God's unstoppable, unthwartable sovereign purpose....[64]

Piper then quotes Isaiah 46:9-10, Daniel 4:35, Job 42:2, and Psalm 115:3, and on page 330 of this same work writes:

> One of the most precious implications of this confidence in God's inviolable sovereign will is that it provides the foundation of the "new covenant" hope for the holiness without which we will not see the Lord (Hebrews 12:14). In the old covenant, the law was written on stone and brought death when it met with the resistance of unrenewed hearts. But the new covenant promise is that God will not let his purposes for a holy people shipwreck on the weakness of human will. Instead he promises to do what needs to be done to make us what we ought to be....[65]

Piper's words, "...the weakness of human will," quoted above, followed by, "...he [God] promises to do what needs to be done to make us what we ought to be," confirm that Piper rejects the freedom of the "human will" (especially in regard to the depraved choosing Jesus as Savior) for those living under the "new covenant." He then quotes several verses in an attempt to prove that his ideas are correct:

> ..."And the Lord your God will circumcise your heart and the heart of your offspring, so that you will love the Lord your God with all your heart and with all your soul, that you may live" (Deuteronomy 30:6, RSV). "I will put my spirit within you, and cause you to walk in my statutes and be careful to observe my ordinances" (Ezekiel 36:27, RSV). "I will make with them an everlasting covenant, that I will not turn away from doing good to them; and I will put the fear of me in their hearts, that they may not turn from me" (Jeremiah 32:40, RSV). "Work out your salvation with fear and trembling; for *it is God who is at work in you, both to will and to work for His good pleasure*" (Philippians 2:12-13). "Now the God of peace...equip you in every good thing to do His will, working in us that which is pleasing in His sight, through Jesus Christ, to whom *be* the glory forever and ever. Amen" (Hebrews 13:20-21).[66]

Is Piper correct in his analysis of these passages, or has his Calvinistic mindset caused him to read into these verses something that does not exist? I agree with the second scenario for reasons addressed in the following rebuttal.

Rebuttal:

My rebuttal is much the same as the one associated with Proverbs 16:9, 19:21, and 20:24. Man most definitely can make choices by means of his free will while, at the same time, God *"directs his steps"* through the variables of daily living. Remember Balaam and his donkey, for they serve as a wonderful example of the principle addressed here!

As part of the rebuttal, let's take a moment to consider some of the ramifications of the theology embraced by the Reformed movement. Reformed theologians (such as Piper) desperately need to believe that God is the cause of all things, for they must credit Him with predetermining who will be saved/justified. Hence, the number of contradictions associated with their approach is overwhelming—as will be further confirmed as we proceed.

Reformed theologians (extreme and hyper-Calvinists) must view God as the cause of all things, especially in the realm of who is or is not part of the elect—that is, if He is to retain (within their system of thought) His position as the one and only Sovereign. This mentality, however, makes God the cause of sin—a subject addressed earlier in this study. Such thinking also generates additional inconsistencies that affect a number of doctrinal matters. For instance, if God alone (according to the Reformed view) has determined from eternity past who makes up the elect, and the elect make up the church under the new covenant, where does this leave the nation of Israel during the church age? How the majority of Reformed theologians answer this question is quite intriguing, so engage your mind and follow closely. The necessity of understanding what follows is critically important if our view of God is to be based on a literal (rather than allegorical) interpretation of His Word.

Many extreme and hyper-Calvinists view the nation of Israel as a nonentity (of no significance) in today's world. They conclude that God is no longer dealing with physical Israel as a nation, relieving Him of the responsibility of fulfilling His unconditional covenants promised to the Jews. They argue that under the new covenant there can be only one elect people of God, the one elect people of God being the church. Therefore, they view the church as fulfilling all of God's unconditional covenants promised to the Hebrew people. However, they must interpret the Scriptures allegorically rather than literally to do so, ushering in a surplus of contradictions impossible to reconcile.

This improper thinking is apparent in Piper's earlier argument by how he interprets Deuteronomy 30:6, Jeremiah 32:40, and Ezekiel 36:27. Let me demonstrate by repeating a portion of his previous quote from *The Pleasures of God:*

> One of the most precious implications of this confidence in God's inviolable sovereign will is that it provides the foundation of the "new covenant" hope for the holiness without which we will not see the Lord (Hebrews 12:14). In the old covenant, the law was written on stone and brought death when it met with the resistance of unrenewed hearts. But the new covenant promise is that God will not let his purposes for a holy people shipwreck on the weakness of human will. Instead he promises to do what needs to be done to make us what we ought to be. "And the Lord your God will circumcise your heart and the heart of your offspring, so that you will love the Lord your God with all your heart and with all your soul, that you may live" (Deuteronomy 30:6, RSV). "I will put my spirit within you, and cause you to walk in my statutes and be careful to observe my ordinances" (Ezekiel 36:27, RSV). "I will make with them an everlasting covenant, that I will not turn away from doing good to them; and I will put the fear of me in their hearts, that they may not turn from me" (Jeremiah 32:40, RSV). "Work out your salvation with fear and trembling; for *it is God who is at work in you, both to will and to work for His good pleasure*" (Philippians

> 2:12-13). "Now the God of peace...equip you in every good thing to do His will, working in us that which is pleasing in His sight, through Jesus Christ, to whom *be* the glory forever and ever. Amen" (Hebrews 13:20-21).[67]

Is Piper's analysis of these Scriptures based on the full counsel of God's Word, or does he allow his Calvinistic background to affect His thinking? I view his conclusions as unacceptable.

As we continue, realize that I included these quotes from Piper for a specific purpose. Every believer must know what to look for when reading materials (or listening to messages) that attempt to interpret God's Word. If the writer, or teacher, downplays (or never mentions) the significance of the physical Israel of our day, and how God is fulfilling a wealth of prophecies (this very moment) through Israel's 1948 return to her land, the writer probably interprets the Old Testament allegorically rather than literally. And what do I mean by the "allegorical" method of interpretation? This method does not view the "literal" Old Testament covenants given to the physical Jewish nation as being eventually fulfilled by physical Israel, but as presently being fulfilled by the church. Neither does such a method consider all of the Old Testament prophecies, especially those pointing to the Jewish nation, as prophecies requiring a literal fulfillment. This system leaves the literal text of the Old Testament at the mercy of the teacher, for it seeks a "deeper," "allegorical" meaning rather than a historical, contextual interpretation. People who agree with this view have great difficulty when dealing with verses such as Luke 24:27:

> *And beginning with Moses and with all the prophets, He explained to them the things concerning Himself in all the Scriptures.* (Luke 24:27)

This verse proves that Jesus interpreted the Old Testament *"Scriptures"* literally, also confirmed by His words of Matthew 24:15:

> *"Therefore when you see the abomination of desolation which was spoken of through Daniel the prophet, standing in the holy place (let the reader understand),* (Matthew 24:15)

Jesus verifies, beyond doubt, that Daniel was a real man whose words were to be interpreted literally. (An overabundance of additional passages could be cited, but we must move on. The *Isaiah* commentary, produced by this ministry, provides a wealth of verses that validate this position.)

How then can John Piper view Deuteronomy 30:6, Jeremiah 32:40, and Ezekiel 36:27, verses that relate specifically to the physical Jewish nation, as making reference to the church? Piper is a Calvinist and has, therefore, been highly influenced by Calvin. Further, Calvin and Luther, the great Reformers, were highly influenced by Augustine. Yet, Augustine used the allegorical method of interpretation to indoctrinate the Catholic Church with heretical dogmas, such as:

1. The rejection of the one-thousand-year reign of Christ on the earth, with the Church now reigning instead
2. Satan is, during the church age, bound
3. Infant baptism for regeneration, with all unbaptized babies excluded from the kingdom
4. Salvation through the Catholic Church by means of the sacraments
5. Purgatory
6. The right to persecute those in disagreement with the Catholic Church
7. The Catholic Church alone is the body of Christ
8. The Lord's supper is the physical presence of Christ's body and blood
9. The apostolic succession from Peter—that Peter was the first Pope
10. God is the cause of all things
11. The predestination of some individuals to salvation and others to damnation
12. Saving faith is irresistible and a gift from God
13. Augustine was one of the first to place tradition on an equal plane with the Scriptures
14. Baptism is necessary for the remission of sins

Dave Hunt covers this subject in greater depth on pages 53-60 of *What Love Is This?* We addressed Augustine's influence on Calvin and Luther in our previous study of *God's Heart as it Relates to Foreknowledge/Predestination*, so a review of those notes might be helpful at this time.

Do you now see why Piper would view Deuteronomy 30:6, Jeremiah 32:40, and Ezekiel 36:27 as being fulfilled by the church rather than the physical Jewish nation (read Piper's previous quote)? But if Deuteronomy 30:6 is interpreted in context, it must point to physical Israel rather than the church. Why? Deuteronomy 30:6 is part of the unconditional covenant known as the Palestinian Covenant, a covenant that God made with the Jewish nation in Moses' day. The covenant verifies (when taken through all of the verses in God's Word) that every Jew living on the earth at the end of the Tribulation will inhabit Canaan after having chosen to exercise personal repentance and faith in Christ while depraved. They return to the land in conjunction with Jesus' Second Coming, which ushers in the Messianic Kingdom. This order of events is easily seen through a careful reading of Deuteronomy 30:1-6:

> *"So it shall be when all of these things have come upon you, the blessing and the curse which I have set before you, and you call them to mind in all nations where the LORD your God has banished you, and you return to the LORD your God and obey Him with all your heart and soul according to all that I command you today, you and your sons, then the LORD your God will restore you from captivity, and have compassion on you, and will gather you again from all the peoples where the LORD your God has scattered you. If your outcasts are at the ends of the earth, from there the LORD your God will gather you, and from there He will bring you back. And the LORD your God will bring you into the land which your fathers possessed, and you shall possess it; and He will prosper you and multiply you more than your fathers. Moreover the LORD your God will circumcise your heart and the heart of your descendants, to love the LORD your God with all your heart and with all your soul, in order that you may live.* (Deuteronomy 30:1-6)

Undeniably, the pronouns *"you"* and *"your"* in these verses point to the physical Jewish nation—not the church. After all, God established the promise of *"the blessing and the curse"* of Deuteronomy 27-28 with physical Israel. She was also promised *"the land"*:

> *And the LORD your God will bring you into the land which your fathers possessed, and you shall possess it;...* (Deuteronomy 30:5)

This promise will be fulfilled at the end of the Tribulation when every Jew living on the earth (at that time) will choose to accept Christ as Savior (Romans 11:26). These Jews will be ushered into the Millennial Kingdom to control and inhabit the land promised to the nation, the parameters of which are specified in Genesis 15:18—real estate that physical Israel will not control and inhabit in its entirety until that time. The Jewish patriarchs, such as Abraham, Isaac, and Jacob, along with all Old Testament believers, will also inhabit the land while living in their resurrected bodies. It is no accident, therefore, that the portion of the land that each Israeli tribe will possess is described in minute detail in Ezekiel 48—a different tribal arrangement than was implemented in the days of Joshua. Piper's allegorical view of the Scriptures, however, depicts the church as fulfilling all of the conditions laid out in Deuteronomy 30:1-6 (verified by his previous quote). He could not be more mistaken. Nor could he be more incorrect in viewing Deuteronomy 30:6 as disproving the free will of man. Why? Deuteronomy 30:6 describes God's circumcision of the hearts of the Jews living on the earth at the end of the Tribulation—after they have chosen to repent and believe while depraved.

Piper also implements the allegorical method while interpreting Jeremiah 32:40. Note the verse:

> *"And I will make an everlasting covenant with them that I will not turn away from them, to do them good; and I will put the fear of Me in their hearts so that they will not turn away from Me.* (Jeremiah 32:40)

Let's examine this verse in its context by including the four verses that precede it—Jeremiah 32:36-39:

> *"Now therefore thus says the LORD God of Israel concerning this city of which you say, 'It is given into the hand of the king of Babylon by sword, by famine, and by pestilence.' "Behold, I will gather them out of all the lands to which I have driven them in My anger, in My wrath, and in great indignation; and I will bring them back to this place and make them dwell in safety. "And they shall be My people, and I will be their God; and I will give them one heart and one way, that they may fear Me always, for their own good, and for the good of their children after them. "And I will make an everlasting covenant with them that I will not turn away from them, to do them good; and I will put the fear of Me in their hearts so that they will not turn away from Me.* (Jeremiah 32:36-40)

These verses address the return of the Jews in a state of belief at the end of the Tribulation (in preparation for the Messianic Kingdom) after banishment into Gentile lands due to unbelief. Considering what was covered in relation to Deuteronomy 30:6, Jeremiah 32:40 cannot, by any stretch of the imagination, point to God's present dealings with the church. Thus, contextually, Piper is drastically incorrect in attempting to apply Deuteronomy 30:6 and Jeremiah 32:40 in an allegorical sense to the church. His ideas (logic) just won't fit. Neither will his view of Ezekiel 36:27 apply void of contradiction, for Ezekiel is addressing an event that transpires at the end of the Tribulation—once every Jew living on the earth at that time repents and believes while depraved:

> *"And I will put my Spirit within you and cause you to walk in My statutes, and you will be careful to observe My ordinances. (Ezekiel 36:27)*

Piper quotes Deuteronomy 30:6, Ezekiel 36:27, Jeremiah 32:40, Philippians 2:12-13, and Hebrews 13:20-21 earlier in an effort to prove that in every case God (not the free will of man) causes a person to believe. (We will discuss Philippians 2:12-13 and Hebrews 13:20-21 later.) Taking what we have addressed regarding Deuteronomy 30:6, Ezekiel 36:27, and Jeremiah 32:40 through the full counsel of God's Word, we find that a choice on the part of the Jews at the end of the Tribulation will cause Christ to return. They will choose to believe on Christ (while depraved), resulting in their calling Him back for the purpose of saving them from the Antichrist and his armies. These facts are confirmed by Hosea 5:15:

> *I will go away and return to My place Until they acknowledge their guilt and seek My face; In their affliction they will earnestly seek Me.* (Hosea 5:15)

The Scriptures verify that Jesus came to the earth and returned to the Father—that He returned to His *"place"* in heaven after His death, burial, and resurrection. He will not return at His Second Coming until specific events transpire, events foretold in the prophetic section of God's Word. Follow closely.

When the Antichrist is on the verge of exterminating the Jews at the end of the Tribulation, *"all Israel"* (Romans 11:26), all Jews on the earth at that time, will repent and call Christ back. In other words, they will repent and exercise faith in Jesus in the midst of their depravity—resulting in God saving them and giving *"them one heart"* to *"fear"* Him *"always"* (Jeremiah 32:39). This national salvation of the Jewish people will result in Jesus' return not only to save them from physical danger, but to usher them into the Messianic Kingdom. Consequently, a free choice, made by depraved Jews, opens the door for God's fulfillment of Deuteronomy 30:6, Ezekiel 36:27, and Jeremiah 32:40—not a programmed manipulation where God causes the Jews (or anyone else) to believe. Thus, Deuteronomy 30:6, Ezekiel 36:27, and Jeremiah 32:40 are not fulfilled through God causing the elect to believe during the church age, a fact that refutes Piper's argument altogether.

As stated earlier, many Reformed theologians perceive the church as replacing the nation of Israel (ethnic Israel) as God's covenant people. They claim that the land promised to Abraham and his descendants is possessed (allegorically) by spiritual Israel, the church (made up of believing Jews and Gentiles alike). As a result, they view the present migration of Jews to their homeland (which began in 1948) as insignificant. In fact, they perceive the secular state of Israel as having no advantage over the Arabs regarding the ownership of the land. Thus, they advocate that Washington

Many verses in God's Word must be interpreted allegorically, rather than literally, for the Reformed theologian's view to survive.

should seek a just settlement between the Arabs and the Jews. This ideology is problematic both scripturally and historically because God promised, in Genesis 12:3, to *"bless"* individuals and nations who *"bless"* physical Israel and *"curse"* those who don't. Consequently, the number of nations who have lost supremacy due to their mistreatment of the Jews is staggering—validating the exactness of the Scriptures.

Numerous verses in God's Word must be interpreted allegorically, rather than literally, for Piper's view to survive. The Scriptures "literally" teach that Israel will return to her homeland in a state of unbelief prior to controlling and inhabiting the land in its entirety in a state of belief. This worldwide regathering in unbelief began in 1948 and continues today. In fact, it will pave the way for the Antichrist to attempt to exterminate the Jews during the Tribulation, shortly before Christ's Second Coming. At the end of the Tribulation, the Jews (all Jews on the earth at that time) will recognize their error in the midst of their depravity, repent of their sin, and accept Jesus as Messiah (Romans 11:26). They will call Him back (Hosea 5:15), after which Jesus will return and defeat the Antichrist and his armies (Revelation 19:11-21). Christ's one-thousand-year reign on the earth (Revelation 20:4) will then begin. Isaiah 11:11 relates to these miraculous events and disproves the allegorical mindset which advocates that the church has replaced ethnic Israel as the rightful owner of the land:

> *Then it will happen on that day that the Lord Will again recover the second time with His hand the remnant of His people, who will remain, From Assyria, Egypt, Pathros, Cush, Elam, Shinar, Hamath, And from the islands of the sea.* (Isaiah 11:11)

The worldwide regathering of the Jews in belief (in faith) is discussed here. This regathering is the *"second"* one. The first worldwide regathering, in unbelief, began in 1948 and continues today. The worldwide regathering in unbelief is also discussed in passages such as Ezekiel 20:33-38, Ezekiel 22:17-22, and Zephaniah 2:1-2, and is climaxed by the Jews in the land (and throughout the world) choosing to exercise faith in Christ at the end of the Tribulation. The subsequent worldwide regathering in belief will be for the purpose of entering and enjoying the Millennium, a regathering assisted by the Gentile nations (validated by Isaiah 11:10, 14:2, 49:22, and 66:18-21). Note: The regathering of the Jews from Babylon in the Old Testament was not a worldwide regathering. Therefore, it cannot be viewed as the worldwide regathering in unbelief.

To comprehend how a *"second"* worldwide regathering of the Jews is to occur (in a state of belief), we must first understand how the Jews are driven out of the land of Canaan after their worldwide regathering in unbelief (their first worldwide regathering). The following input addresses this subject matter.

When a large portion of the Jews sign a *"covenant"* with the Antichrist (Daniel 9:27), the Tribulation will begin. Yet, in the *"middle"* of the seven years of Tribulation, the Antichrist will break the *"covenant"* and seek to destroy every Jew on the earth (Daniel 9:27; Revelation 12:1-6, 13-17). When these events transpire, the Jews will *"flee to the mountains"* (Matthew 24:15-22) in *"the wilderness"* (Revelation 12:6, 14). *"Bozrah,"* located in modern day southern Jordan, is a mountainous wilderness and the location of the Second Coming. These facts are based on Isaiah 34:1-8, Isaiah 63:1-6, Micah 2:12 (the phrase, *"in the fold,"* is interpreted, *"Bozrah,"* in the King James Bible), and Habakkuk 3:3 (*"Teman"* and *"Mount Paran"* are both in the vicinity of Bozrah).

After Jesus returns to save the believing remnant of the Jews at Bozrah and defeats the Antichrist and his armies, the Jews from throughout the world (all of whom will have exercised personal repentance and faith while depraved) will be regathered to the holy land to enjoy the blessings of the Messianic Kingdom. Thus, all Jews on the earth at the end of the Tribulation will be followers of Christ. These events will fulfill Romans 11:26, which states that *"all Israel will be saved"*—ushering in the fulfillment of the *"new covenant"* of Jeremiah 31:31-34. So, Jesus established the New Covenant (through His death, burial, and resurrection), and the church was birthed in Acts 2—and now lives under this covenant. The New Covenant will not be fulfilled in totality, however, until the end of the Tribulation—when every Jew living on the earth repents and believes while depraved. The church will have been raptured (and taken to heaven) before these amazing events transpire.

I desired to include several quotes from two of John Piper's sermons. My request was denied, so a paraphrased version is presented below.

Piper views the church as having replaced the nation of Israel as God's covenant people. Consequently, he views the promises made to Abraham, including those regarding the land, as inherited allegorically by the church, "spiritual Israel" in Piper's mind. He teaches, in fact, that being born of Jewish descent does not make a person heir of the land or any other promise of God. Therefore, after stating that Arab nations have no right to molest Israel, he maintains that secular Israel today cannot claim a divine right to the land. Hence, he advocates that physical Israel seek a peaceful settlement based on justice, mercy, and practical feasibility. In turn, he stresses that Washington (our representatives) seek a just settlement in accord with the historical and social claims of both peoples. He then, holding fast to his allegorical view of the Scriptures, teaches that all Jewish and Gentile believers will inherit the land through inheriting the world (the new heavens and the new earth)—which includes the land.

Piper overlooks a vital truth from Isaiah 11:11:

> *Then it will happen on that day that the Lord Will again recover the second time with His hand the remnant of His people, who will*

> *remain, From Assyria, Egypt, Pathros, Cush, Elam, Shinar, Hamath, And from the islands of the sea.* (Isaiah 11:11)

Note the phrase *"...again recover the second time with His hand the remnant of His people..."* The fact that the Jews will be regathered a *"second time"* from throughout the world means that a first regathering is required. The contextual view of Isaiah 11:11-16 confirms that this *"second"* regathering of Israel (from throughout the world) occurs after *"all Israel will be saved"* (Romans 11:26) at the end of the Tribulation. Thus, a regathering in belief must occur. If a *"second"* regathering is required, a regathering in belief, the present regathering, the first which began in 1948 and continues today, is a regathering in unbelief—as shown by the spiritual climate among Jews in the land today. This Scriptural sequence leaves room for a majority of the Jewish nation, presently being regathered in a state of unbelief, to be driven out of the land in association with the events of the second half of the Tribulation—eventually resulting in every Jew who remains on the earth at the end of the Tribulation choosing Jesus as Messiah. In conjunction with Christ's Second Coming, these Jewish believers will be regathered from throughout the world to inhabit the land originally promised to Abraham and his descendants. They will inhabit the land in their physical bodies, living alongside Jews such as Abraham, Moses, and Joshua in resurrected bodies. This view is obtained through a literal interpretation of the Scriptures, not an allegorical one. The Scriptural fact is that the unbelieving Jews occupying the land today have every right to that piece of real estate, especially since their return in unbelief was prophesied in passages such as Ezekiel 20:33-38, Ezekiel 22:17-22, and Zephaniah 2:1-2. We should be elated that Israel is presently in the land. In fact, their return is one of the greatest (as well as most significant) miracles of the modern era—that is, if you view the Old Testament Scriptures literally, as did Jesus.

In *Tabletalk,* Ligonier Ministries, Inc., spring of 1999, page 2, R.C. Sproul Jr., another Reformed theologian, writes regarding Israel:

> We're not dispensationalists here....We believe that the church is essentially Israel. We believe that the answer to, "What about the Jews?" is, "Here we are." We deny that the church is God's "plan B." We deny that we are living in God's redemptive parenthesis.
>
> There, we are again one people. In His holy and heavenly temple there is neither Jew nor Greek, male nor female, pre-mil nor post-mil. There, we are all together, the Israel of God, princes with God, and the *ekklesia*, the set apart ones. [68]

If Piper and Sproul, along with the majority of their extreme and hyper-Calvinist associates (and some moderate Calvinists as well), are correct in their beliefs regarding the present state of Israel (that physical Israel has no more right to the land than the Palestinians or anyone else), then to support the Jews above any other nation is improper. However, such a mindset would breed contempt against physical Israel should she pursue her rightful ownership of the land. Can you see how a distorted view of Israel in the present state of affairs could result in a lack of support from the church in particular and the United States in general? History has proven what would occur should America turn her back on the Jewish people, especially since God has promised to bless those who bless physical Israel and curse those who don't (Genesis 12:3)—Egypt in the book of Exodus, for example, and Germany under Hitler. Hence, how believers in America perceive Israel greatly affects the future of this nation!

The body of Christ must be aware of this error within Calvinism. If a large number of Calvinists view the present Jewish state as irrelevant, and in some cases a menace to society, how will the Jews be viewed by the church of the future should Calvinism have its way—especially if Calvinism goes unchallenged by those who disagree with its distorted logic and irresponsible reasoning?

Our study is revealing how the different schools of thought within Christendom view God's heart. We have a great need to heed Paul's admonishment to the church at Corinth:

> *Brethren, do not be children in your thinking; yet in evil be babes, but in your thinking be mature.* (1Corinthians 14:20)

If we remain *"children in"* our *"thinking,"* we will be swept away by every wind of doctrine that permeates the post-modern society of our day. We must graduate from "milk" to the "meat" of the Word (Hebrews 5:14), the one thing capable of leading us into a deeper understanding of the God we serve. What the Spirit of God can do with truth etched on the mind of the passionate student of God's Word is nothing short of amazing. In fact, Paul addresses this very issue in 2Timothy 2:7:

> *Consider what I say, for the Lord will give you understanding in everything.* (2Timothy 2:7)

Paul, writing to the church at Corinth in 1Corinthians 2:16, desired that they take the mind the Lord had given them, *"the mind of Christ,"* and use it to think through what they believed regarding God's heart. Why? How a believer views God is everything. Thus, a proper *"understanding"* (2Timothy 2:7) of the Scriptures is vital if God is to be correctly perceived. John Piper, in his DVD series, *TULIP,* Disk 1, Session 1, INTRODUCTION TO TULIP, Title 5, Chapter 2, states:

> Bad theology dishonors God and hurts people....Right doctrine honors God and blesses people.[69]

I could not agree with him more. The issue is not who wins the argument, or debate, or who influences the most people to consider a different way of thinking. The issue is whose mindset, perspective, theology, or point of view lines up with every word of every verse included in the Scriptures. Undoubtedly, "bad theology dishonors God and hurts people." The converse is true as well, for "right doctrine honors God and blesses people." My prayer is that, above all things in life, we might view God as the Scriptures portray Him—nothing more, nothing less. To Him be the glory!

Few sections of Scripture are more highly debated than Ephesians 1:1-12. Topics such as predestination and election (the believer's chosenness) create a hornets' nest of dissension. We covered verses 1-12 of Ephesians 1 in considerable depth in the first book of this series, *God's Heart as it Relates to Foreknowledge/Predestination*, where we focused mainly on how these passages relate to foreknowledge and predestination. We will deal primarily with Ephesians 1:4 and 1:11 here, taking what we discussed in *God's Heart as it Relates to Foreknowledge/Predestination* and linking it to new areas of discussion. The fresh input should be enjoyable.

Ephesians 1:4

> *just as He chose us in Him before the foundation of the world, that we should be holy and blameless before Him....*

John Piper (a Reformed theologian), in his work, *The Pleasures of God*, page 136, writes regarding his view of election:

> ...God chooses freely who will belong to his people. God does not simply elect Christ and then wait on human self-determination, to govern who will be "in Christ."...Your union with Christ is the choice and work of God. Election is not God's choice of an unknown group of people who come to Christ by virtue of their self-determining power. Election is the act of God by which he determines who will be in Christ....[70]

Piper adds the following concerning Ephesians 1:4 in his footnote on that same page:

> ...Is this Paul's way of saying that God did not choose specific individuals? ...There is nothing about the phrase "chose us in Christ" that demands a nonindividual interpretation. On the contrary, there are numerous passages that demand an individual view of election, e.g. Matthew 22:14; 1Corinthians 1:27-28; James 2:5; John 6:37, 39, 10:16, 26; 13:18; 17:6, 9, 24; Romans 8:28-33; 11:4-7, etc....neither does the literal wording of Ephesians 1:4 fit the corporate interpretation: "[God] chose us in him before the foundation of the world." The ordinary meaning of the word for "choose" in verse 4 is to "select" or "pick out" of a group (see Luke 6:13; 14:7; John 13:18; 15:16, 19). The object of this "selection" is said to be "us." So the natural meaning of the verse is that God selects his people from all humanity, before the foundation of the world; and he does this "in Christ," that is, by viewing them in relation to Christ their redeemer.[71]

Does Piper properly evaluate the phrase, "in Christ," or, *"in Him"* (Ephesians 1:4) in the last sentence of his previous quote? Or does, "in Christ," or, *"in Him,"* (Ephesians 1:4) mean much more? In other words, is Piper correct in stating "that God selects his people from all humanity, before the foundation of the world; and he does this 'in Christ,' that is, <u>by viewing them in relation to Christ their redeemer</u>" (emphasis added)? Is something missing in Piper's evaluation of Ephesians 1:4? Does being chosen *"in Him,"* "in Christ," mean that God only views the elect "in relation to Christ," as Piper advocates? Or does it mean to be actually placed into Christ, God's *"chosen one"* (Isaiah 42:1; Luke 9:35), subsequent to exercising personal repentance and faith while depraved, to reap the wonderful blessings associated with living inside God's Son? I am in agreement with the second sequence because of verses such as 2Corinthians 5:17, Colossians 2:10, Ephesians 2:6, Colossians 2:11, and 2Corinthians 5:21. Note the blessings associated with being placed *"in Him"* (*"in Christ"*) <u>after</u> believing on Him:

> *Therefore if any man is in Christ, he is a new creature; the old things passed away; behold, new things have come.* (2Corinthians 5:17)

> *and in Him you have been made complete, and He is the head over all rule and authority;* (Colossians 2:10)

> *and raised us up with Him, and seated us with Him in the heavenly places, in Christ Jesus,* (Ephesians 2:6)

> *and in Him you were also circumcised with a circumcision made without hands, in the removal of the body of the flesh by the circumcision of Christ;* (Colossians 2:11)
>
> *He made Him who knew no sin to be sin on our behalf, that we might become the righteousness of God in Him.* (2Corinthians 5:21)

We will expose the error in Piper's interpretation shortly. The subsequent quotes from John MacArthur Jr. and John Calvin, when exposed to the same questioning, also fall short.

John MacArthur, Jr., in his work, *The Love of God*, page 161, states:

> The plan of redemption was made not after Adam fell but before the beginning of creation. This is consistent with everything Scripture says about election. The saved are chosen in Christ "before the foundation of the world" (Eph. 1:4)....[72]

MacArthur confirms that he perceives believers as having been elected to salvation "in Christ 'before the foundation of the world'"—a theological mindset found contradictory in our study of *God's Heart as it Relates to Foreknowledge/Predestination.*

John Calvin comments on Ephesians 1:4 in *Institutes*, Book 2, Chapter 17, Section 2:

> The nature of this mystery is to be learned from the first chapter to the Ephesians, where Paul, teaching that we were chosen in Christ, at the same time adds, that we obtained grace in him. How did God begin to embrace with his favour those whom he had loved before the foundation of the world, unless in displaying his love when he was reconciled by the blood of Christ? As God is the fountain of all righteousness, he must necessarily be the enemy and judge of man so long as he is a sinner. Wherefore, the commencement of love is the bestowing of righteousness, as described by Paul: "He has made him to be sin for us who knew no sin; that we might be made the righteousness of God in him," (2Co 5: 21). He intimates, that by the sacrifice of Christ we obtain free justification, and become pleasing to God, though we are by nature the children of wrath, and by sin estranged from him....[73]

Calvin classifies as "mystery" the contradiction inundating Calvinism—that God chose/elected the elect to salvation "in Christ" from eternity past, by means of an eternal decree. Because election must be preceded by God's foreknowledge (1Peter 1:1-2), such an arrangement is impossible (nothing can precede an eternal decree, as was verified in *God's Heart as it Relates the Foreknowledge/Predestination*, the first book of this *God's Heart* series). Ephesians 1:4 teaches, rather, that believers are chosen to office once they are placed in Christ subsequent to repenting and exercising faith while depraved—a truth that will be examined more thoroughly in *God's Heart as it Relates to Election/Atonement/Grace/Perseverance*, the fourth book of this *God's Heart* series.

James White, in *The Potter's Freedom*, also gives commentary regarding Ephesians 1:4. He attempts unsuccessfully to prove that we were chosen to salvation in Christ *"before the foundation of the world."* (Permission was requested to quote this resource, but permission was denied.)

Rebuttal:

Will the quotes from Piper, MacArthur, and Calvin stand without contradiction when taken through all of God's Word? In other words, is their view of the phrase, *"just as He chose us in Him,"* (Ephesians 1:4) proper, or could the phrase point to something else? It points to something totally different than what these men suppose.

The argument presented by Piper, MacArthur, Calvin, and White (along with other Calvinists) is highly contradictory due to their extreme view of sovereignty, which disallows man the freedom of choice, especially in respect to the depraved choosing Christ as Savior. Consequently, they view God as having chosen certain individuals to salvation, His choice occurring before man arrives on the earth—in fact, from eternity past by means of an eternal decree. This mindset has caused them to either miss, or ignore, some amazingly vital truths. Warning: The following rebuttal presents the same truth in a variety of ways, redundancy being necessary for a clear understanding.

The title of our present study is *God's Heart as it Relates to Sovereignty/Free Will*. Serious questions must be answered if we are to come away with a healthy view of these subjects. For instance, did God sovereignly choose (from eternity past, and therefore, before man exists in his mother's womb) who will be the recipient of eternal life? Or does man possess a free will that allows him (in his depravity) to make that choice for himself while being drawn by God—since God draws all, every human being, desiring that all be saved (John 1:9; 6:44; 12:32; 16:8; 1Timothy 2:4; 2Peter 3:9)? The subsequent commentary attempts to properly answer these questions by viewing Ephesians 1:4 based on all of the verses in

God's Word instead of a select few interpreted out of context.

Are believers chosen in Christ solely as a result of God's sovereign choice, His choice occurring from eternity past by means of an eternal decree and, thus, before an individual is born? Or are New Testament believers chosen in Christ once God places them in Christ, His *"chosen one"* (Isaiah 42:1; Luke 9:35), after they have repented and believed while depraved? We will allow Scripture alone to determine which mindset is correct.

All New Testament believers are chosen by God. Ephesians 1:4 validates this truth, especially since the *"us"* in the verse points to believers:

> *just as He chose us in Him....* (Ephesians 1:4)

The question, therefore, is where, when, and how New Testament believers are chosen. As to where they are chosen, they are chosen *"in Him,"* that is, "in Christ." So, New Testament believers are not chosen to be placed into Christ; for Ephesians 1:4 states that they are chosen once they are *"in Him,"* that is, once they are "in Christ." Hence, New Testament believers are chosen once they are in Christ, after they repent and believe while depraved. This fact verifies the impossibility of Ephesians 1:4 teaching that God chose the elect to salvation in Christ (*"in Him"*) from eternity past (by means of an eternal decree). View Diagrams 2 and 8 in the Reference Section for additional input.

Now that we have determined where a New Testament believer is chosen, we must determine when and how a New Testament believer is chosen. The Calvinist would say that New Testament believers were chosen/elected to salvation (not to office) from eternity past, and therefore, before they (the elect) experience physical birth (read the preceding quotes from Piper, MacArthur, and Calvin). They use the phrase, *"before the foundation of the world"* (Ephesians 1:4), in an attempt to prove that God did this (so called) choosing to salvation from eternity past (by means of an eternal decree) and, thus, well before the chosen/elect arrive on the earth. However, the phrase, *"just as He chose us in Him before the foundation of the world,"* when taken through all of the Scriptures, can be found to mean something totally different. Consider the following:

God's Word teaches that Christ is the New Testament believer's *"life"*:

> *When Christ, who is our life, is revealed, then you also will be revealed with Him in glory.* (Colossians 3:4)

1John 5:11 states that eternal life is in God's *"Son,"* and that this *"life"* has been given to the New Testament believer:

> *And the witness is this, that God has given us eternal life, and this life is in His Son.* (1John 5:11)

John 3:15 validates the same truth:

> *that whoever believes may in Him have eternal life.* (John 3:15)

Romans 6:23 confirms the identical fact:

> *For the wages of sin is death, but the free gift of God is eternal life in Christ Jesus our Lord.* (Romans 6:23)

And lastly, 1John 5:20:

> *And we know that the Son of God has come, and has given us understanding, in order that we might know Him who is true, and we are in Him who is true, in His Son Jesus Christ. This is the true God and eternal life.* (1John 5:20)

Clearly, *"eternal life"* is *"in Christ Jesus our Lord"* (Romans 6:23).

Suddenly our study becomes extremely captivating, for the Scriptures also teach that the depraved (during the church age) who exercise repentance and faith are then *"baptized into"* the eternal Christ through the power of the eternal Holy *"Spirit"* (1Corinthians 12:13), *"crucified with Christ"* (Romans 6:3; 6:6; Galatians 2:20), *"buried with Him"* (Colossians 2:12), made *"new"* (2Corinthians 5:17), and *"raised...up with Him"* (Ephesians 2:6). Thus, believers during the church age are placed into Christ (the moment they make the choice to repent and believe while depraved), crucified, buried, made new, and raised with Christ. Therefore, when they are placed in Christ and made new, they receive His kind of life, a special type of life, eternal life, life with no beginning and no end. As a result of the type of life received, New Testament believers are perceived by the Father as having always been in Christ, even from eternity past—although their point of entry into Christ occurred the moment they repented and believed. This truth significantly impacts the interpretation of the phrase, *"just as He chose us in Him before the foundation of the world,"* (Ephesians 1:4). In fact, it verifies that the depraved can choose Christ prior to spiritual regeneration, meaning that God does <u>not</u> make the choice for any New Testament believer to be saved/justified. This view also allows a hoard of additional Scriptures to be interpreted void of contradiction. The same harmony does not exist within Calvinism's perception of the passage, as confirmed by the subsequent comments.

All forms of Calvinism teach that God, from eternity past, and by means of an eternal decree, chose the elect in Christ. They believe that His choice and His alone determined who would or would not be saved. Could the Scriptures teach, however, that a New Testament believer, once he makes the choice to repent and believe while depraved, is placed into Christ, the Father's *"chosen one"* (Isaiah

42:1; Luke 9:35), and at that time is chosen/elected? In other words, is it possible that depraved individuals who live during the church age, through choosing to exercise faith in Christ, are chosen/elected "in Christ" (*"in Him"*—Ephesians 1:4) after repenting and believing? I deem the Scriptures to be teaching exactly that, and Scripture alone will be employed to validate these findings.

If the preceding paragraphs seem difficult to comprehend, don't be concerned. Help is on the way. We will first address how New Testament believers are placed into Christ and follow with what this placement "in Christ" (*"in Him"*—Ephesians 1:4) means.

The eternal *"Holy Spirit...baptized"* [placed] us into Christ's *"body"* once we exercised repentance and faith while depraved:

> *For by one Spirit we were all baptized into one body, whether Jews or Greeks, whether slaves or free, and we were all made to drink of one Spirit.* (1Corinthians 12:13)

> *Or do you not know that all of us who have been baptized into Christ Jesus...?* (Romans 6:3a)

Yes, once we repented and believed while depraved, we were *"baptized into one body"* (the *"body"* of *"Christ Jesus"*) through the Person of the eternal *"Spirit"* (1Corinthians 12:13; Romans 6:3a). This truth means that our old self, sinful nature, old man, Adamic nature, etc. (all synonymous) was *"baptized into His* [Christ's] *death"* (Romans 6:3b), a significant truth to recognize and understand:

> *Or do you not know that all of us who have been baptized into Christ Jesus have been baptized into His death?* (Romans 6:3)

These thoughts line up perfectly with Paul's words recorded in Romans 6:6 and Galatians 2:20, again confirming that our *"old self"* (sinful nature, old man, Adamic nature, etc.) was *"crucified with Christ"*:

> *knowing this, that our old self was crucified with Him,...* (Romans 6:6a)

> *"I have been crucified with Christ; and it is no longer I who live, but Christ lives in me; ...* (Galatians 2:20a)

Our old self (sinful nature, old man, Adamic nature, etc.) was also *"buried"* with Christ:

> *Therefore we have been buried with Him through baptism into death,...* (Romans 6:4a)

> *having been buried with Him in baptism,...* (Colossians 2:12a)

After the old self (old man, Adamic nature, sinful nature, etc.) was crucified and buried with Christ, we were also *"raised up with"* Christ:

> *and raised us up with Him, and seated us with Him in the heavenly places, in Christ Jesus,* (Ephesians 2:6)

> *having been buried with Him in baptism, in which you were also raised up with Him through faith in the working of God, who raised Him from the dead.* (Colossians 2:12)

The person raised from the grave is the *"new creature"* (new man) of 2Corinthians 5:17, the holy and blameless saint who replaced the old man (sinful nature, Adamic nature, old self, etc.) we used to be:

> *Therefore if any man is in Christ, he is a new creature; the old things passed away; behold, new things have come.* (2Corinthians 5:17)

"In Christ" we also received *"every spiritual blessing"*:

> *Blessed be the God and Father of our Lord Jesus Christ, who has blessed us with every spiritual blessing in the heavenly places in Christ,* (Ephesians 1:3)

According to Ephesians 1:13, we were also *"sealed in Him"* once we were placed *"in Him"*:

> *In Him, you also, after listening to the message of truth, the gospel of your salvation-- having also believed, you were sealed in Him with the Holy Spirit of promise,* (Ephesians 1:13)

New Testament believers are *"sealed in Him"* (in Christ) after they repent and exercise faith while depraved. Consequently, for God to have chosen believers *"in Him"* (to salvation) from eternity past by means of an eternal decree is impossible. (Please read the following sentence multiple times before continuing; its content is critical.) The depraved can choose to accept Christ while on earth and, due to the eternal life they instantaneously receive through becoming new creations in Christ, be viewed by God as having been in Christ from eternity past (review Diagram 8 in the Reference Section). Colossians 3:4, 1John 5:11, John 3:15, Romans 6:3-4, and

1John 5:20 confirm this truth.

New Testament believers also become *"the righteousness of God"* through being placed *"in Him,"* in Christ:

> *He made Him who knew no sin to be sin on our behalf, that we might become the righteousness of God in Him.* (2Corinthians 5:21)

New Testament believers are *"made complete" "in Him"*:

> *and in Him you have been made complete, and He is the head over all rule and authority;* (Colossians 2:10)

Once New Testament believers are *"in Him,"* they are *"circumcised with a circumcision made without hands"*:

> *and in Him you were also circumcised with a circumcision made without hands, in the removal of the body of the flesh by the circumcision of Christ;* (Colossians 2:11)

Those *"in Christ"* receive *"no condemnation"* from God:

> *There is therefore now no condemnation for those who are in Christ Jesus.* (Romans 8:1)

Interestingly, Paul viewed some of his fellow New Testament believers as being *"in Christ before"* him:

> *Greet Andronicus and Junias, my kinsmen, and my fellow prisoners, who are outstanding among the apostles, who also were in Christ before me.* (Romans 16:7)

Note that *"Andronicus and Junias...were in Christ before"* Paul. Therefore, they had to be placed *"in Christ"* and chosen/elected *"in Christ"* after repenting and believing while depraved—after arriving on the earth. Had they been chosen/elected in Christ to salvation from eternity past, by means of an eternal decree, with no choice in the matter (Calvinism's view), Paul could not have known that they had been placed *"in Christ"* and chosen/elected *"in Christ"* before him. These undeniable facts again verify the importance of considering every word, of every phrase, of every verse, before drawing conclusions regarding what we are to believe.

New Testament believers are *"sanctified"* in their person (in soul and spirit), not in their behavior, the moment they are placed *"in Christ Jesus"*:

> *to the church of God which is at Corinth, to those who have been sanctified in Christ Jesus, saints by calling, with all who in every place call upon the name of our Lord Jesus Christ, their Lord and ours*: (1Corinthians 1:2)

"Grace" is given to church saints *"in Christ Jesus"*:

> *I thank my God always concerning you, for the grace of God which was given you in Christ Jesus,* (1Corinthians 1:4)

1Corinthians 1:30 relates very well with the present subject matter:

> *But by His doing you are in Christ Jesus, who became to us wisdom from God, and righteousness and sanctification, and redemption,* (1Corinthians 1:30)

God placed us *"in Christ Jesus,"* which lines up perfectly with 1Corinthians 12:13 (where we earlier discovered that God, the Holy Spirit, was responsible for baptizing us into Christ once we chose to repent and believe while depraved). Keep in mind that our point of entry into Christ was after physical birth and after we chose to accept Him while depraved.

We, while living on the earth, are also privileged to be seated *"in the heavenly places, in Christ"* (Ephesians 2:6):

> *and raised us up with Him, and seated us with Him in the heavenly places, in Christ Jesus,* (Ephesians 2:6)

Those who are placed *"in Christ"* are *"created"* into a totally new person *"in Christ":*

> *For we are His workmanship, created in Christ Jesus for good works....* (Ephesians 2:10)

We were made *"alive"* spiritually in conjunction with being placed *"in Christ Jesus"*:

> *Even so consider yourselves to be dead to sin, but alive to God in Christ Jesus.* (Romans 6:11)

These verses provide ample leeway for the New Testament believer to repent and believe while depraved, a subject addressed extensively in *God's Heart as it Relates to Depravity*, the third book of this *God's Heart* series.

The New Testament believer is granted *"life"* only in conjunction with being placed *"in Christ Jesus"*:

> *For the law of the Spirit of life in Christ Jesus has set you free from the law of sin and of death.* (Romans 8:2)

And finally, Peter wrote the following regarding the *"Peace"* made available to *"all who are in Christ"*:

> *Greet one another with a kiss of love. Peace be to you all who are in Christ.* (1Peter 5:14)

The verses just cited only partially describe what New Testament believers receive once placed *"in Christ,"* for an abundance of additional passages could have been incorporated. They are sufficient proof, however, to render unacceptable the idea that God chose/elected certain persons to salvation *"in Christ"* from eternity past by means of an eternal decree, as Piper, MacArthur, White, Calvin, and other Calvinists suppose. Note again MacArthur's previous quote:

> The plan of redemption was made not after Adam fell but before the beginning of creation. This is consistent with everything Scripture says about election. The saved are chosen in Christ "before the foundation of the world" (Eph. 1:4)....[74]

Such statements present an insurmountable problem for the Calvinists when taken through all the verses that relate to the believer's chosenness "in Christ." For example, let's assume for a moment that Piper, MacArthur, and their contemporaries are correct in concluding that God chose/elected the elect to salvation "in Christ" from eternity past. Should this be the case, then all of the elect would be *"new"* creations (2Corinthians 5:17), *"blessed...with every spiritual blessing"* (Ephesians 1:3), and made *"the righteousness of God"* (2Corinthians 5:21) prior to physical birth. Scripture teaches, however, that no one is chosen "in Christ" (from eternity past) to be saved (the Arminian, Calvinist, and Reformed view). New Testament believers are chosen to "office" (given a *"special"* spiritual *"gift"*—1Peter 4:10) once they are placed "in Christ" after repenting and believing while depraved. Of course, as was mentioned earlier, the eternal life received by New Testament believers in conjunction with being placed "in Christ" and made new (after repenting and believing while depraved) allows God to view them as having always been "in Christ." Thus, our point of entry into Christ was in time (after repenting and exercising faith while depraved), yet God perceives us as having always been "in Christ" due to the type of life we received in conjunction with being saved—life with no beginning or end. Amazing!

Let's again read Ephesians 1:4:

> *just as He chose us in Him before the foundation of the world, that we should be holy and blameless before Him....* (Ephesians 1:4)

New Testament believers are chosen *"in Him,"* that is, in Christ, and are instantaneously made *"holy and blameless before Him"* (*"before"* the Father) as a result of being placed in the Father's holy and blameless Son. Recognize, once again, that New Testament believers are not chosen to be placed *"in Him,"* but rather are chosen once they are *"in Him."* Therefore, this verse is not communicating that those who are chosen in Christ will, at some point after being chosen, become holy and blameless. Instead, it communicates that the moment a person is placed in Christ he is chosen (to office) and made *"holy and blameless."* Consequently, had the "elect" been chosen/elected in Christ to salvation from eternity past, they would have been made *"holy and blameless"* in eternity past—saved in eternity past. Thus, Reformed Theology's theory relating to the believer's chosenness/election presents a variety of contradictions impossible to reconcile (as is also the case with Arminianism and all forms of Calvinism—consult Diagram 8 in the Reference Section). For these systems to be valid, all inconsistencies regarding the believer's chosenness must be resolved—a total impossibility without yielding to mystery, which is no solution at all.

All men and women, including believers, are born in rebellion to God—in fact, born as *"children of wrath"* (Ephesians 2:3). Paul writes in Ephesians 2:3:

> *Among them we too all formerly lived in the lusts of our flesh, indulging the desires of the flesh and of the mind, and were by nature children of wrath, even as the rest.* (Ephesians 2:3)

The fact that all of Adam's sons (all persons) are born *"children of wrath"* (Ephesians 2:3) is confirmed on numerous occasions in the Scriptures, so let's observe how Ephesians 2:3 fits the context of Ephesians 2:1-7:

> *And you were dead in your trespasses and sins, 2 in which you formerly walked according to the course of this world, according to the prince of the power of the air, of the spirit that is now working in the sons of disobedience. 3 Among them we too all formerly lived in the lusts of our flesh, indulging the desires of the flesh and of the mind, and were by nature children of wrath, even as the rest. 4 But God, being rich in mercy, because of His great love with which He loved us, 5 even when we were dead in our*

> *transgressions, made us alive together with Christ (by grace you have been saved), 6 and raised us up with Him, and seated us with Him in the heavenly places, in Christ Jesus, 7 in order that in the ages to come He might show the surpassing riches of His grace in kindness toward us in Christ Jesus.* (Ephesians 2:1-7)

These verses teach that even New Testament believers, when they arrive on the earth as unbelievers, are born *"dead in trespasses and sins"* (v.1). New Testament believers also *"walked according to the course of this world, according to the prince of the power of the air, of the spirit that is now working in the sons of disobedience"* in their spiritually unregenerated state (v.2). They *"lived in the lusts of"* their *"flesh," "indulging the desires of the flesh and of the mind, and were by nature children of wrath, even as the rest"* (v.3). *"But God"* in His *"mercy"* and *"love"* (v.4), *"even when we were dead in our transgressions, made us alive together with Christ (by grace you have been saved)* (v.5), *and raised us up with Him, and seated us with Him in the heavenly places, in Christ Jesus* (v.6), *in order that in the ages to come He might show the surpassing riches of His grace in kindness toward us in Christ Jesus"* (v.7).

Paul clearly teaches (here and elsewhere in Scripture) that all persons are born dead (spiritually separated from God) and rebellious toward God—yet possess enough truth (light) to exercise repentance and faith while depraved (a subject discussed in great depth in *God's Heart as it Relates to Depravity*, the third book of this *God's Heart* series). If the Calvinists' perception of the believer's chosenness/election in Christ (Ephesians 1:4) is correct (the elect, in their opinion, having been chosen <u>to salvation</u> in Christ from eternity past), then those chosen (in Christ) to salvation from eternity past are born hostile to God and *"children of wrath"* (Ephesians 2:3). Thus, Calvinism's perception of the New Testament believer's chosenness *"in Him"* (in Christ) can't withstand the litmus test of the full counsel of God's Word, as verified below:

1. Based on all forms of Calvinism (including Reformed Theology), the elect are chosen to salvation *"in Him"* (in Christ) from eternity past, by means of an eternal decree. Read MacArthur's previous quote. Also note Piper's previous quote.

2. The Scriptures teach, however, that all who are chosen *"in Him"* (Ephesians 1:4) are simultaneously made *"holy and blameless"* (Ephesians 1:4).

3. A New Testament believer is not in Christ until he is baptized into Christ through the avenue of the Holy Spirit subsequent to repenting and believing while depraved (1Corinthians 12:13).

4. Also consider that one cannot be chosen *"in Him"* (Ephesians 1:4) before one is *"in Him"*—a Biblical fact.

5. The Scriptures teach that to be *"in Christ,"* or *"in Him,"* means that a person has been made *"new"* (2Corinthians 5:17), *"complete"* (Colossians 2:10), *"the righteousness of God"* (2Corinthians 5:21), and is *"seated...in the heavenly places, in Christ Jesus"* (Ephesians 2:6).

6. The Scriptures also communicate that all persons are born *"children of wrath"* (Ephesians 2:3).

7. Holding Calvinism (including Reformed Theology) accountable to the entire body of truth contained in the Scriptures, we detect the error in their ideology. Had we been chosen *"in Him"* (Ephesians 1:4) to salvation before we were born (Calvinism's view), we would have arrived on the earth as *"new"* creations (2Corinthians 5:17) yet *"children of wrath"* (Ephesians 2:3). Impossible!

8. If the elect could somehow possess this blessed standing prior to physical birth, yet lose it through physical birth, how could they gain it back—having lost that which only Christ, through dying once (Hebrews 6:1-6; 10:10, 14), can provide? Impossible again!

Can a non-contradictory interpretation of Ephesians 1:4 be found? Of course! Free will permits the depraved the opportunity to exercise personal repentance and faith and instantaneously receive salvation—through being placed *"in Christ"* (2Corinthians 5:17). This choice made by the depraved results in the Holy Spirit placing them in Christ (1Corinthians 12:13), into the Father's *"chosen one"* (Isaiah 42:1; Luke 9:35), Christ Himself. They are not only saved at that point, but are also chosen (Ephesians 1:4) to function in a special office/position within Christ's body as a result of having been placed in God's *"chosen one"* (Isaiah 42:1; Luke 9:35), Jesus the Messiah. Being God's perfect Son, Jesus wasn't chosen to salvation. He was chosen to the office of Messiah. Hence, when a New Testament believer is placed into Christ, he is not only saved/justified, but chosen to office as well.

The previous input allows us to understand that the disciples weren't chosen to salvation from eternity past. They were chosen to office/position (chosen as apostles—during Christ's First Coming) according to John 6:70:

> *Jesus answered them, "Did I Myself not choose you, the twelve, and yet one of you is a devil?"* (John 6:70)

How could Judas, described by Christ as *"a devil,"* have been chosen to salvation? Contradictions would abound in such an arrangement!

Let's take a moment to review what Ephesians 1:4 confirms regarding the New Testament believer:

> Once New Testament believers are placed in Christ (after repenting and believing while depraved), they are viewed by the Father as having always been in Christ—even from *"before the foundation of the world"* (Ephesians 1:4), although they arrived on earth in rebellion to God. How can this be? They receive eternal life, life with no beginning or end, once they repent and believe (while depraved) and are placed in the eternal Son. The Father then sees them as having always been "in Christ." (Review Diagram 8 in the Reference Section.) This sequence allows Ephesians 1:4 to be interpreted void of contradiction.

The chosenness addressed in Ephesians 1:4 is an individual chosenness, not a "corporate" one. Why would I mention this subject? Arminianism holds to a corporate chosenness, as verified by the following quote from, *Why I am not a Calvinist,* written by Jerry L. Walls and Joseph R Dongell, page 76:

> ...As Markus Barth expresses it, "Election in Christ must be understood as the election of God's people. Only as members of that community do individuals share in the benefits of God's gracious choice." This view of election most fully accounts for the corporate nature of salvation, the decisive role of faith and the overarching reliability of God's bringing his people to their desired end.[75]

Walls and Dongell, agreeing with Barth and his Arminian view of the Scriptures, believe that the church was chosen to salvation in Christ from eternity past. In our previous study of *God's Heart as it Relates to Foreknowledge/Predestination,* we addressed why this view is unacceptable. The Scriptures teach that New Testament believers are placed into Christ, and chosen individually (one at a time) in Christ, once they repent and believe while depraved. Therefore, God did not look into the future to see who would believe and, as a result, elect (choose) those individuals to salvation as a corporate body by means of an eternal decree—as the Arminian believes. (Review Diagrams 4 and 5 in the Reference Section.)

When Calvinists are challenged to address the previously mentioned inconsistencies within Calvinism, their answer, for the most part, is that the "elect" do not become righteous, holy, blameless, new creations, who are blessed with every spiritual blessing, etc., when they are elected to salvation in Christ from eternity past (note that they view the elect as having been elected to salvation from eternity past instead of being elected to office after repenting and believing while depraved). They would say that these blessings are received later—when they are saved/justified. The Scriptures will not allow such an interpretation. Based on Ephesians 1:4, for example, the person who is placed in Christ, and as a result chosen in Him (to office), is also made *"holy and blameless before Him."* Additional verses, such as 1Corinthians 12:13, 2Corinthians 5:17, Ephesians 2:6, Colossians 2:10, and 2Corinthians 5:21 have been cited to confirm that the New Testament believer is granted a wealth of blessings the moment he is placed into Christ, and chosen/elected to office in Christ—Christ being God's *"chosen one"* (Isaiah 42:1; Luke 9:35) Who was chosen to the office of Messiah. The previous Scriptures have proven that Calvinism's dogma will not stand—the idea that the "elect" were chosen to salvation "in Christ" from eternity past, by means of an eternal decree, so that after arriving on the earth they might become members of God's family through God's irresistible grace.

2Timothy 1:9 is used by Calvinists in an attempt to support their view of Ephesians 1:4:

> *who has saved us, and called us with a holy calling, not according to our works, but according to His own purpose and grace which was granted us in Christ Jesus from all eternity,* (2 Timothy 1:9)

Many Calvinists view this verse in the following manner: God chose the "elect" to salvation (*"in Christ"*) from eternity past (by means of an eternal decree) so He might draw them to Himself through irresistible grace at some point after their physical birth. This belief stems from the falsehood that man, in his depravity, is incapable of choosing Christ. However, our present study confirms that free will fits flawlessly into 2Timothy 1:9; for once a person chooses (while depraved) to accept Jesus as Savior, he receives His kind of life, eternal life (through being placed in the eternal Son), and the Father perceives that individual as having always been in Christ. Therefore, the New Testament believer can be viewed as having been *"in Christ Jesus from all eternity"* (2Timothy 1:9), in Christ when He was *"crucified"* (Romans 6:6; Galatians 2:20), in Christ when He was resurrected (Colossians 2:12), in Christ when He ascended (Ephesians 2:6), and in Christ at this present moment (Colossians 3:3).

2Timothy 1:9 can also be perceived as follows: God purposed the plan of salvation through His holy Son *"from all eternity,"* no one being saved until personal repentance and faith are exercised while depraved.

God can't have a relationship with an idea, especially since a person does not exist until he is conceived in the womb (reference the notes on Jeremiah 1:5 in *God's Heart as it Relates to Foreknowledge/Predestination*, the first book of this

God's Heart series). Disregarding this fact, Piper writes in his previous quote relating to Ephesians 1:4:

> ...So the natural meaning of the verse is that God selects his people from all humanity, before the foundation of the world; and he does this "in Christ," that is, by viewing them in relation to Christ their redeemer.[76]

How can God select "his people from all humanity," and "in Christ," before they become a people? Yet the Calvinists consider this mindset plausible in an effort to disregard the fact that the depraved can repent and believe—as well as protect their unhealthy view of sovereignty. We addressed this subject in *God's Heart as it Relates to Foreknowledge/Predestination*. We will examine it in greater depth in *God's Heart as it Relates to Depravity*, the third book of this *God's Heart* series.

This present discussion exposes the error in John Piper's words from *TULIP,* Disk 2, Session 7, UNCONDITIONAL ELECTION: GOD CHOSE INDIVIDUALS, Title 5, Chapter 1:

> Before the foundation of the world, as God contemplated the world to come, He [God] chose who would be rescued from the fall and who wouldn't be, without respect to their having met any conditions as the basis of His choice.[77]

Piper follows later with this next statement, which contradicts all that he has taught regarding the Reformed view of God's sovereignty and how it (Reformed Theology) perceives man as totally incapable of choosing Christ while depraved:

> Whether you are among the elect depends on one thing–will you submit to Jesus, period. And then you may know.[78]

Do you see the inconsistencies in Piper's thinking? On the one hand, he teaches that God's choice, not man's choice, determines who will be part of the elect. On the other hand, he states that being part of the elect is dependent upon one's willingness to "submit" (make a choice) to follow Christ. So which is it? Both can't be true, being diametrically opposed. I realize that many Calvinists would view Piper's words as communicating that God first spiritually regenerates the elect and gives them repentance and faith, after which they are free to choose to repent and believe. In this case, however, spiritual regeneration would precede repentance and faith, a direct violation of verses such as John 1:12, Acts 16:31, Acts 26:18, Romans 10:9-10, and 2Corinthians 3:16—which verify that repentance and faith precede spiritual regeneration. Should spiritual regeneration precede repentance and faith, followed by salvation, the "elect" of Calvinism would be saved twice—

since Scripture equates spiritual regeneration with salvation. John 1:12, Acts 16:31, Acts 26:18, Romans 10:9-10, and 2Corinthians 3:16 will be examined in detail later in this series.

Another serious problem exists within Calvinism. How does a Calvinist's view of election help those persons who perceive themselves as part of the non-elect, yet desire to become part of the elect? What could these individuals possibly do to become part of the elect should God have failed to elect them to salvation from eternity past? In fact, how can any Calvinist be sure of his election when he must persevere in order to prove that his election is certain? What sort of works would need to be performed to validate that he has been elected/chosen? Calvinism doesn't define such matters for its followers because Scripture doesn't teach such matters, leaving the Calvinists uncertain about their destiny to the very end.

In *God's Heart as it Relates to Depravity*, the third book of this *God's Heart* series, we will confirm even further that a depraved man can choose Christ—a truth that lines up perfectly with our present study of Ephesians 1:4. Thus, he can accept Jesus, after which God baptizes (places) him (the old man) into Christ through the power of the Holy Spirit (1Corinthians 12:13), kills him (Romans 6:3; 6:6; Galatians 2:20), buries him (Colossians 2:12), and makes him *"new"* (2Corinthians 5:17). This new man is *"in Christ"* (2Corinthians 5:17), in the Father's *"chosen one"* (Isaiah 42:1 and Luke 9:35), and is chosen/elected to office (given *"a special gift"* to function within Christ's body—1Peter 4:10). He is the possessor of eternal life as well, life with no beginning or end, and is viewed by the Father as having always been in Christ and chosen/elected. Hence, Paul was free to write, *"just as He chose us in Him before the foundation of the world"* (Ephesians 1:4).

Let's once again review what we have gleaned regarding this subject matter to make certain we have it. A great difference exists between understanding a topic versus possessing the ability to express it with clarity. For this reason, I have chosen to be redundant—having learned the value of repetitiveness while teaching these truths over the past three decades.

Jesus, God's chosen one, was chosen to the office of Messiah – not to salvation. The New Testament believer, having been placed into the chosen one, is chosen to office as well.

Jesus is God's *"chosen one"* of Isaiah 42:1 and Luke 9:35, Who was chosen/elected to office, the office of Messiah—not to salvation. Therefore, once the New Testament believer is placed into God's *"chosen"* Son (subsequent to exercising repentance and faith while depraved) he is chosen/elected to office as well. The Father then perceives that individual as having always been in Christ, and chosen in Christ, as a result of the eternal life he received once placed in Christ (after repenting and believing while depraved). Thus, we were not chosen from eternity past to be saved, but were chosen to office once we were placed in Christ after repenting and believing while depraved. By means of this special office/position within Christ's body, God has opportunity to bring glory to Himself through our unique gifting. With this mindset, all contradictions vanish, and Ephesians 1:4 fully validates free will.

We will examine additional positive ramifications of this wonderful truth when we address the New Testament believer's "chosenness" in *God's Heart as it Relates to Election/ Atonement/ Grace/ Perseverance*, the fourth book of this *God's Heart* series. I, in the meantime, sense a need to encourage you by giving you a taste of what is to come.

Can you comprehend the inconsistencies associated with the Calvinists' argument relating to the believer's chosenness/election, which they must uphold in an attempt to validate their improper view of God's sovereignty—a view which forces them to perceive the depraved as void of a free will to choose Christ? The following quote from Dave Hunt's, *What Love is This?*, page 237, addresses this error within Calvinism:

> The Canons of Dort explained this tenet as "the unchangeable purpose of God, whereby, before the foundation of the world, he hath out of mere grace, according to the sovereign good pleasure of his own will, chosen, from the whole human race...a certain number of persons to redemption in Christ...." Unconditional Election is the outworking of Calvinism's extreme view of sovereignty, which allows man no freedom of choice or action even to sin. That being the case, if anyone is to be saved, God must choose for them. Out of Unconditional Election, then, comes predestination to salvation.[79]

Properly interpreting *"just as He chose us in Him before the foundation of the world"* (Ephesians 1:4) is tremendously important. The first button in an improper buttonhole in this instance communicates a totally different salvation (and God) than is portrayed in the Scriptures. Are you seeing, to even a greater degree, the need for God's people to understand what is communicated here? One of the purposes of this study is to expose believers, in fact, all who are interested in this subject matter, to the truth that Calvinism is easily refuted. It has become increasingly amazing to me the degree to which the principles of Romans 1-8, especially the verses relating to the believer's identity in Christ, have assisted in this process. We are seeking a proper view of God's heart. Misinterpret the believer's chosenness (election), however, and you misinterpret His heart. Yes, it is that critical!

We must be equipped to answer the following questions pertaining to Ephesians 1:4 before moving forward. Feel free to reference the previous materials should you need them.

1. Are individuals chosen (elected) to salvation from eternity past by means of an eternal decree? If not, to what are New Testament believers chosen/elected?

2. How can a person, who chooses to accept Christ while depraved, be viewed by God as having been in Christ from eternity past?

3. The Calvinists believe that the Father has chosen the elect "in Christ" to salvation from eternity past (by means of an eternal decree)—that being the beginning point (so to speak) of their chosenness in Christ (read John MacArthur's previous quote). How does the fact that all persons arrive on the earth as enemies of God refute such thinking?

4. Describe how the free will of man (man's ability to choose Christ in his depraved state) fits into Ephesians 1:4, *"just as He chose us in Him before the foundation of the world, that we should be holy and blameless before Him,"* without contradiction.

Before moving to Ephesians 1:11, let's consider for a moment how our study of *God's Heart as it Relates to Foreknowledge/Predestination* (the first book of this *God's Heart* series) relates to our present observations. We discovered there that believers could not have been predestined or chosen/elected to salvation (as the Calvinists suppose) from eternity past by means of an eternal decree. After all, God's decrees are eternal. In other words, they have always existed in His eternal mind and heart. Because Romans 8:29 requires foreknowledge ("foreknowledge" meaning, "to know beforehand") to precede the New Testament believer's predestination, and 1Peter 1:1-2 requires foreknowledge to precede the New Testament believer's election/chosenness, the Calvinists' view (which has believers predestined and elected/chosen to salvation from eternity past by means of an eternal decree) allows no room for foreknowledge to precede either predestination or election in this arrangement (refer to the diagrams in the Reference Section, especially Diagram 2). What then is the solution? The Scriptures teach that a person (during the church age) is predestined (to receive a glorified body) and chosen/elected (to office) when he is placed into the eternal Son, the Father's *"chosen one"* (Isaiah 42:1) and made new—after having made a choice while depraved to repent and believe. God then perceives that individual as having always been in Christ due to his having been placed in His eternal Son—the very Source of life with no beginning or end. Great news! (Review Diagram 8 in the Reference Section if necessary.)

Ephesians 1:11c

> *...who works all things after the counsel of His will,* (Ephesians 1:11c)

We addressed this phrase in our previous study of *God's Heart as it Relates to Foreknowledge/Predestination,* but we will add to that discussion.

Many Calvinists perceive Ephesians 1:11 as teaching that God wills all things that occur, as confirmed by Arthur Pink's words from *The Attributes of God*, page 39:

> The absolute and universal supremacy of God is affirmed with equal plainness and positiveness in the New Testament. There we are told that God "worketh all things after the counsel of his own will" (Eph. 1:11)–the Greek for "worketh" means "to work effectually."...
>
> Here then is a sure resting-place for the heart. Our lives are neither the product of blind fate nor the result of capricious chance, but every detail of them was ordained from all eternity, and is now ordered by the living and reigning God....[80]

Pink's interpretation of Ephesians 1:11 depicts God as ordaining, from eternity past, all things that transpire.

Alvin L. Baker, *Berkouwer's Doctrine of Election: Balance or Imbalance*? (Phillipsburg, NJ: Presbyterian and Reformed Publishing Co., 1981), page 174, writes regarding Ephesians 1:11:

> "God works 'all things,' including sin, according to His eternal will."[81]

John MacArthur (a Reformed theologian), in *The Love of God*, page 109, records:

> What God has purposed, He will also do....God is not at the mercy of contingencies. He is not subject to His creatures'

> choices. He "works all things after the counsel of His will"....Nothing occurs but that which is in accord with His purposes....Nothing can thwart God's design, and nothing can occur apart from His sovereign decree....He does all His good pleasure....[82]

On page 165 of that same work, MacArthur states:

> ...God is sovereign, but He is by no means impersonal or irrational. The difference between fatalism and the biblical doctrine of divine sovereignty is really quite profound. It is true, as Scripture teaches, that "God works all things after the counsel of His will" (Eph. 1:11)...But He does not govern arbitrarily or whimsically.
>
> Nor does God impose His sovereign will in a way that does violence to the will of the creature. The outworking of His eternal plan in no way restricts the liberty of our choices or diminishes our responsibility when we make wrong choices. Unbelief is forced on no one. Those who go to a Christless eternity make their own choice in accord with their own desires. They are not under any compulsion from God to sin....People who choose unbelief make that choice in full accord with their own desires.[83]

Reformed Theology perceives Ephesians 1:11 as teaching that God decrees all things. Yet, according to MacArthur, God does not "impose His sovereign will in a way that does violence to the will of the creature." Do you detect the contradiction? He goes on to say, "Unbelief is forced on no one." Again, do you perceive the contradiction? Nor are the non-elect of Reformed Theology "under any compulsion from God to sin" (MacArthur). Once again, do you see the contradiction? MacArthur's words are pointless, hollow, and meaningless because the non-elect of Reformed Theology walk in "unbelief" because God, being the cause of all things (based on their ideology), never grants them opportunity to believe.

Rebuttal:

If the Calvinists are correct in their interpretation of Ephesians 1:11, it leads to one of the most horrific conclusions imaginable. We will continue to discover, therefore, as we progress, the need to take every thought through all the Scriptures rather than a select few. The following is a much-needed lesson if the name of the Sovereign Ruler of the universe is to be protected.

Does Ephesians 1:11c teach that all events are determined by God's will?

> *...who works all things after the counsel of His will,* (Ephesians 1:11c)

We must consider a variety of issues before drawing our conclusions. First, *"works,"* from the root word *energeo* ("to be at work, to work, to do"), can also be interpreted "energizes." Thus, God *"energizes all things after the counsel of his will."*

In Colossians 1:29 we read:

> *And for this purpose also I labor, striving according to His power, which mightily works within me.* (Colossians 1:29)

"Works" in this case is also *energeo*, so the verse can be rendered:

> *And for this purpose also I labor, striving according to His power, which mightily energizes within me.*

This positive energizing is brought about by God. Even in Philippians 2:13, as well as a variety of additional passages, Paul teaches that God works in (energizes) those who are His. Note Paul's words in 1Corinthians 12:6:

> *And there are varieties of effects, but the same God who works all things in all persons.* (1Corinthians 12:6)

"Persons" in this verse is in italics in the NASB, meaning that it was inserted for "clarification." This insertion can cause confusion, for some individuals have used this passage in an attempt to prove that God works (energizes) all things in all people—the redeemed and unredeemed alike. Paul is not teaching that all "energizing" comes from God. In fact, when 1Corinthians 12:6 is studied in context with surrounding verses, you find that Paul is addressing God's energizing of believers only within the realm of the spiritual gifts.

This truth lines up perfectly with 2Thessalonians 2:9, for Satan has the ability to energize as well:

> *that is, the one whose coming is in accord with the activity of Satan, with all power and signs and false wonders.* (2Thessalonians 2:9)

"Activity" in 2Thessalonians 2:9 can be viewed as an "energizing," being derived from the Greek *energeia,* meaning "operative power."

Even in Ephesians 2:1-2, and in agreement with Paul's words of 2Thessalonians 2:9, we find that *"working"* is from the Greek *energeo:*

> *And you were dead in your trespasses and sins, in which you formerly walked according to the course of this world, according to the prince of the power of the air, of the spirit that is now working* [energizing] *in the sons of disobedience.* (Ephesians 2:1-2)

Satan energizes whomever he can in an attempt to thwart God's ultimate plan, the plan that Paul describes so vividly below:

> *He made known to us the mystery of His will, according to His kind intention which He purposed in Him with a view to an administration suitable to the fulness of the times, that is, the summing up of all things in Christ, things in the heavens and things upon the earth....* (Ephesians 1:9-10)

Paul's words of Colossians 1:16-20 also tie in well here:

> *For by Him all things were created, both in the heavens and on earth, visible and invisible, whether thrones or dominions or rulers or authorities-- all things have been created by Him and for Him. And He is before all things, and in Him all things hold together. He is also head of the body, the church; and He is the beginning, the first-born from the dead; so that He Himself might come to have first place in everything. For it was the Father's good pleasure for all the fullness to dwell in Him, and through Him to reconcile all things to Himself, having made peace through the blood of His cross; through Him, I say, whether things on earth or things in heaven.* (Colossians 1:16-20)

The Father's *"will"* is to one day sum *"up all things in Christ, things in the heavens and things upon the earth..."* (Ephesians 1:9-10)—and in so doing, *"reconcile all things to Himself...through"* Christ (Colossians 1:20). This *"summing up"* (Ephesians 1:10) is fulfilled <u>after</u> the unredeemed are judged and ushered away to eternal punishment. After *"all things"* that remain *"in the heavens...and earth"* are summed up *"in Christ"* (Ephesians 1:10), the Son will present *"all"* these *"things"* to the Father, *"that God may be all in all"*:

> *But now Christ has been raised from the dead, the first fruits of those who are asleep. For since by a man came death, by a man also came the resurrection of the dead. 22 For as in Adam all die, so also in Christ all shall be made alive. But each in his own order: Christ the first fruits, after that those who are Christ's at His coming, then comes the end, when He delivers up the kingdom to the God and Father, when He has abolished all rule and all authority and power. For He must reign until He has put all His enemies under His feet. The last enemy that will be abolished is death. For He has put all things in subjection under His feet. But when He says, "All things are put in subjection," it is evident that He is excepted who put all things in subjection to Him. And when all things are subjected to Him, then the Son Himself also will be subjected to the One who subjected all things to Him, that God may be all in all.* (1Corinthians 15:20-28).

Through what means will this chain of events come to fruition? God *"works"* (Ephesians 1:11), or energizes, *"all things"* in that direction, and according to His plan, without in any way violating man's free will. In other words, God has the ability to strengthen individuals in such a way that His ultimate plan can be fulfilled without removing their freedom of choice—some people choosing to continue in disobedience and dying lost and condemned, other people accepting Jesus as Savior while depraved and receiving eternal life.

A perfect example of this truth is God's dealings with Pharaoh. After Pharaoh chose to disregard Moses' request, through listening to Satan's lies and being influenced by Satan's energizing, God hardened (strengthened) Pharaoh's heart so Pharaoh might carry out (have the courage to walk in) what he (Pharaoh) had originally chosen. (We will address this subject in more detail later). God is sovereign enough, however, to use Pharaoh's unwise choices as a means to bring about His desired end. After all, Pharaoh's disobedience, which resulted in Israel's eventual release from Egypt, paved the way for Jesus' birth in Bethlehem later in the nation's history. This series of events illustrates sovereignty at its best, unfolding with every person on God's earth possessing the freedom to choose as he pleases. Truly, what a sovereign God we serve! With these facts in mind, consider the following input which, by the way, agrees perfectly with what we have previously gleaned from Ephesians 1:11.

Since both God and Satan are in the business of energizing, we must make certain to attach ourselves to the proper energy source. This proper attachment requires a choice, as validated by James 4:7:

> *Submit therefore to God. Resist the devil and he will flee from you.* (James 4:7)

The terms *"Submit"* and *"Resist"* demand that man possess the ability to choose between good and evil. Proper choices, however, require large quantities of discernment, discernment obtained through one avenue only—the Word of God activated by the Spirit of God (Hebrews 5:13-14). Consequently, a lack of passion for truth yields a deficiency of discernment. Without discernment, *"the devil"* (James 4:7) makes certain that our unwise choices prevent us from experiencing the abundant life made available through Christ.

We next need to consider the words, *"all things,"* in the phrase, *"who works all things after the counsel of His will"* (Ephesians 1:11). Paul cannot be teaching that God causes "all events" or "all that transpires," for Luke 7:30 states:

> *But the Pharisees and the lawyers rejected God's purpose for themselves, not having been baptized by John.* (Luke 7:30)

> *But the Pharisees and lawyers rejected the counsel of God against themselves, being not baptized of him.* (Luke 7:30 KJV)

We learn here that God's ultimate *"purpose"* (*"counsel"*) for the universe will stand even though some individuals refuse to participate in it. However, as God's *"purpose"* unfolds, He desires that not one person *"perish"*:

> *"The Lord is not slow about His promise, as some count slowness, but is patient toward you, not wishing* [willing] *for any to perish but for all to come to repentance"* (2Peter 3:9).

Therefore, if a man perishes, he does so as a result of his own choice—that is, unless God sometimes wills what He does not desire, a total impossibility (yet an idea accepted by Reformed Theology). Should God sometimes will what He doesn't desire (the Reformed view), He would on occasion desire what He does not bring to pass—a mindset that abolishes rather than establishes His sovereignty.

2Timothy 2:26 adds interesting input to our present topic of discussion:

> *and they may come to their senses and escape from the snare of the devil, having been held captive by him to do his will.* (2Timothy 2:26)

Should God will *"all things"* (Ephesians 1:11) that come to pass, as Reformed Theology maintains, and Satan (at the same time) hold individuals *"captive...to do his will"* (2Timothy 2:26), we could conclude that (1) God's will is equivalent to

Satan's will, making Satan God's ally or (2) Satan's will is stronger than God's will, stripping Him of His sovereignty. Is this a correct picture of our omnipotent and righteous God? Of course not! Thus, the Calvinists' unhealthy view of God's sovereignty, which perceives God as willing all things, ends up tarnishing His sovereignty while dishonoring His character. Again we observe the tumultuous end result when a system of thought is allowed to rest on a faulty foundation.

The Father would be thrilled should all mankind choose to accept His Son. They could then become part of *"the summing up of all things in Christ"* (addressed in Ephesians 1:9-10) and the wonderful events that follow—bringing much pleasure to the Father. But verses such as John 1:11-12 and John 5:40 teach that the depraved must choose Christ before becoming part of God's family, an option which most individuals have disregarded.

Now we arrive at yet another interesting topic—*"the counsel of God's will,"* addressed in Ephesians 1:11c:

> *...who works all things after the counsel of His will.* (Ephesians 1:11c)

The word *"counsel"* is tremendously important, for without it the verse would read, "who works all things after His will." But if God should work all things after His will, sin would be God's will and Satan His friend and ally. So, Paul inserts *"counsel"* to make certain he communicates otherwise.

The phrase, *"The counsel of His will,"* is best understood by realizing that God made a decision, with no one holding Him hostage, to grant man the freedom of choice. Yet, even with man possessing this freedom, God's purposes will stand. How can this be? God *"works"* ("energizes") all things, but *"works"* doesn't point to a controlled or rigid manipulation but rather to a God-energized stimulation (as was the case with Pharaoh, a subject addressed earlier). Hence, God can grant man a free will—yet strengthen man to carry out man's choices without violating man's freedom of choice. In this arrangement, *"all things"* are worked according to *"the counsel of His will"* without requiring God to will sin. Should God will sin, He would judge man for committing the very sin He willed. Impossible—that is, if He is to remain just. God's sovereignty is truly amazing!

Matthew 23:37 further substantiates that God's will can be rejected by man:

> *"O Jerusalem, Jerusalem, who kills the prophets and stones those who are sent to her! How often I wanted to gather your children together, the way a hen gathers her chicks under her wings, and you were unwilling.* (Matthew 23:37)

Isaiah 65:12 is in agreement:

> *I will destine you for the sword, And all of you shall bow down to the slaughter. Because I called, but you did not answer; I spoke, but you did not hear. And you did evil in My sight, And chose that in which I did not delight."* (Isaiah 65:12)

Numerous Scriptures confirm man's free will. Regardless of the number of people who choose to obey or disobey, however, God's sovereign will cannot be thwarted—His will being to eventually sum up *"all things in Christ, things in the heavens and things upon the earth"* (as we addressed earlier in our discussion of Ephesians 1:9-10). Thus the phrase, *"who works all things after the counsel of His will"* (Ephesians 1:11), relates to the fulfillment of His ultimate will and plan addressed in Ephesians 1:9-10—man all the while possessing the freedom of choice. By no stretch of the imagination is Paul communicating that men are robots, unable to choose anything but what God has ordained to come to pass. Such an arrangement would strip God of His justice, making Him the cause of man's disobedience while requiring that man obey.

If Paul, in Ephesians 1:11, were teaching that God wills all things that come to pass, then God would cause the believer's sin while willing the "non-elect's" disobedience. God would also mandate Satan's disobedience. Should such an arrangement be valid, Satan would be God's assistant, ally, and helper. The Scriptures teach otherwise: Matthew 16:23; Mark 8:33; Luke 4:1-13; 13:10-17; 22:3; Acts 5:3; 13:10; 26:18; Romans 16:20; 2Corinthians 2:11; 11:14; 1Thessalonians 2:18; 2Thessalonians 2:8-10; 1Timothy 5:14-15; Revelation 12:9; 20:7-10.

Are you seeing, to even a greater degree, the need for this study? We must never allow ourselves to experience the following:

> "Men stumble over the truth from time to time, but most pick themselves up and hurry off as if nothing happened." (Winston Churchill)[84]

I trust you will not "hurry off" from this study as though "nothing happened" due to a resolute commitment to an opposing, yet contradictory ideology.

Romans 9:10-23

The remainder of *God's Heart as it Relates to Sovereignty/Free Will* focuses on Romans 9:10-23. Reformed theologians rely heavily upon this section of Scripture while attempting to validate their view of God's sovereignty, especially as to how it (their brand of sovereignty) relates to Reformed Theology's unconditional election to salvation. However, these passages teach the free will of man, while maintaining God's sovereignty, in a most captivating fashion. (The *Romans 9* study produced by this ministry addresses all thirty-three verses of this remarkable chapter should you be interested in additional input.)

Many believers fear these passages due to the seemingly endless debate surrounding their content. Yet, they are easily understood when taken through the full counsel of God's Word. Paul, in fact, continues answering the questions he received from the unbelieving Jews in Romans 3:1-8—Paul's response proving that a person's salvation is independent of lineage or good works and totally dependent on whether he has exercised faith in Christ. Thus, the backdrop of Romans 3:1-8 will be examined first before basking in the truths of Romans 9:10-23.

The Awesome Backdrop of Romans 3:1-8

The first eight verses of Romans 3 are covered in more detail in two resources produced by this ministry: (1) *The Foundational Truths of Romans 1-8* and (2) *Advancing in Romans 1-8*. In these eight passages we discover the fundamental error of Paul's Jewish opponents' theology: They incorrectly defined the word "chosen." Instead of viewing themselves as having been chosen as the nation through which the Father would bear the Messiah (and taking that wonderful truth to the Gentiles), they perceived the entire nation as having been chosen (by God) to salvation prior to physical birth. They perceived God's choice as having determined the destiny of the Jews—never their own choices. Therefore, refusing to change their definition of "chosen" caused them to consistently reject Paul's gospel. Why would they need to repent and exercise faith in Christ for salvation (as Paul prescribed) had Jehovah sealed their salvation prior to their being born? Hence, in Romans 9:10-23, Paul continues disproving and exposing his Jewish opponents' contradictory theology (which began surfacing in this epistle through their questions of Romans 3:1-8), by confirming that the nation's chosenness/election had nothing to do with salvation but everything to do with the special "office" to which Israel (the nation) had been called—that of bearing the Messiah and taking the news of His coming to the Gentiles.

We will now transition into Romans 9:10, keeping in mind that in Romans 9:1-9 Paul mentions: (1) The abundant blessings God has poured out upon the nation of Israel—the Jews (2) God's choice of Abraham as the father of the Jewish nation (3) The Messiah would be born through Isaac's lineage rather than Ishmael's—Isaac being Abraham's son of faith, Ishmael Abraham's son of the flesh.

Paul picks up with Jacob and Esau (the sons of Isaac through Rebekah) in Romans 9:10, and through verse 23 presents some of the most debated (and misunderstood) passages in the entirety of God's Word. Actually, they are easily understood when studied in context, so enjoy our trek through this most amazing segment of God's Word.

Romans 9:10 *And not only this, but there was Rebekah also, when she had conceived twins by one man, our father Isaac;*

Paul mentions Rebekah and her "*twins*" (Jacob and Esau) born through Isaac. As we examine this passage (along with Romans 9:11-23), we must not lose sight of Paul's emphasis. He stresses, time after time, that God's spiritual blessings (and promises) are never received on the basis of lineage or good works. He proves, in fact, that believers alone are Abraham's spiritual children (Galatians 3:29), whether Jew or Gentile. This truth in no way implies that God's blessings and promises were removed from physical Israel and given exclusively to the church (which began in Acts 2). Thus, Paul is not teaching that God is finished with physical Israel and is concerned with the church alone. Paul is communicating that the believers within physical Israel have obtained blessings that the unbelievers within the nation have not. 1Peter 2:1-10 verifies this fact, for First Peter was written to Jews who had accepted Jesus as Messiah.

Some theologians view Romans 9:10-13 as teaching that God chose Jacob (the individual) to salvation over Esau (the individual) prior to physical birth. John Piper (a follower of Reformed Theology) in, *The Justification of God*, page 62, is in agreement with this unbiblical mindset. Let's read Romans 9:10-13 along with some of Piper's comments:

> *And not only this, but there was Rebekah also, when she had conceived twins by one man, our father Isaac; for though the twins were not yet born, and had not done anything good or bad, in order that God's purpose according to His choice might stand, not because of works, but because of Him who calls, it was said to her, "THE OLDER WILL SERVE THE YOUNGER" Just as it is written, "JACOB I LOVED, BUT ESAU I HATED."* (Romans 9:10-13)

Note Piper's words:

> Paul's purpose in referring to God's choice of Jacob over Esau is to show that there is no way to evade the implications of God's unconditional election here....God's choice of Jacob over Esau cannot be due to any human distinctives possessed by birth (like Jewishness) or action (like righteousness). It is based solely on God's own free and sovereign choice.[85]

On page 73 of this same work, Piper states:

> ...God maintains his sovereign purpose of election by determining before they are born who will belong to the "saved"

> among Israel. And this determination is not based on what any man is or wills or does ([Rom.] 9:11, 12, 16), but solely on God whose word or call effects what he purposes (9:12b). For this reason Paul is confident that God's word had not fallen but is in fact working out God's sovereign purpose even in the unbelief of Paul's kinsmen.[86]

Piper records the following on page 175 of this same work. Remember these words for future reference:

> ...the divine decision to "hate" Esau was made "before they were born or had done anything good *or evil*" (9:11)....[87]

On pages 203-204, Piper pens:

> ...So Paul gives the better example of Jacob and Esau who had exactly the same parents, occupied the same womb at the same time and were appointed for their respected destinies before they were born....[88]

John Calvin, in *Institutes*, Book 3, Chapter 22, Section 4, states:

> Paul, while he concedes that in respect of the covenant they were the holy offspring of Abraham, yet contends that the greater part of them were strangers to it, and that not only because they were degenerate...but because the principal point to be considered was the special election of God, by which alone his adoption was ratified. If the piety of some established them in the hope of salvation, and the revolt of others was the sole cause of their being rejected, it would have been foolish and absurd in Paul to carry his readers back to a secret election. But if the will of God (no cause of which external to him either appears or is to be looked for) distinguishes some from others, so that all the sons of Israel are not true Israelites, it is vain for any one to seek the origin of his condition in himself. He afterwards prosecutes the subject at greater length, by contrasting the cases of Jacob and Esau. Both being sons of Abraham, both having been at the same time in the womb of their mother, there was something very strange in the change by which the honor of the birthright was transferred to Jacob, and yet Paul declares that the change was an attestation to the election of the one and the reprobation of the other.[89]

Yet, note what Genesis 25:21-23 states regarding the twin brothers:

> *21. And Isaac prayed to the LORD on behalf of his wife, because she was barren; and the LORD answered him and Rebekah his wife conceived. 22. But the children struggled together within her; and she said, "If it is so, why then am I this way?" So she went to inquire of the LORD. And the LORD said to her, 23. "Two nations are in your womb; And two peoples shall be separated from your body; And one people shall be stronger than the other; And the older shall serve the younger."* (Genesis 25:21-23)

By using the phrases, *"Two nations," "two peoples,"* and *"one people"* in Genesis 25:23, God confirms that He is speaking of nations (Israel and Edom)—not individuals (Jacob and Esau). Most theologians who believe that God determines man's destiny from eternity past make only a passing reference to Genesis 25:23 because it negates their argument for "individuals" in Romans 9:10-13. Therefore, John MacArthur (a Reformed theologian) only comments on the phrase, *"the older will serve the younger,"* in *The MacArthur Study Bible*. He totally sidesteps the phrase, *"Two nations are in your womb,"* because his Reformed view cannot withstand the truth of the entire passage.

Should Romans 9:10-13 teach that God elected and predestined all of the elect to salvation in eternity past, Romans 8:30 would communicate that the elect not yet born are already *"called," "justified,"* and *"glorified"* due to *"predestined," "called," "justified,"* and *"glorified"* being in the past tense in the Greek:

> *and whom He predestined, these He also called; and whom He called, these He also justified; and whom He justified, these He also glorified.* (Romans 8:30)

Be sure to digest what is stated in the previous paragraph regarding Romans 8:30 before continuing. Our *Romans 1-8* course has much more to say about the subject should you need additional input.

The total impossibility of God having elected a portion of mankind to salvation prior to physical birth becomes increasingly apparent.

Romans 9:11 *for though the twins were not yet born and had not done anything good or bad, so that God's purpose according to His choice would stand, not because of works but because of Him who calls,*

Let's allow our findings regarding Romans 9:10 to assist our study of Romans 9:11. Because Paul is addressing nations here (instead of individuals), two truths are necessary to take into account: (1) The Jews (the nation of Israel) descended from Jacob (2) The Edomites descended from Esau. In Romans 9:11, Paul confirms that God's *"choice"* of Jacob (Israel) over Esau (the Edomites) was made while both Jacob and Esau were in their mother's womb.

Reformed Theology advocates that God chose Jacob (the individual) to salvation but rejected Esau (the individual) prior to either child experiencing physical birth—an error exposed by passages such as Genesis 25:23). Remember, nations are the issue here, not individuals. We will observe in Romans 9:12-13 that God's choice of Israel (the nation) to become His wife and bear the Messiah had nothing to do with her merit, for she was sinful. Thus, He didn't choose Israel for the purpose of granting every Jew salvation (as some Jews have erroneously concluded)—also validated by Paul in Romans 1-8. God chose Israel to bless the world through bearing the Messiah, Jesus Christ (a Jew in His humanity), and to take the news of His coming to the Gentiles. Consequently, Romans 9:11 doesn't present information relating to where Jacob and Esau would spend eternity (as some individuals wrongly suppose). Romans 9:11 speaks of God's choice of the nation of Israel as the nation through which the Messiah would be born. She was to take this incredible news to the Gentiles, which she has yet to do.

A "key" to unlocking the confusion associated with terms such as election and predestination is presented next. This "key" is covered in detail in *God's Heart as it Relates to Foreknowledge/Predestination*, the first book of this *God's Heart* series; so I will be brief. Pay close attention, reading the following more than once if necessary—and it will probably be necessary!

The words, *"according to,"* in Romans 9:11 are employed 790 times in the New American Standard Bible, 725 in the King James, and on occasion are found more than once in some verses. "*According to*" is used in relation to predestination in Ephesians 1:11, an intriguing passage indeed:

> *... having been predestined according to His purpose who works all things after the counsel of His will,* (Ephesians 1:11)

(Remember that words and phrases are underlined for emphasis, and input inserted in brackets [ ] for clarification, in certain verses included in this study.)

Ephesians 3:11, which teaches that God's purposes are "*eternal*," adds critical insight into Ephesians 1:11:

> *This was in accordance with the eternal purpose which He carried out in Christ Jesus our Lord,* (Ephesians 3:11)

Coupling Ephesians 1:11 with Ephesians 3:11, we can conclude: (1) The New Testament believer is *"predestined according to His* [God's] *purpose"* (Ephesians 1:11) (2) God's *"purpose,"* which is *"eternal"* (Ephesians 3:11), must precede the believer's predestination. How can this conclusion be valid? Should you reference the 790 instances where *"according to"* is used in the NASB, you would find that in each case the action or entity that follows *"according to"* (such as God's *"purpose"* in Ephesians 1:11) must occur (or exist) before the action or entity that precedes *"according to"* (such as *"predestined"* in Ephesians 1:11). Consequently:

If **A** is according to **B**

Then **B** precedes **A**

Let's combine our findings and draw some reliable conclusions:

(1) God's purposes are eternal (Ephesians 3:11)—they have no beginning.

(2) Because man is "*predestined* [A] *according to God's purpose* [B]" (Ephesians 1:11), God's purpose (as it relates to predestination) must precede man's predestination ("*according to*" causes B to always precede A).

(3) Predestination, therefore, could not have occurred in eternity past by means of an eternal decree, for such an arrangement disallows predestination to follow God's eternal purpose—as required by Romans 9:11. Stated differently, God's eternal purpose could not precede an eternal predestination. Thus, predestination could not have occurred in eternity past by means of an eternal decree—refuting all forms of Calvinism and Arminianism. (*God's Heart as it Relates to Foreknowledge/Predestination,* the first book of this *God's Heart* series, provides more input regarding the subject.)

Let's take our gleanings and dig deeper into Romans 9:11:

> *for though the twins were not yet born, and had not done anything good or bad, in order that God's purpose according to His choice might stand,...* (Romans 9:11)

The wording of this verse differs from the norm. On the surface it seems to communicate that God's *"choice"* precedes His *"purpose,"* but it actually confirms that His *"purpose"* precedes His *"choice."* Because *"might stand"* relates to *"purpose,"* Paul is saying that God's *"choice"* was made after His *"purpose"* already existed—and that it was made so His *"purpose...might stand."* John Piper (a Reformed theologian) agrees (note that he renders "*choice*" as election):

> ...In Rom 9:11c Paul says that God elected Jacob and not Esau "in order that the purpose of God according to election might remain."... (*The Justification of God*, page 49)[90]

Even the English Standard Version renders this phrase as:

> *...in order that God's purpose of election might continue,...* (Romans 9:11 ESV)

John MacArthur, a Reformed theologian, is in agreement. Note his commentary on Romans 9:11 in *The MacArthur Study Bible*:

> ...Rather, God's choice of Jacob resides solely in His own sovereign plan....[91]

Wayne Grudem, also a Reformed theologian, is likewise in agreement. Note his words from page 287 of *Bible doctrine*:

> ...Nothing that Jacob or Esau would do in life influenced God's decision; it was simply in order that his purpose of election might continue.[92]

Romans 9:11 lines up perfectly with Ephesians 3:11, which teaches that God's purposes are "*eternal.*" Romans 9:11 verifies, in fact, that God's "*purpose*" precedes His "*choice.*" Romans 9:11, therefore, cannot be communicating that God chose certain individuals to salvation from eternity past by means of an eternal decree. Such an arrangement would prevent God's eternal purpose from preceding His choice. Thus, Romans 9:11 disproves Calvinism's "*unconditional election*" to salvation by means of an eternal decree.

Conclusion: Romans 9:11 teaches that God is free to choose nations (in time) to fulfill His "*purpose*" without removing the free will of the individuals who make up those nations. God chose Israel (the Jews) over the Edomites to be the nation through which the blessed Messiah would be born. This chosenness of Israel guaranteed no one within the nation passage to heaven.

Romans 9:12 *it was said to her, "THE OLDER WILL SERVE THE YOUNGER."*

This verse further confirms that Paul is addressing nations rather than individuals, for Esau (the "*older*" brother) never served Jacob (the "*younger*" brother).

However, Esau's descendants, the Edomite nation, consistently served Jacob's descendants, the nation of Israel. In fact, the Old Testament prophet Obadiah rebuked Edom for her elation over Israel's misfortune (Obadiah 1-14), an elation that resulted from Israel's consistent dominance over the Edomites.

Unsurprisingly, John MacArthur gives no commentary on this passage in *The MacArthur Study Bible* other than referencing Genesis 25:23. His theology cannot withstand the truth recorded here.

Romans 9:13 *Just as it is written, "JACOB I LOVED, BUT ESAU I HATED."*

Knowledge gained from Romans 9:11-12 makes John Piper's words from page 175 of *The Justification of God* extremely intriguing:

> ...the divine decision to "hate" Esau was made "before they were born or had done anything good *or evil*" (9:11).... [93]

God does not at any place in His Word teach that He hated Esau the individual. Hence, Piper's words are inaccurate. In Malachi 1:2-3, however, God does speak of hating "*Esau,*" the name "Esau" in this case pointing to the Edomites:

> *"I have loved you," says the LORD. But you say, "How have You loved us?" "Was not Esau Jacob's brother?" declares the LORD. "Yet I have loved Jacob; but I have hated Esau, and I have made his mountains a desolation and appointed his inheritance for the jackals of the wilderness."* (Malachi 1:2-3)

God, speaking through Malachi to the Jewish nation long after (hundreds of years after) He had spoken to Rebekah in Genesis 25:23, is not saying that He *"hated"* Esau the individual. Esau was dead by then. God *"hated"* Esau's descendants, the Edomite nation—*"hated"* meaning to "love less," as will be confirmed shortly. God is dealing with nations in these passages, not individuals, verified by *"us"* in Malachi 1:2:

> *"I have loved you," says the LORD. But you say, "How hast Thou loved us?" "Was not Esau Jacob's brother?" declares the LORD. "Yet I have loved Jacob;* (Malachi 1:2)

The context here is extremely important. God is speaking to the Jewish nation through His prophet Malachi. Consequently, the use of "*us*" in the phrase, "*How hast Thou loved us?*," which points to the Jewish nation, coupled with the phrase,

"Yet I have loved Jacob," proves that *"Jacob"* in this case points to the nation of Israel, not to Jacob the individual. Let's take this input and apply it to the subsequent verse:

> *but I have hated Esau, and I have made his mountains a desolation, and appointed his inheritance for the jackals of the wilderness."* (Malachi 1:3)

Just as *"Jacob"* is synonymous with the nation of Israel in Malachi 1:2, *"Esau"* is synonymous with the Edomite nation, Esau's descendants, in Malachi 1:3. This interpretation ties in perfectly with the overall body of Scripture, for God married Israel in Exodus 24—meaning that He loves Israel more than any other nation. We will soon prove that *"hated"* in the phrase, *"I have hated Esau"* (Malachi 1:3), means "to love less." This fact will confirm even more so that *"Esau"* points to the Edomite nation—not to Esau the individual.

Genesis 25:19-26 adds additional support to our findings, for the circumstances surrounding Rebekah's pregnancy, along with Jacob and Esau's birth, are recorded in these passages. Verse 23 is especially relevant to our present topic of interest:

> *And the LORD said to her, "Two nations are in your womb; And two peoples will be separated from your body; And one people shall be stronger than the other; And the older shall serve the younger."* (Genesis 25:23)

Don't miss the fact that Paul quotes from this verse in Romans 9:12:

> *it was said to her, "The older will serve the younger."* (Romans 9:12)

Even the phrase, *"it was said to her"* (Romans 9:12), confirms that Paul is referring to Genesis 25:23 (*"And the Lord said to her"*—Genesis 25:23). Note that *"hated"* is nowhere to be found in Romans 9:12 or Genesis 25:23! Theologians who view Romans 9:10-13 as addressing individuals rather than nations make a perilous contextual mistake by associating the phrase, *"before they were born or had done anything good or evil"* (Romans 9:11), with *"hated"* in Malachi 1:3. This connection is impossible, for nations are the issue in Malachi 1:2-3 (as in Romans 9:11-13), not individuals, further exposing Reformed Theology's error. Consider as well that Jacob and Esau were born centuries before God spoke through His prophet Malachi. Yet John Piper, a Reformed theologian, writes (as recorded previously):

> ...the divine decision to "hate" Esau was made "before they were born or had done anything good *or evil*" (9:11).... [94]

Let's again read Romans 9:13:

Just as it is written, "Jacob I loved, but Esau I hated." (Romans 9:13)

We have established that Paul quotes Malachi 1:2-3 in Romans 9:13. Keep in mind that God (through Paul) is addressing nations rather than individuals (review the notes associated with Romans 9:10-12 if needed), for we have already proven that *"Esau"* is a synonym for Edom and *"Jacob"* a synonym for Israel. Note the transition from *"Esau"* and *"Jacob"* in Malachi 1:1-3 to *"Edom"* and *"Israel"* in Malachi 1:4-5:

*1 The oracle of the word of the LORD to Israel through Malachi. 2 "I have loved you," says the LORD. But you say, "How hast Thou loved us?" "Was not **Esau** Jacob's brother?" declares the LORD. "Yet I have loved **Jacob**; 3 but I have hated **Esau**, and I have made his mountains a desolation, and appointed his inheritance for the jackals of the wilderness." 4 Though **Edom** says, "We have been beaten down, but we will return and build up the ruins"; thus says the LORD of hosts, "They may build, but I will tear down; and men will call them the wicked territory, and the people toward whom the LORD is indignant forever." 5 Your eyes will see this and you will say, "The LORD be magnified beyond the border of **Israel**!"* (Malachi 1:1-5)

Nations (Israel and Edom) are the issue here, not individuals (Jacob and Esau)! Therefore, *"hated"* in Romans 9:13 should not cause concern. The following truth verifies why.

In Genesis 29:31, *"unloved"* (NASB) is translated *"hated"* in the KJV. Combining Genesis 29:30 and 31, however, we understand that *"hated"* actually means "to love less."

*So Jacob went in to Rachel also, and indeed he **loved Rachel more than Leah,** and he served with Laban for another seven years. Now the LORD saw that Leah was **unloved**, and He opened her womb, but Rachel was barren.* (Genesis 29:30-31 NASB)

*And he went in also unto Rachel, and **he loved also Rachel more than Leah**, and served with him yet seven other years. And when the LORD saw that Leah was **hated**, he opened her womb: but*

> *Rachel was barren.* (Genesis 29:30-31 KJV)

Nowhere in the Genesis account do we find Jacob actually despising Leah. He just *"loved...Rachel more than Leah"* (Genesis 29:30).

Luke 14:26 and Matthew 10:37 support our findings regarding *"hate"*:

> *"If anyone comes to Me, and does not hate his own father and mother and wife and children and brothers and sisters, yes, and even his own life, he cannot be My disciple.* (Luke 14:26—NASB)

> *"He who loves father or mother more than Me is not worthy of Me; and he who loves son or daughter more than Me is not worthy of Me.* (Matthew 10:37—NASB)

Should *"hate"* in Luke 14:26 mean to literally despise, then the believer is to *"hate"* (despise) every member of his family for the sake of Christ. This idea is not what Matthew 10:37-38 suggests. Neither do Exodus 20:12, Matthew 15:4, and Ephesians 6:2-4 imply such an outlandish notion:

> *"Honor your father and your mother, that your days may be prolonged in the land which the LORD your God gives you.* (Exodus 20:12—NASB)

> *"For God said, 'Honor your father and mother,' and, 'He who speaks evil of father or mother, let him be put to death.'* (Matthew 15:4—NASB)

> *HONOR YOUR FATHER AND MOTHER (which is the first commandment with a promise), THAT IT MAY BE WELL WITH YOU, AND THAT YOU MAY LIVE LONG ON THE EARTH. And, fathers, do not provoke your children to anger; but bring them up in the discipline and instruction of the Lord.* (Ephesians 6:2-4—NASB)

Scripture is void of the error that a believer is to literally *"hate"* his family.

God loved *"Esau"* (the Edomites) less than *"Jacob"* (the nation of Israel), as indicated by Malachi 1:1-5, due to having married Israel in Exodus 24 so the "blessed" Messiah could be born a Jew. Hence, Israel possessed a higher position in God's strategy for mankind than did the Edomites. Israel sits in this elevated position even today, for she is to take the amazing news of the Messiah to the Gentile world—a calling she has yet to fulfill.

Conclusion: Romans 9:13 in no way teaches that God predetermines a person's destiny before birth. Nations are addressed in this passage, not individuals!

Romans 9:14 *What shall we say then? There is no injustice with God, is there? May it never be!*

Reformed theologians (extreme and hyper-Calvinists) use this verse in an attempt to prove that Paul, in Romans 9:10-13, is addressing Jacob and Esau's individual destinies. They incorrectly assume, therefore, that Paul is in agreement with their view of unconditional election. Their mindset causes them to conclude that the accusation of Romans 9:14 would come forth from those viewing God as unjust should He have chosen Jacob (the individual) to salvation over Esau (the individual). Remember: Reformed Theology (extreme and hyper-Calvinism) views Jacob as having been chosen (elected) to salvation over Esau prior to either boy exiting the womb. Thus John Piper, a Calvinist (Reformed theologian), in *The Justification of God*, page 93, writes:

> We will not be far off, therefore, if we infer that the offense of 9:6-13 which evoked the charge of divine unrighteousness is Paul's assertion that God, indetermining the beneficiaries of his mercy, does not base his decisions on any human distinctives that a person may claim by birth or effort. Therefore, the view of divine righteousness which the objection presupposes is that a righteous God must elect persons on the basis of their real and valuable distinctives, whether racial (Jewishness) or moral (keepers of the law). On this assumption God would indeed be unrighteous to elect Jacob over Esau "before they were born or had done anything good or evil."[95]

Piper suggests that man would be in error by accusing God of unrighteousness should He have elected Jacob (the individual) to salvation over Esau (the individual) "...before they were born..." The following rebuttal explains why his conclusions regarding election are invalid.

Rebuttal:

Paul, in Romans 9:1-5, addresses the special position the nation of Israel (Jacob's descendants) holds in God's overall plan for man. As a result of Jehovah choosing (electing) Israel as His wife (Exodus 24:1-8), she would bear the Messiah—a message she has, thus far, failed to take to the Gentiles although chosen (elected) by God to do so. Hence, God did not choose (elect) Israel for the purpose of securing the salvation of any Jew. He chose (elected) Israel as His wife to bring the Messiah into the world so she, in turn, could take the news of His coming to the Gentiles—an opportunity she has thus far basically neglected. Israel has received an abundance of blessings from her Husband, but her rebellion has caused countless Jews to die void of salvation. In fact, the nation bypassed a wealth of additional blessings due to disobedience. Again, none of the blessings granted to physical Israel guaranteed a single Jew passage to heaven.

God bestows salvation to Israelites in the same way He bestows salvation to Gentiles—through making them part of His family once they repent and exercise faith while depraved (a truth Paul's Jewish opponents vehemently opposed). Consequently, Israel's position in God's strategy did nothing to grant the individuals within the nation a righteous standing before Jehovah. Paul's Gentile readers in Rome needed to understand this truth. Had they not, they might have accused Paul of teaching that God chose (elected) Jacob (the individual) to salvation (prior to physical birth) and withheld from Esau (the individual) the freedom to believe—a falsehood impossible for Romans 9:13 to communicate.

The same Jewish critics of Romans 3 continued their argument against Paul's teaching by asking, *"…There is no injustice with God, is there?…"* (Romans 9:14). Being Jews, they would have never accused God of *"injustice"* had He chosen (elected) Jacob (the individual) to salvation prior to physical birth over Esau (the individual)—for Jacob was a Jew, Esau a Gentile. Remember, Paul's Jewish opponents believed that Jews were chosen to be saved before birth. They also perceived Gentiles as needing to exercise their free will and become proselytes to Judaism if they were to become part of God's family. Paul's Jewish challengers would have also known that *"hated"* means "to love less" in this instance—proving that Paul was not addressing Jacob and Esau's individual destinies in Romans 9:13, but the fact that God loved Israel more than the Edomites.

Paul taught that Israel (the nation) was chosen to office (to bear the Messiah and take the news of His coming to the Gentiles) rather than to salvation—a truth which infuriated his Jewish critics. They could never accept this teaching—that is, unless they perceived themselves as sinners and accepted Jesus as Messiah.

The theology of the unbelieving Jews contained two lethal flaws: (1) They viewed themselves as having been chosen to salvation prior to physical birth—that their eternal destiny was secured by a choice Jehovah made before they were born (2) They considered the works of the Law as eventually validating their righteous standing before God. In their minds, once the Law was obeyed according to Jehovah's standard, they would be ushered into heaven—their righteous behavior and acceptance into heaven confirming God's previous choice of them to salvation. The Law, however, requires perfection (Matthew 5:48; James 2:10). Therefore, Paul taught that no person can achieve access into God's presence through the deeds of the Law (Romans 3:20; 5:20). Yes, contradictory assumptions are consistently exposed when placed alongside the full counsel of God's Word.

Because Paul taught that God accepts Jews and Gentiles into His presence on the basis of faith rather than the works of the Law, the unbelieving Jews had no alternative but to accuse Paul of promoting a God Who is unjust (Romans 9:14). A complete theological makeover would have been required for Paul's Jewish critics to admit that God remains just while accepting individuals who have not earned their passage to heaven through the deeds of the Law. Hence, Paul's major purpose in recording Romans 9:14 was to expose the improper theology of his Jewish opponents who began testing him as early as Romans 3:1. Let's again read Romans 9:14:

> *What shall we say then? There is no injustice with God, is there? May it never be!* (Romans 9:14)

As has already been determined, unsaved Jews in Paul's day viewed God as having chosen (elected) the Jews to salvation through His Old Testament covenant enacted with the Hebrew people. Thus, they perceived themselves as having been chosen to salvation prior to physical birth. Consequently, to choose Jacob (the ancestor of the Israelites) to salvation (prior to physical birth) over Esau (the ancestor of the Edomites—a Gentile nation) would have been in agreement with the Jewish mindset that rejected Jesus' Messiahship—for they viewed all Gentiles (including Esau) as free to accept or reject God's offer of salvation after physical birth.

Paul did a masterful job of refuting his Jewish opponents, for he taught that God remains righteous (and just) while accepting Jews and Gentiles who exercise faith in Christ. Paul also refuted his critics' arguments by teaching that God remains just while rejecting Jews and Gentiles who disregard His free offer of salvation. Paul's Jewish enemies disagreed, accusing God of *"injustice"* should He accept only a portion of the Jews rather than all—a mindset that resulted from their viewing Israel as having been chosen to destiny rather than to office. Yet, these ill-informed Jewish critics got one thing right: If God's choice should determine where Jews spend eternity, He would be totally unjust had He chosen only a few Jews to be saved when He was capable of choosing all. Therefore, they would have immediately detected the error within Reformed Theology—a movement which came on the scene quite some time after their encounter with Paul. Hence, Paul was not teaching the Reformed view of the Scriptures as Reformed theologians incorrectly suggest!

We continue to observe that an improper view of one's chosenness/election (as was the case with Paul's Jewish critics) results in an inaccurate view of the Godhead. Paul's Jewish opponents, refusing to discard their contradictory view of election (that God had chosen the Israelites to be saved), short-circuited when exposed to Paul's gospel—which taught that only Jews who exercise faith in Christ will become part of God's family. Yet, Paul's Jewish critics possessed the insight to understand that had God's choice determined the destiny of all Jews, He would be both unjust and unloving had He chosen only a portion of the nation to salvation when He was capable of choosing all.

The Hebrew people have most definitely *"blasphemed"* God's *"name"* (Romans 2:24) through misunderstanding their chosenness/election:

> *For "THE NAME OF GOD IS BLASPHEMED AMONG THE GENTILES BECAUSE OF YOU," just as it is written.* (Romans 2:24)

The Israelites were chosen/elected to office, never destiny. (In times past I have viewed unbelieving Gentiles as presenting the questions recorded in Romans 9:14 and 19. Further study seems to indicate, however, that the questions were offered by the same unbelieving Jews who generated the questions of Romans 3:1-8.)

Instead of addressing man's eternal destiny in passages such as Romans 9:10-13, Paul describes God's selection (choice) of certain nations for the purpose of accomplishing His overall purpose for man—without removing the free will of the individuals who make up those nations. Thus, in Romans 9:14 (by stating, *"May it never be!"*), Paul teaches that God was anything but unjust in choosing (electing) Israel over the Edomites as the nation privileged to birth the Messiah (Jesus' Father, of course, being the heavenly Father). Neither is God unjust by saving only a portion of national Israel and a portion of the Gentiles—the portion in both instances that exercises faith in Christ. Had Jehovah predestined (from eternity past, by means of an eternal decree) Jacob (the individual—a Jew) to salvation over Esau (the individual—a Gentile), as some theologians incorrectly assume, He could rightly have been accused of *"injustice,"* forfeiting His sovereign right to rule. God cannot remain just and condemn a man to eternal punishment who is never given an opportunity (choice) to believe.

Individuals who view God as having determined man's destiny from eternity past would disagree with my conclusions. Their perception of Paul's teaching is that God elected and predestined Jacob (the individual) to salvation over Esau (the individual), granting neither party a choice in the matter. Genesis 25:23 refutes such thinking, for it confirms that Paul addresses *"nations"* rather than individuals in Romans 9:10-13. Paul taught that God, instead of predetermining where Jacob and Esau (as individuals) would spend eternity, predetermined that Israel (descendants of Jacob) would play a larger role in His overall strategy for man than would the Edomites (descendants of Esau)—giving every member of Israel and the Edomite nation the freedom to repent and believe. This contextual view of these passages causes contradiction to flee, preventing us from blaspheming God's name as we share the gospel with those who are without Christ.

Before transitioning into Romans 9:15, let's summarize why Paul's Jewish opponents so struggled with his theology, accusing him in Romans 9:14 of portraying God as unjust:

1. Paul taught that God chose the nation of Israel to office—not to salvation (destiny).

2. Paul's Jewish opponents perceived the entire nation of Israel as having been chosen to salvation (destiny)—not to office.

3. Paul taught that only those Jews (and Gentiles) who repent and believe while depraved will be saved (justified)—that their salvation is <u>not</u> based on works.

4. Paul's Jewish opponents concluded that should Gentiles be saved (justified) by faith rather than by the works of the Law, God would be unjust by accepting a people who had not earned their salvation through good deeds. After all, these unbelieving Jews had performed countless deeds under the Law while the Gentiles had not.

5. Paul's Jewish opponents also concluded that should God save (justify) only a portion of Israel, He would be unjust should He not save all—especially since God, in their minds, was capable of saving the entire nation.

6. Interestingly, Paul's Jewish opponents would have had no problem with God electing Jacob (the individual—a Jew) to salvation prior to physical birth over Esau (the individual—a Gentile) had Paul been addressing individuals in Romans 9:13. Their opposition to Paul's theology, in fact, proves that Paul was referencing nations in Romans 9:13 (Israel and Edom)—not individuals (Jacob and Esau). The nation of Israel, having been chosen to <u>office</u> over the Edomite nation (with no Jew being saved who rejects Jesus' Messiahship), was truth Paul's Jewish critics could not accept—again refuting Reformed Theology's view of "individuals" in verses 13 and 14, and thus, the "U" of the TULIP, Unconditional Election.

Romans 9:15 *For He says to Moses, "I WILL HAVE MERCY ON WHOM I HAVE MERCY, AND I WILL HAVE COMPASSION ON WHOM I HAVE COMPASSION."*

As we examine this passage, we must realize that the phrases, *"I will have mercy on whom I have mercy, and I will have compassion on whom I have compassion,"* are taken from Exodus 33:19. God stated these words to Moses shortly after Israel worshipped the golden calf in Exodus 32—a fact that greatly affects the interpretation of Romans 9:15-16.

As mentioned earlier, Reformed Theology (extreme and hyper-Calvinism) views the names *"Jacob"* and *"Esau"* (Romans 9:13) as pointing to individuals rather than nations in an attempt to justify their view of unconditional election (a view that perceives God as having elected certain persons to salvation from eternity past by means of an eternal decree). Once this error is committed, they must perceive Paul as addressing man's eternal destiny in Romans 9:15-16. Consequently, until they rectify their improper interpretation of Romans 9:13 (in relation to the names *"Jacob"* and *"Esau"*), they have no alternative but to perpetuate their error by viewing Romans 9:15-16 as teaching unconditional election to salvation. As a result of elevating God's sovereignty above all of His other amazing attributes (including His love), they are forced to attempt to prove that God elects and predestines certain individuals to salvation prior to physical birth—in fact, that God is the cause of all things. They must totally disallow free will (especially as it relates to mans' ability to choose Christ while depraved) if their view of sovereignty is to stand. The following quotes validate the previous statements.

John Piper, in his work, *The Justification of God*, page 103, is quoted at this time. Note how his inaccurate view of sovereignty tarnishes his perception of the free will of man:

> ...Paul presupposed that God's righteousness is his unswerving commitment to preserve and display the glory of his name. If this is the case the quotation of Ex 33:19 in Rom 9:15 as an argument for the righteousness of God in his unconditional election becomes more intelligible; for, as we saw, Ex 33:19 is a proclamation of God's *name* and a manifestation of his *glory*—the glory of his sovereign freedom in having mercy on whomever he wills....[96]

On page 157 of that same work Piper states:

> ...Therefore, since according to Ex 33:19 God's glory or name consists basically in his sovereign freedom in the bestowal of mercy..., there is no unrighteousness with God when his decision to bless one person and not another is based solely on his own will rather than on any human distinctive.
> On the contrary, he *must* pursue his "purpose of election" in this way in order to remain righteous, for only in his sovereign, free bestowal (and withholding) of mercy on whomever he wills is God acting out of a full allegiance to his name and esteem for

> his glory. ..."willing and running" cannot legitimately be limited in such a way that *some* willing, like the act of trusting Christ does ultimately determine God's bestowal of mercy, namely, the mercy of salvation....[97]

R.C. Sproul (a Reformed theologian), in *Chosen by God*, page 151, comments on Romans 9:16:

> ...This is the Word of God that requires all Christians to cease and desist from views of predestination that make the ultimate decision for salvation rest in the will of man....[98]

Sproul follows on pages 154-155 with these words:

> Unconditional election means that our election is decided by God according to his purpose, according to his sovereign will....It is not based on our willing or on our running, but upon the sovereign purpose of God.[99]

Clearly, Piper and Sproul use Romans 9:15-16 in an attempt to prove that God has elected and predestined certain individuals to salvation prior to physical birth. They must totally disallow free will in their beliefs (especially as it relates to man's ability to choose Christ while depraved) if their improper view of sovereignty is to stand.

Rebuttal

Paul addresses God's strategy with nations in Romans 9:15—not His selection of certain individuals to salvation, leaving the remainder to the consequence of their sin (or condemned to damnation), as Reformed Theology teaches.

In Romans 1-8, Paul proved that the deeds of the Law make no one righteous—not even the Jews (Romans 3:20; 5:20). He also verified that faith in the *"seed"* of Genesis 3:15, Jesus the Messiah (Galatians 3:16), must be exercised by man (while depraved) before the Father will bestow salvation (Romans 5:1). In Romans 9, Paul teaches that Israel was chosen by God, not due to any worth on her part, but strictly as an instrument to bring about His desired end. In fact, Deuteronomy 7:6-7 states that Israel was the smallest and most insignificant nation on the earth when God chose her as His wife. God's overall plan for Israel was that the *"seed"* of Genesis 3:15 (Jesus, the Messiah—Galatians 3:16) be born through her lineage. He also desired that she, as a kingdom of priests (Exodus 19:6), exercise faith in the Messiah and, as a result, take the good news of the Messiah to the Gentiles—a calling she has rejected thus far but will later fulfill.

A misunderstanding of Paul's gospel among his Jewish critics prompted Paul to address yet another situation in the Scriptures besides Jacob and Esau. In Romans 9:15-18, Paul speaks of two men, one evil and one good, who were used significantly by God to shape Israel's early history. These men are Moses and Pharaoh. Let's begin by addressing Paul's words in Romans 9:15:

> *For He says to Moses, "I WILL HAVE MERCY ON WHOM I HAVE MERCY, AND I WILL HAVE COMPASSION ON WHOM I HAVE COMPASSION."* (Romans 9:15)

Romans 9:15 does not teach that God chose (elected) Israel (or any individual within the nation) to salvation. Neither does it teach that God chose (elected) certain Gentiles to salvation. Rather, it speaks of God's *"mercy"* and *"compassion"* displayed toward His chosen, sinful people (Israel), by not personally dwelling among them and, in turn, consuming them after their sin with the golden calf.

To comprehend the previous statement, as well as the context of Romans 9:15, we must first read Exodus 33:12-23:

> *12 Then Moses said to the LORD, "See, Thou dost say to me, 'Bring up this people!' But Thou Thyself hast not let me know whom Thou wilt send with me. Moreover, Thou hast said, 'I have known you by name, and you have also found favor in My sight.' 13 "Now therefore, I pray Thee, if I have found favor in Thy sight, let me know Thy ways, that I may know Thee, so that I may find favor in Thy sight. Consider too, that this nation is Thy people." 14 And He said, "My presence shall go with you, and I will give you rest." 15 Then he said to Him, "If Thy presence does not go with us, do not lead us up from here. 16 For how then can it be known that I have found favor in Thy sight, I and Thy people? Is it not by Thy going with us, so that we, I and Thy people, may be distinguished from all the other people who are upon the face of the earth?"*
>
> *17 And the LORD said to Moses, "I will also do this thing of which you have spoken; for you have found favor in My sight, and I have known you by name." 18 Then Moses said, "I pray Thee, show me Thy glory!" 19 And He said, "I Myself will make all My goodness pass before you, and will proclaim the name of the LORD before you; and I will be gracious to whom I will be gracious, and will show compassion on whom I will show compassion." 20 But He*

> *said, "You cannot see My face, for no man can see Me and live!" 21 Then the LORD said, "Behold, there is a place by Me, and you shall stand there on the rock; 22 and it will come about, while My glory is passing by, that I will put you in the cleft of the rock and cover you with My hand until I have passed by. 23 Then I will take My hand away and you shall see My back, but My face shall not be seen."* (Exodus 33:12-23)

Moses desired that God dwell among the Jewish people (note Moses' use of *"us"* in Exodus 33:15-16) after Israel's gross involvement with the golden calf. Yet, God desired that His presence dwell with Moses (note Jehovah's use of *"you"* in verse 14, pointing to Moses alone). What prompted God's response? The answer is the key to properly interpreting Romans 9:15. Had God dwelt among the people, especially after their sin with the golden calf in Exodus 32, they would have been consumed:

> *For the LORD had said to Moses, "Say to the sons of Israel, 'You are an obstinate people; should I go up in your midst for one moment, I would destroy you. Now therefore, put off your ornaments from you, that I may know what I will do with you.'"* (Exodus 33:5)

Even after seeing God's glory in Exodus 34:1-7, Moses remained committed to God dwelling in the midst of the nation. Observe Moses' use of *"our"* in Exodus 34:9.

> *He said, "If now I have found favor in Thy sight, O Lord, I pray, let the Lord go along in <u>our</u> midst, even though the people are so obstinate, and pardon our iniquity and our sin, and take us as Your own possession."* (Exodus 34:9)

God's *"mercy"* (Romans 9:15) caused Him to refuse Moses' request. Had God lived among His people, as Moses desired, He would have destroyed the nation (Exodus 33:5). Instead, He permitted His presence to enter the Israelite camp through His representative Moses:

> *It came about when Moses was coming down from Mount Sinai (and the two tablets of the testimony were in Moses' hand as he was coming down from the mountain), that Moses did not know that the skin of his face shone because of his speaking with Him. 30 So when Aaron and all the sons of Israel saw Moses, behold, the skin of his face shone, and they were afraid to come near him. 31 Then*

> *Moses called to them, and Aaron and all the rulers in the congregation returned to him; and Moses spoke to them. 32 Afterward all the sons of Israel came near, and he commanded them to do everything that the LORD had spoken to him on Mount Sinai. 33 When Moses had finished speaking with them, he put a veil over his face. 34 But whenever Moses went in before the LORD to speak with Him, he would take off the veil until he came out; and whenever he came out and spoke to the sons of Israel what he had been commanded, 35 the sons of Israel would see the face of Moses, that the skin of Moses' face shone. So Moses would replace the veil over his face until he went in to speak with Him.* (Exodus 34:29-35)

What a brilliant demonstration of God's *"mercy"* and *"compassion"* (Romans 9:15), for He spared Israel by refusing Moses' request! In other words, God displayed *"mercy"* and *"compassion"* (Romans 9:15) by exhibiting His glory through *"Moses' face"* (Exodus 34:29-35) rather than personally dwelling in the *"midst"* of the people (Exodus 33:5). By doing so, He confirmed His words of Exodus 33:19, *"I will be gracious to whom I will be gracious, and will show compassion on whom I will show compassion."* Yes, He was very "*gracious*" and compassionate, for had His presence dwelt among the people in the manner that Moses requested, the nation would have become extinct (Exodus 33:5)!

Viewing Romans 9:15 in context (by applying it to the events recorded in Exodus 32-34), we find that it has nothing to do with God choosing (electing) Moses, Israel, or anyone else to salvation. Rather, it pertains to God showing *"mercy"* and *"compassion"* toward His chosen, sinful people (Israel) by not personally dwelling among them and, in turn, consuming them.

This account illustrates that we sometimes make less than excellent requests of God. At these times Romans 8:26-27 comes into play, for *"the Spirit...intercedes...according to the will of God"* when our desires and will conflict with His.

The physical nation of Israel remains God's chosen people, for she was chosen to bring the Messiah into the world (which she did) and to spread the good news of His coming to the Gentiles (which she has yet to do). She was not chosen to salvation in eternity past. Therefore, God will surely fulfill His original promise to Abraham (the father of the nation)—that in Abraham *"all the families of the earth shall be blessed"* (Genesis 12:3). Through Abraham's lineage, the Messiah (the *"seed"* of Genesis 3:15 and Galatians 3:16) would be born, saving/justifying all who choose to repent and believe while depraved. Thus the phrases, *"and I will be gracious to whom I will be gracious, and will show compassion on whom I will show compassion"* (Exodus 33:19) confirm that when it comes to the distribution of special favors, Jehovah knows best. God's choice of Israel, for the purpose of bringing the Messiah into the world (along with other unique purposes), was a gracious and compassionate favor granted to an unworthy people. It by no means meant that God had chosen (elected) Israel (or anyone else) to salvation. Even though a remnant within Israel walked with God, a significant number of Israelites were sinful. Yet Israel remained, and still remains, God's chosen nation. Hence, by rejecting Moses' unwise request (that He dwell in the midst of Israel), God displayed mercy and compassion (Romans 9:15) toward a sinful people by staying away—appearing to Moses instead, with His glory entering the camp on Moses' face. Had He entered the camp as Moses desired, Israel would have been wiped off the face of the earth!

Romans 9:16 *So then it does not depend on the man who wills or the man who runs, but on God who has mercy.*

What we have addressed thus far sheds considerable light on Romans 9:16. Moses' *"will"* was that God dwell in the midst of Israel, an unwise choice indeed. God's *"mercy"* prevailed in that His glory entered the camp on Moses' face. Consequently, the result was not dependent upon what *"man"* (Moses in this instance) willed, *"but on God who has mercy."* God's mercy was displayed due to Israel's chosenness to office (that of bringing the Messiah into the world and telling the Gentiles of His coming). Had God honored Moses' request, the unconditional Abrahamic covenant (Genesis 12:1-3) would have become extinct—making God a liar in the process. Knowing that Moses' motives were right (righteous), even though he had misread the situation, allowed God to display His glory on Moses' face as an act of mercy. The previous thought brings encouragement considering the number of times we have misread God's perfect will and begged Him for what would bring harm!

Paul picks up this theme in 2Corinthians 3:1-18. These verses, along with Exodus 34:29-35, verses that were addressed earlier, confirm that the glory beaming from Moses' face was not permanent. In fact, it faded, verifying its temporary status. Paul uses this truth to prove that the old covenant of Law (symbolized by Moses), which was conditional and unable to make anyone right with God (Romans 3:20), would eventually fade and give way to the new covenant, an unconditional covenant of grace brought about through Jesus Christ. Note Paul's words in 2Corinthians 3:1-18:

> *Are we beginning to commend ourselves again? Or do we need, as some, letters of commendation to you or from you? 2 You are our letter, written in our hearts, known and read by all men; 3 being manifested that you are a letter of Christ, cared for by us, written not with ink but with the Spirit of the living God, not on tablets of*

> *stone, but on tablets of human hearts. 4 Such confidence we have through Christ toward God. 5 Not that we are adequate in ourselves to consider anything as coming from ourselves, but our adequacy is from God, 6 who also made us adequate as servants of a new covenant, not of the letter but of the Spirit; for the letter kills, but the Spirit gives life. 7 But if the ministry of death, in letters engraved on stones, came with glory, so that the sons of Israel could not look intently at the face of Moses because of the glory of his face, fading as it was, 8 how shall the ministry of the Spirit fail to be even more with glory? 9 For if the ministry of condemnation has glory, much more does the ministry of righteousness abound in glory. 10 For indeed what had glory, in this case has no glory because of the glory that surpasses it. 11 For if that which fades away was with glory, much more that which remains is in glory.*
>
> *12 Therefore having such a hope, we use great boldness in our speech, 13 and are not as Moses, who used to put a veil over his face so that the sons of Israel might not look intently at the end of what was fading away. 14 But their minds were hardened; for until this very day at the reading of the old covenant the same veil remains unlifted, because it is removed in Christ. 15 But to this day whenever Moses is read, a veil lies over their heart; 16 but whenever a person turns to the Lord, the veil is taken away. 17 Now the Lord is the Spirit, and where the Spirit of the Lord is, there is liberty. 18 But we all, with unveiled face, beholding as in a mirror the glory of the Lord, are being transformed into the same image from glory to glory, just as from the Lord, the Spirit.*
> (2Corinthians 3:1-18)

Paul's words, *"but whenever a person turns to the Lord, the veil is taken away"* (verse 16), are extremely compelling. After all, a choice is required on behalf of those who come to Christ (in this particular case, the Jews) prior to the *"veil"* being *"taken away."* This rock solid fact confirms that the depraved can choose Christ, resulting in God revealing Himself to an ever-increasing degree through His truth, activated by the Holy Spirit, once the choice is made. This passage also refutes the idea that spiritual regeneration must precede faith—a popular, yet incorrect teaching promoted by Reformed Theology (consult Diagrams 10 and 11 in the Reference Section). It also disproves the doctrine of unconditional election (that God elected certain persons to salvation from eternity past by means of an eternal decree)—another popular, yet inaccurate assumption of our day. Unsurprisingly, many theologians who adhere to the improper above-mentioned ideology cite

2Corinthians 3:14-15 and 2Corinthians 3:18 in their commentaries but bypass 2Corinthians 3:16. Such is the case in *The MacArthur Study Bible*, written by the Reformed theologian, John MacArthur. Reformed Theology cannot withstand the truth of 2Corinthians 3:16, for it teaches that man turns to the Lord before he is spiritually regenerated—the exact opposite of the Reformed view which has God spiritually regenerating man before man is capable of turning to the Lord.

Does the phrase, *"But their minds were hardened"* (2Corinthians 3:14), indicate that Paul was a proponent of unconditional election? In other words, was Paul communicating to the church at Corinth that God hardens the non-elect so they might perish—or was he referencing something else? We will examine Romans 9:17-18 shortly to gain additional insight into this subject matter.

Conclusion regarding Romans 9:15-16: Moses willed that God enter Israel's camp after she sinned with the golden calf. Moses' heart was right before God (he desired that the nation be blessed), but his understanding regarding the consequence of such an action on God's part was inadequate. God's mercy caused Him to reject Moses' request for the good of the nation—in fact, for the good of mankind. Had God's presence entered the midst of the camp the nation would have perished, no Messiah would have been born, and the Abrahamic Covenant would have become extinct—a covenant enacted by God for the purpose of blessing mankind through the blessed Messiah. Hence, God's strategy *"...does not depend on the man who wills* [Moses in this case] *or the man who runs, but on God who has mercy"* (Romans 9:16). Moses incorrectly viewed God as confirming Israel's chosenness through entering the camp. God, on the other hand, confirmed Israel's chosenness by staying away—by allowing His glory to enter on Moses' face, thus displaying His mercy. Paul is not teaching that man is void of a free will to repent and believe while depraved. Neither is Paul communicating that a work is performed should the depraved will to repent and exercise faith (read Romans 3:27-28, 4:4-5, and 9:32 for verification). Scripture consistently stresses that the depraved must choose (will) to repent and believe if God is to impart salvation.

Romans 9:17 and 18, amazingly intriguing passages, will be studied as a block rather than separately.

Romans 9:17 *For the Scripture says to Pharaoh, "FOR THIS VERY PURPOSE I RAISED YOU UP, TO DEMONSTRATE MY POWER IN YOU, AND THAT MY NAME MIGHT BE PROCLAIMED THROUGHOUT THE WHOLE EARTH."*

Romans 9:18 *So then He has mercy on whom He desires, and He hardens whom He desires.*

A huge theological gulf exists between the Calvinists and the followers of free will in regard to these passages. Calvinism's view will be studied first.

We must keep in mind that Calvinism is generally divided into three branches—hyper, extreme, and moderate (for lack of better terms). Many Calvinists would take issue with these "labels," but they exist as a means to classify the varying opinions that inundate Calvinism's overall system of thought. The following definitions are not exhaustive, but contain pertinent information regarding the present subject matter.

Hyper-Calvinism

God predestined the elect to salvation and the non-elect to damnation from eternity past by means of an eternal decree. Man, in his depraved state, cannot choose Christ. Consequently, God must spiritually regenerate the elect, as well as give them the gifts of repentance and faith, before they can repent, believe, and be saved. This branch of Calvinism adheres to limited atonement.

Comment: Even though I adamantly disagree with this system of thought, I view the hyper-Calvinists as more straightforward regarding their views than the other branches of Calvinism. I think you will agree as we continue.

Extreme Calvinism

God predestined the elect to salvation from eternity past (by means of an eternal decree) but left the non-elect to the consequence of their sin. Man, in his depraved state, cannot choose Christ. As a result, God must spiritually regenerate the elect, as well as give them the gifts of repentance and faith, before they can repent, believe, and be saved. This branch of Calvinism adheres to limited atonement.

Comment: Bottom line, extreme and hyper-Calvinists believe the same thing. What difference exists between God leaving the non-elect to the consequence of their sin, with no opportunity to believe (extreme Calvinism), versus predestining the non-elect to damnation in eternity past (hyper-Calvinism), if only the elect in both cases will be saved? No difference exists, for in extreme Calvinism the non-elect are predestined to damnation by default (that is, if extreme Calvinism is held accountable to its bottom line).

Moderate Calvinism

The depraved can repent and exercise faith in Christ due to possessing a free will. However, only the elect, chosen to salvation by God from eternity past by means of an eternal decree, can, and will, choose to believe. This branch of Calvinism normally adheres to unlimited atonement.

Comment: What difference would it make for the depraved to possess a free will to choose Christ should only the elect be capable of repenting and believing? Under such an arrangement, God, not man, would determine where man spends eternity. Therefore, bottom line, moderate Calvinism eliminates free will altogether in regard to salvation and inadvertently places itself in the same category as extreme and hyper-Calvinism. Note: Diagram 11 in the Reference Section portrays the three branches of Calvinism in graphic form.

Keep these definitions in mind as we continue. Also, remember that Reformed Theology consists of extreme and hyper-Calvinism.

The extreme and hyper-Calvinists differ in their view of Romans 9:17-18, especially in relation to the word *"hardens."* The extreme Calvinists, who believe that God predestined the elect to salvation from eternity past but left the non-elect to the consequence of their sin, must interpret *"hardens"* in Romans 9:18 as God merely leaving the non-elect in a condition outside of salvation. The hyper-Calvinists, on the other hand, who teach that God elects the elect to salvation from eternity past, but damns the non-elect from eternity past, perceive the term *"hardens"* in Romans 9:18 as pointing to God causing the evil that flows from the hardened heart. Yet, both extreme and hyper-Calvinists use these same verses (Romans 9:17-18) in an attempt to uphold their differing views.

If you are confused, just choose to persevere. The pieces of the puzzle will soon come together.

We will first examine the extreme Calvinists' view of *"hardens"* in Romans 9:18. I have included several quotes for the purpose of presenting an accurate picture of their interpretation of God's dealings with Pharaoh.

John Piper, an extreme Calvinist, in *The Pleasures of God*, page 321, states:

> ...In Exodus 8:1 the Lord says to Moses, "Go in to Pharaoh and say to him, 'Thus says the Lord, "Let my people go, that they may serve me."'" In other words, God's command, that is, his *will*, is that Pharaoh let the Israelites go. Nevertheless, from the start he also willed that Pharaoh *not* let the Israelites go. In Exodus 4:21 God says to Moses, "When you go back to Egypt, see that you do all those wonders before Pharaoh, which I have put in your hand; but *I will harden his heart,*

> *so that he will not let the people go."* At one point Pharaoh himself acknowledges that his unwillingness to let the people go is sin: "Now therefore, please forgive my sin" (Exodus 10:17). Thus, what we see is that God commands Pharaoh to do a thing which God himself wills not to allow. The good thing that God commands, God himself prevents. And the thing he brings about involves sin.[100]

Is Piper serious? "...God commands Pharaoh to do a thing which God himself wills not to allow. The good thing that God commands, God himself prevents." Wow! Must we cease using rational thought as we pursue God's truth?

RC Sproul (also an extreme Calvinist) writes the following on pages 74-75 of *Chosen by God* and disregards the obvious contradiction:

> Fallen man is flesh. In the flesh he can do nothing to please God. Paul declares, "The fleshly mind is enmity against God; for it is not subject to the law of God, nor indeed *can* be. So then, those who are in the flesh *cannot* please God." (Rom. 8:7, 8)
>
> ...People who are in the flesh have not been reborn. Unless they are first reborn, born of the Holy Spirit, they cannot be subject to the law of God. They cannot please God.
>
> Fallen man has the natural ability to make choices but lacks the moral ability to make godly choices.[101]

Consider where this thinking takes the Reformed theologian, especially in light of the fact that Moses (in obedience to God's instruction) asked Pharaoh to grant Israel the freedom to worship in the wilderness (Exodus 8:27). Had Pharaoh complied, he would have made a choice in agreement with God's will—a total impossibility based on the extreme and hyper-Calvinists' view of total depravity. Therefore, the Calvinists (especially extreme and hyper) must conclude that God required something of Pharaoh that Pharaoh (being depraved) could not perform—which lines up perfectly with Piper and Sproul's preceding quotes. But such an arrangement would make God enormously less than the all-wise, just, and loving Sovereign He claims to be! In fact, such an arrangement would make Him irrational. Again, we witness the impossibility of reconciling the contradictions within Calvinism. No wonder "mystery" is used (misused actually) so frequently by the proponents of Reformed Theology!

In *The Justification of God*, pages 158-159, John Piper records:

> In Rom. 9:17 Paul quotes Exodus 9:16 as his second Old Testament support for the righteousness of God in unconditional election....

> I am suggesting, therefore, that Paul employs Ex 9:16 (=Rom 9:17) as he did Ex 33:19—to further support his initial claim in 9:14 [Romans 9:14] that God is not unrighteous in the absoluteness of his unconditional election....[102]

On page 179, Piper also writes:

> The one task remaining in this chapter is to complete our exposition of *how* Paul intends for Rom 9:15-18 to defend the claim that God is not unrighteous in unconditionally predestining some Israelites to salvation and some to condemnation....[103]

Although difficult at times to determine if Piper is an extreme or hyper-Calvinist, he seems to perceive Romans 9:17-18 as teaching extreme Calvinism's definition of unconditional election—which according to his view, in no way makes God unrighteous "in unconditionally predestining some Israelites to salvation and some to condemnation."

On page 160 of that same work, Piper writes regarding Paul's use of *"hardens"* (Romans 9:18) in an attempt to prove extreme Calvinism's view of the term—which differs greatly (on the surface at least) from that of hyper-Calvinism (the different branches of Calvinism were addressed earlier should you need additional input). Keep in mind that three core Hebrew words are used in Exodus 4-14 to describe how Pharaoh's heart was hardened (my upcoming rebuttal will discuss these words in much detail). Note Piper's comments:

> In all likelihood when Paul uses the word [*"hardens"* NASB] in Romans 9:18 he is adopting the word from the LXX which corresponds to not just one of the three main Hebrew words, but to the synonymous import of each....[104]

How the LXX renders *"hardens"* (Romans 9:18) will be addressed later. The Septuagint (LXX) is a translation of the Old Testament Hebrew Scriptures into Greek. Don't overlook Piper's use of the phrase, "the synonymous import of each."

On pages 161-162, Piper writes concerning the three main Old Testament Hebrew words used in Exodus 4-14 to describe the hardening of Pharaoh's heart:

> I conclude, therefore, that the narrator of Ex 4-14 does not see [in the three main Hebrew words used for *"harden"*] terms with fundamentally different meanings. They all [the three main Hebrew words for *"harden"*] point to a condition of heart which

> renders it insensible to promptings and inflexible of will, and thus, in Pharaoh's case, adamantly opposed to God's demands....[105]

On page 161 of that same work, Piper makes reference to "Forster and Marston," the authors of *God's Strategy in Human History*—a book that portrays Paul as addressing nations rather than individuals in Romans 9:10-13. Forster and Marston also believe that the depraved possess the ability to repent and exercise faith prior to spiritual regeneration, and that *"hardens"* can also mean "to strengthen" rather than to "make hard." Note Piper's words:

> ...From wider usage and from the theological premise that Pharaoh's evil choice must be autonomous, they argue that to harden means to strengthen someone in his chosen course....[106]

On page 163, Piper attempts to refute the fact that *"hardens"* can mean "to strengthen" rather than to "make hard":

> ...A precise analysis of the verb forms...reveals that before the first active assertion of God's hardening in Ex 9:12 there are two assertions that Pharaoh hardened his own heart...and after 9:12 there are two assertions that he hardened his own heart.... What follows from this is that Pharaoh's "self-hardening" is equally well-attested before *and after* the first statement that God has hardened him. From this it cannot be inferred that Pharaoh's "self-hardening" represents his prior, independent sin for which God's hardening is the punishment. In view of the subsequent "self-hardening" (9:34; 13:15) it is just as probable that "the hardening of man by God appears as self-hardening."
>
> Concerning the six passive references to Pharaoh's "being hardened," five occur before Ex 9:12 and one (9:35) afterwards. But the most important question here is: Who *is* doing the hardening? Forster and Marston *assume* it is Pharaoh and not God. But in view of the prediction of 4:21 ("I will harden") this assumption loses its plausibility....[107]

Piper views the phrase, *"I will harden"* (Exodus 4:21), as confirming that God hardened Pharaoh's heart in every instance where the word *"harden"* or *"hardened"* is used in reference to Pharaoh, even his own "self-hardening." However, verses such as Exodus 8:15, 32, 9:34, and 13:15 (*"stubborn"*), clearly teach that Pharaoh hardened his own heart. Because of Piper's improper assumption, he is forced to credit God with hardening Pharaoh's heart (according to his definition of *"hardening"*) in instances such as Exodus 7:13, 14, 22, 8:19, 9:7, and 9:35 as well. How Piper defines *"harden"* is our next topic of discussion.

Even though Piper argues that God hardened Pharaoh's heart, never Pharaoh, you might be surprised at how he defines *"hardens"* of Romans 9:18. In *The Justification of God*, page 178, Piper writes:

> In 9:14-18 [of Romans] Paul is answering an objector who says that if God acts this way he is unrighteous. The thread of Paul's thoughts, therefore, requires that 9:14-18 concern itself with the divine action described in 9:6-13, namely with God's choosing to save some within Israel while rejecting others, or as 9:13 puts it, with his loving some and hating others. Nothing else but the demands of this flow of thought explains so clearly why Paul in 9:14-18 treats the two sides of God's sovereign activity and why he chooses to use the word "harden" in 9:18. Must we not conclude, therefore, that the hardening in Rom 9:18 has reference, just as the hardening in 11:7, to the action of God whereby a person is left in a condition outside salvation and thus "prepared for destruction" (9:22)?[108]

Piper concludes that Paul's use of *"hardens"* in Romans 9:18 points to God leaving a person "in a condition outside of salvation and thus 'prepared for destruction.'" Such a mindset would allow Piper's view of depravity and unconditional election to stand within extreme Calvinism at least. The error associated with this mindset will be revealed later.

RC Sproul, in *Chosen by God*, pages 144 and 147, writes along these same lines, first speaking against "active hardening" and following with his approval of "passive hardening":

> Active hardening would involve God's direct intervention within the inner chambers of Pharaoh's heart. God would intrude into Pharaoh's heart and create fresh evil in it. This would certainly insure that Pharaoh would bring forth the result that God was looking for. It would also insure that God is the author of sin.
>
> Passive hardening is a totally different story. Passive hardening involves a divine judgment upon sin that is already present. All that God needs to do to harden the heart of a person whose heart is already desperately wicked is to "give him over to his sin."...

> In God's ultimate act of judgment he gives sinners over to their sins. In effect, he abandons them to their own desires. So it was with Pharaoh. By this act of judgment, God did not blemish his own righteousness by creating fresh evil in Pharaoh's heart. He established his own righteousness by punishing the evil that was already there in Pharaoh.[109]

These quotes confirm that Piper and Sproul (extreme Calvinists) do not view *"hardens"* (Romans 9:18) as pointing to God creating evil in Pharaoh's heart (as the hyper-Calvinists have concluded). Neither do Piper and Sproul believe that *"harden"* points to God strengthening Pharaoh to accomplish what Pharaoh had already chosen to do (a subject addressed shortly). Instead, they view *"harden"* as God giving Pharaoh over to his sin—giving Pharaoh over, in the midst of his spiritual depravity, to the consequence of his sin. Note: Always keep in mind that in Reformed Theology (extreme and hyper-Calvinism) the non-elect, due to their depravity, cannot obey God by choosing absolute good. Reformed Theology even supposes that the elect cannot accept Christ while depraved—that they must be freed from their depravity through spiritual regeneration before they can exercise faith in Christ (along with repentance) and be saved.

Are Piper and Sproul correct in their assumptions? We will address this issue shortly.

Request was made to quote James R. White's, *The Potter's Freedom*, pages 211-212, but the request was denied. Paraphrased, he states that Pharaoh's heart was hardened in the sense that he was chosen (by God's plan) for destruction. According to White, no other view is plausible. Is no other view plausible? Shortly, we will allow Scripture alone to answer this question.

John Calvin's words in Book 1, Chapter 18, Section 2, of *Institutes* are somewhat difficult to follow but much-needed input if we are to understand Calvin's view of *"hardened*":

> ...He is said to have hardened the heart of Pharaoh, to have hardened it yet more, and confirmed it. Some evade these forms of expression by a silly cavil, because Pharaoh is elsewhere said to have hardened his own heart, thus making his will the cause of hardening it; as if the two things did not perfectly agree with each other, though in different senses viz., that man, though acted upon by God, at the same time also acts. But I retort the objection on those who make it. If to harden means only bare permission, the contumacy will not properly belong to Pharaoh. Now, could any thing be more feeble and insipid than to interpret as if Pharaoh had only allowed himself to be hardened? We may add, that Scripture

> cuts off all handle for such cavils: "I," saith the Lord, "will harden his heart," (Exo 4: 21). So also, Moses says of the inhabitants of the land of Canaan, that they went forth to battle because the Lord had hardened their hearts, (Jos 11: 20)....In like manner, in Isaiah, he says of the Assyrian, "I will send him against a hypocritical nation, and against the people of my wrath will I give him a charge to take the spoil, and to take the prey," (Isa 10: 6) not that he intends to teach wicked and obstinate man to obey spontaneously, but because he bends them to execute his judgments, just as if they carried their orders engraven on their minds. And hence it appears that they are impelled by the sure appointment of God. I admit, indeed, that God often acts in the reprobate by interposing the agency of Satan; but in such a manner, that Satan himself performs his part, just as he is impelled, and succeeds only in so far as he is permitted. The evil spirit that troubled Saul is said to be from the Lord, (1Sa 16: 14) to intimate that Saul's madness was a just punishment from God. Satan is also said to blind the minds of those who believe not (2Co 4: 4). But how so, unless that a spirit of error is sent from God himself, making those who refuse to obey the truth to believe a lie?...
>
> ...since the will of God is said to be the cause of all things, all the counsels and actions of men must be held to be governed by his providence; so that he not only exerts his power in the elect, who are guided by the Holy Spirit, but also forces the reprobate to do him service. [110]

Calvin, in *Institutes*, Book 3, Chapter 23, Section 1, also writes:

> ...God is said to have raised up Pharaoh, and to harden whom he will. Hence it follows, that the hidden counsel of God is the cause of hardening....[111]

Arthur Pink, in *The Sovereignty of God*, page 91, has this to say:

> ...Upon the wicked, God exerts a restraining, softening, directing, and hardening, and blinding power, according to the dictates of His own infinite wisdom and justice and unto the outworking of His own eternal purpose....[112]

Undoubtedly, the Calvinists are in disagreement over Paul's use of *"hardens"* (Romans 9:18). Some Calvinists view *"hardens"* as God giving man over to his sin, leaving man to the consequence of his error. Other Calvinists perceive *"hardens"* as God actively producing the hardening by causing the evil that flows from the hardened heart. Are any Calvinists correct in their assumptions? Consider the following rebuttal.

Rebuttal:

We have addressed how extreme Calvinists (such as Piper and Sproul) view the word *"hardens."* They basically perceive it as God giving Pharaoh over to his sin—giving Pharaoh over, in the midst of his spiritual depravity, to the consequence of his sin. Piper, Sproul, and other Reformed theologians seem to view *"hardens"* from this vantage point to distance themselves from the hyper-Calvinists. The hyper-Calvinists' view of *"hardens"* portrays God as producing the hardening by causing the evil that flows from the hardened heart. Note RC Sproul's words from page 143 of his work, *Chosen by God*:

> The dreadful error of hyper-Calvinism is that it involves God in coercing sin....[113]

Should Sproul and Piper be correct, they, along with all extreme Calvinists, destroy their definition of total depravity. The hyper-Calvinists are guilty of the same contradiction. How so? Both extreme and hyper-Calvinism define total depravity as the total inability of the depraved to make a willing choice according to God's will. They hold to this definition in an attempt to maintain their view of the "T" of the TULIP, Total Depravity, a view which leaves the depraved with an inability to willingly choose to believe. If their definition is correct, why would God be required to harden Pharaoh's heart (based on extreme or hyper-Calvinism's definition of the term "harden") if Pharaoh's heart was, in its natural state, incapable of performing God's will? In other words, how could God's hardening cause a totally depraved heart to become more hardened—especially if, according to extreme and hyper-Calvinism, the depraved are spiritual corpses? Why would God need to supply additional aid to an individual incapable of choosing His will? Should such be the case, Pharaoh was a pretty lively corpse before experiencing Reformed Theology's brand of hardening they assume is addressed in the book of Exodus—disproving extreme and hyper-Calvinism's definition of total depravity altogether.

Extreme and hyper-Calvinism's view of *"hardens"* (Romans 9:18) fails to properly interpret the different applications of the word in the Hebrew language. Dave Hunt, who disagrees with all forms of Calvinism, writes on pages 334-335 of *What Love is This?*:

> We gain a better understanding of God's dealings with Pharaoh through the Hebrew words translated "harden" or "hardened" in the King James. In the sense of hardening one's own heart, *kabed* is used four times: Exodus 7:14, 8:15, 9:7 and 9:34. *Qashah*, only used once (Exodus 7:3), means to become stiff-necked or stubborn. *Chazaq* (Exodus 4:21; 7:13, 22; 8:19; 9:12, 35; 10:20, 27; 11:10; 14:4, 8, 17) means to strengthen or give courage, indicating that God was not causing Pharaoh to be an evil man or to do evil actions, but was giving Pharaoh the strength and courage to stand by his intent not to let Israel go, even when the plagues became overwhelmingly terrifying....[114]

Forster and Marston, in *God's Strategy in Human History*, pages 169-170, state:

> The Bible does not teach that God made Pharaoh unrepentant. The main word used for the hardening of Pharaoh's heart is *chazaq*, and it seems to mean that God emboldened or encouraged Pharaoh's heart so that he had the stubborn courage to stand even in the face of very frightening miracles.
>
> The verb *qashah* occurs only twice in the context of the hardening of Pharaoh's heart, and refers to the effects of the whole process of God's dealings and Pharaoh's reactions.
>
> The phrase "made heavy" [*kabed*] his heart is used only once with God as the agent of making heavy [Exodus 10:1]. This comes just after Pharaoh himself has rejected his final solemn warning, and has made his own heart heavy. It seems to indicate that God was actively involved in stimulating and allowing the process.
>
> God never prevents anyone from repenting.[115]

With this input in mind, we will go to the Scriptures to examine the meaning of *chazaq,* the main Hebrew word used to describe the hardening of Pharaoh's heart. Be sure to draw your conclusions as to how it (*chazaq*) relates to Pharaoh after you have read all of the verses. These Scriptures provide crucial input regarding this frequently misunderstood truth. Note the number of times that *chazaq* points to God strengthening or encouraging the subject on which the action is performed (the English equivalent of *chazaq* is recorded in bold print in each of the passages). Reading the underlined verses first would serve you well.

Several Instances of the Use of Chazaq

Deuteronomy 1:38—*'Joshua the son of Nun, who stands before you, he shall enter there;* ***encourage*** *him, for he shall cause Israel to inherit it.*

Deuteronomy 3:28—*'But charge Joshua and* ***encourage*** *him and strengthen him; for he shall go across at the head of this people, and he shall give them as an inheritance the land which you will see.'*

Joshua 11:20—*For it was of the LORD to* ***harden*** *their hearts, to meet Israel in battle in order that he might utterly destroy them, that they might receive no mercy, but that he might destroy them, just as the LORD had commanded Moses.*

Judges 3:12—*Now the sons of Israel again did evil in the sight of the LORD. So the LORD* ***strengthened*** *Eglon the king of Moab against Israel, because they had done evil in the sight of the LORD.*

Judges 16:28—*Then Samson called to the LORD and said, "O Lord GOD, please remember me and please* ***strengthen*** *me just this time, O God, that I may at once be avenged of the Philistines for my two eyes."*

1Samuel 23:16—*And Jonathan, Saul's son, arose and went to David at Horesh, and* ***encouraged*** *him in God.*

2Samuel 11:25—*Then David said to the messenger, "Thus you shall say to Joab, 'Do not let this thing displease you, for the sword devours one as well as another; make your battle against the city stronger and overthrow it'; and so* ***encourage*** *him."*

2Kings 12:5—*let the priests take it for themselves, each from his acquaintance; and they shall* ***repair*** *the damages of the house wherever any damage may be found.*

2Kings 12:6, 7, 8, 12, and 14, as well as 2Kings 22:5-6—The words "***repair***" and "***repaired***" in these passages are from the Piel form of Chazaq.

1Chronicles 26:27—*They dedicated part of the spoil won in battles to* ***repair*** *the house of the LORD.*

1Chronicles 29:12—*Both riches and honor come from Thee, and Thou dost rule over all, and in Thy hand is power and might; and it lies in Thy hand to make great, and to* ***strengthen*** *everyone.*

2Chronicles 11:11—*He also* ***strengthened*** *the fortresses and put officers in them and stores of food, oil and wine.*

2Chronicles 11:12—*And he put shields and spears in every city and* ***strengthened*** *them greatly. So he held Judah and Benjamin.*

2Chronicles 11:17—*And they* ***strengthened*** *the kingdom of Judah and supported Rehoboam the son of Solomon for three years, for they walked in the way of David and Solomon for three years.*

2Chronicles 24:5—*And he gathered the priests and Levites, and said to them, "Go out to the cities of Judah, and collect money from all Israel to* ***repair*** *the house of your God annually, and you shall do the matter quickly." But the Levites did not act quickly.*

2 Chronicles 24:12—*And the king and Jehoiada gave it to those who did the work of the service of the house of the LORD; and they hired masons and carpenters to restore the house of the LORD, and also workers in iron and bronze to* ***repair*** *the house of the LORD.*

2Chronicles 26:9—*Moreover, Uzziah built towers in Jerusalem at the Corner Gate and at the Valley Gate and at the corner buttress and* ***fortified*** *them.*

2Chronicles 29:3—*In the first year of his reign, in the first month, he opened the doors of the house of the LORD and* ***repaired*** *them.*

2Chronicles 29:34—*But the priests were too few, so that they were unable to skin all the burnt offerings; therefore their brothers the Levites* ***helped*** *them until the work was completed, and until the other priests had consecrated themselves....*

2Chronicles 32:5—*And he took courage and rebuilt all the wall that had been broken down, and erected towers on it, and built another outside wall, and* ***strengthened*** *the Millo in the city of David, and made weapons and shields in great number.*

2Chronicles 34:8—*Now in the eighteenth year of his reign, when he had purged the land and the house, he sent Shaphan the son of Azaliah, and Maaseiah an official of the city, and Joah the son of Joahaz the recorder, to* ***repair*** *the house of the LORD his God.*

2Chronicles 34:10—*Then they gave it into the hands of the workmen who had the oversight of the house of the LORD, and the workmen who were working in the house of the LORD used it to restore and* ***repair*** *the house.*

2Chronicles 35:2—*And he set the priests in their offices and* ***encouraged*** *them in the service of the house of the LORD.*

Ezra 1:6—*And all those about them* ***encouraged*** *them with articles of silver, with gold, with goods, with cattle, and with valuables, aside from all that was given as a freewill offering.*

Ezra 6:22—*And they observed the Feast of Unleavened Bread seven days with joy, for the LORD had caused them to rejoice, and had turned the heart of the king of Assyria toward them to* ***encourage*** *them in the work of the house of God, the God of Israel.*

Nehemiah 2:18—*And I told them how the hand of my God had been favorable to me, and also about the king's words which he had spoken to me. Then they said, "Let us arise and build." So* ***they put*** *their hands to the good work.*

Nehemiah 3:19—*And next to him Ezer the son of Jeshua, the official of Mizpah,* ***repaired*** *another section, in front of the ascent of the armory at the Angle.*

Nehemiah 6:9—*For all of them were trying to frighten us, thinking, "They will become discouraged with the work and it will not be done." But now, O God,* ***strengthen*** *my hands.*

Job 4:3—"*Behold you have admonished many, And you have* ***strengthened*** *weak hands.*

Psalm 64:5—*They* ***hold fast*** *to themselves an evil purpose; They talk of laying snares secretly; They say, "Who can see them?"*

Psalm 147:13—*For He has* ***strengthened*** *the bars of your gates; He has blessed your sons within you.*

Isaiah 22:21—*And I will clothe him with your tunic, And tie your sash securely about him, I will* ***entrust*** *him with your authority, And he will become a father to the inhabitants of Jerusalem and to the house of Judah.*

Isaiah 33:23—*Your tackle hangs slack; It cannot* ***hold*** *the base of its mast firmly, Nor spread out the sail. Then the prey of an abundant spoil will be divided; The lame will take the plunder.*

Isaiah 35:3—*Encourage the exhausted, and* ***strengthen*** *the feeble.*

Isaiah 41:7—*So the craftsman* ***encourages*** *the smelter, And he who smooths metal with the hammer encourages him who beats the anvil, Saying of the soldering, "It is good"; And he* ***fastens*** *it with nails, That it should not totter.*

Isaiah 54:2—"*Enlarge the place of your tent; Stretch out the curtains of your dwellings, spare not; Lengthen your cords, And* ***strengthen*** *your pegs.*

Jeremiah 5:3—*O LORD, do not Thine eyes look for truth? Thou hast smitten them, But they did not weaken; Thou hast consumed them, But they refused to take correction.* ***They have mad****e their faces* ***harder*** *than rock; They have refused to repent.*

Jeremiah 10:4—"*They decorate it with silver and with gold; They* ***fasten*** *it with nails and with hammers So that it will not totter.*

Jeremiah 23:14—"*Also among the prophets of Jerusalem I have seen a horrible thing: The committing of adultery and walking in falsehood; And they* ***strengthen*** *the hands of evildoers, So that no one has turned back from his wickedness. All of them have become to Me like Sodom, And her inhabitants like Gomorrah.*

Ezekiel 13:22—"*Because you disheartened the righteous with falsehood when I did not cause him grief, but have* ***encouraged*** *the wicked not to turn from his wicked way and preserve his life,*

Ezekiel 30:24—*'For I will* ***strengthen*** *the arms of the king of Babylon and put My sword in his hand; and I will break the arms of Pharaoh, so that he will groan before him with the groanings of a wounded man.*

Ezekiel 34:4—"*Those who are sickly* ***you have*** *not* ***strengthened****, the diseased you have not healed, the broken you have not bound up, the scattered you have not brought back, nor have you sought for the lost; but with force and with severity you have dominated them.*

Ezekiel 34:16—"*I will seek the lost, bring back the scattered, bind up the broken, and* ***strengthen*** *the sick; but the fat and the strong I will destroy. I will feed them with judgment.*

Daniel 10:18—*Then this one with human appearance touched me again and* ***strengthened*** *me.*

Daniel 10:19—*And he said, "O man of high esteem, do not be afraid. Peace be with you;* ***take courage*** *and* ***be courageous!****" Now as soon as he spoke to me, I* ***received strength*** *and said, "May my lord speak, for* ***you have strengthened*** *me."*

Hosea 7:15—*Although I trained and* ***strengthened*** *their arms, Yet they devise evil against Me.*

Nahum 2:1—*The one who scatters has come up against you. Man the fortress, watch the road;* ***Strengthen*** *your back, summon all your strength.*

Nahum 3:14—*Draw for yourself water for the siege! Strengthen your fortifications! Go into the clay and tread the mortar!* ***Take hold*** *of the brick mold!*

Do you think it feasible to apply the Hebrew word *chazaq,* rendered *"strengthen"* in so much of the Old Testament, in the same manner to Pharaoh? As you read the following verses from the book of Exodus, all of which relate to Pharaoh, replace *"harden"* (or *"hardened"*) with "strengthen" (or "strengthened") and note the transformed perspective.

Exodus 4:21—*And the LORD said to Moses, "When you go back to Egypt see that you perform before Pharaoh all the wonders which I have put in your power; but I will* ***harden*** *his heart so that he will not let the people go.*

Exodus 9:12—*And the LORD* ***hardened*** *Pharaoh's heart, and he did not listen to them, just as the LORD had spoken to Moses.*

Exodus 9:35—*And Pharaoh's heart was* ***hardened****, and he did not let the sons of Israel go, just as the LORD had spoken through Moses.*

Unquestionably, *"hardened" (chazaq)* in Exodus 9:35 is in the passive voice, meaning the subject is being acted upon. Thus, God did the hardening, but it points to God strengthening Pharaoh's heart to do what Pharaoh had previously chosen. However, John Piper writes on page 168 of *The Justification of God*:

> ...Thus behind the passive voice in [Exodus] 9:35 stands Yahweh. But since the hardening of 9:35 is parallel to the self-hardening in 9:34 we are shown again...that for the ancient writer these three events (self-hardening, being hardened, and God hardening) are not three, but one.[116]

Again we observe that Piper (and other Reformed theologians) must interpret *"hardened"* as God doing the hardening in every case, a hardening that gives the non-elect (who, in Piper and his contemporaries' minds, possess a depraved heart incapable of choosing absolute good) over to their sin. From their vantage point, *"hardened"* could never point to God strengthening Pharaoh's heart to do what Pharaoh had previously chosen. Neither can they accept the truth that Pharaoh possessed a heart capable of choosing both evil and God's will (salvation, that is)—a fact that negates the Reformed view of Total Depravity, doing away with the TULIP altogether (T—Total Depravity; U—Unconditional Election; L—Limited Atonement; I—Irresistible Grace; P—Perseverance of the Saints). (The TULIP is addressed in depth in *God's Heart as it Relates to Foreknowledge/Predestination*, the first book of this *God's Heart* series.)

Note how differently these additional passages (where *chazaq* is employed) read when *"hardened"* and *"harden"* are replaced with "strengthened" and "strengthen."

Exodus 10:20—*But the LORD* ***hardened*** [strengthened] *Pharaoh's heart, and he did not let the sons of Israel go.*

Exodus 10:27—*But the LORD* ***hardened*** [strengthened] *Pharaoh's heart, and he was not willing to let them go.*

Exodus 11:10—*And Moses and Aaron performed all these wonders before Pharaoh; yet the LORD* ***hardened*** [strengthened] *Pharaoh's heart, and he did not let the sons of Israel go out of his land.*

Exodus 14:4—"*Thus I will* ***harden*** [strengthen] *Pharaoh's heart, and he will chase after them; and I will be honored through Pharaoh and all his army, and the Egyptians will know that I am the LORD." And they did so.*

Exodus 14:8—*And the LORD* ***hardened*** [strengthened] *the heart of Pharaoh, king of Egypt, and he chased after the sons of Israel as the sons of Israel were going out boldly.*

Exodus 14:17—*And as for Me, behold, I will* ***harden*** [strengthen] *the hearts of the Egyptians so that they will go in after them; and I will be honored through Pharaoh and all his army, through his chariots and his horsemen.*

Other passages such as Ezekiel 3:7-9 confirm that *chazaq* can point to the resolve and determination of a people to complete their chosen course of action. Consider how these verses are rendered in the American Standard Version:

> *7 But the house of Israel will not hearken unto thee; for they will not hearken unto me: for all the house of Israel are of **hard** (chazaq) forehead and of a stiff (qashah) heart. 8 Behold, I have made thy face **hard** (chazaq) against their faces, and thy forehead **hard** (chazaq) against their foreheads. 9 As an adamant harder than flint have I made thy forehead: fear them not, neither be dismayed at their looks, though they are a rebellious house.* (Ezekiel 3:7-9 ASV)

Israel, without reservation, was determined to complete the course of evil she had previously chosen. Her forehead was *"hard" (chazaq),* but God made Ezekiel's forehead just as *"hard" (chazaq)* as he (Ezekiel) stood against the sin of the nation while exercising his freedom of choice. This example (along with a plethora of others) confirms that *chazaq* can point to God strengthening an individual in that individual's chosen course of action. *Chazaq* does not point, therefore, to a hardening of the hearts of the non-elect so they can't believe—an idea found nowhere in Scripture.

Piper and Sproul (Reformed theologians) both seem to indicate that the Greek word for *"hardens"* in Romans 9:18, which is *skleruno* (sklay-roo'-no), points to God giving the non-elect over to their sin. Our study of the Hebrew word *chazaq* disproves such thinking, for *"hardened"* is used on several occasions in the Old Testament to indicate that God strengthened individuals to complete their chosen course of action. Thus, Pharaoh's hardened heart in no way validates the false idea that God made Pharaoh part of the non-elect in eternity past. *"Hardens"* points to God granting Pharaoh the strength to carry out his (Pharaoh's) choices. This fact is confirmed by Exodus 3:19:

> *"But I know that the king of Egypt will not permit you to go, except under compulsion.* (Exodus 3:19)

Notice that before anything is stated in Scripture regarding God's hardening of Pharaoh's heart (later addressed for the first time in Exodus 4:21), God revealed to Moses that Pharaoh would allow (*"permit"*) Israel to leave only *"under compulsion"*—"*permit*" proving that Pharaoh's choice, not God's, determined when the Jews would depart (although God's foreknowledge allowed Him to state previously the number of years Israel would be in exile in Egypt—Genesis 15:13).

Exodus 6:1 states as well:

> *Then the LORD said to Moses, "Now you shall see what I will do to Pharaoh; for under compulsion he shall let them go, and under compulsion he shall drive them out of his land."* (Exodus 6:1)

The phrase, *"shall let them go,"* again confirms that Pharaoh ultimately determined when the Jews would exit the land. This ties in wonderfully with Exodus 12:29-33:

> *Now it came about at midnight that the LORD struck all the first-born in the land of Egypt, from the first-born of Pharaoh who sat on his throne to the first-born of the captive who was in the dungeon, and all the first-born of cattle. 30 And Pharaoh arose in the night, he and all his servants and all the Egyptians; and there was a great cry in Egypt, for there was no home where there was not someone dead. 31 Then he called for Moses and Aaron at night and said, "Rise up, get out from among my people, both you and the sons of Israel; and go, worship the LORD, as you have said. 32 Take both your flocks and your herds, as you have said, and go, and bless me also." 33 And the Egyptians urged the people, to send them out of the land in haste, for they said, "We shall all be dead."* (Exodus 12:29-33)

God had hardened (strengthened) Pharaoh in the midst of horrendous adversity. In fact, God's hardening (His granting Pharaoh the strength to stand) allowed Pharaoh to persist so fervently and consistently. The death of the firstborn in Egypt (Exodus 12:29), however, was the catalyst that resulted in Israel leaving *"under compulsion"*—in fact, at the insistence of Pharaoh and the Egyptians (Exodus 3:19; 12:30-33). This *"compulsion"* resulted from Jehovah strengthening the evil leader during the onslaught of the plagues. Yes, Pharaoh chose (by his own will) to disobey, just as he chose (by his own will) to release Israel. God, however, granted Pharaoh the strength to persevere in the midst of the consequence of his evil choices prior to the evil leader choosing to free the Hebrew people.

Dave Hunt, in *What Love is This?,* page 333, states:

> When God hardened Pharaoh's heart to further His purposes for Israel and Egypt, to manifest His power more fully, and specifically to complete His judgment upon the gods of Egypt, He was, in fact, only helping Pharaoh to do what that tyrant wanted to do. When He sent Moses to Egypt, God declared, "I am sure that the king of Egypt will not let you go..." (Exodus 3:19). This was Pharaoh's disposition before a word was said about God's hardening of his heart. Yet Calvinists are almost unanimous in their avoidance of this scripture. Passing it by, they begin their comments with Exodus 4:21, "I will harden his

> heart, that he shall not let the people go." Like the others, Pink ignores 3:19 and writes, "did not God harden his heart *before* the plagues were sent upon Egypt?—see Exodus 4:21!" [A quote from Arthur W. Pink's, *The Sovereignty of God*, (Grand Rapids, MI: Baker Book House, 2nd printing. 1986), 96.] White, too, avoids 3:19 and also uses 4:21 as foundational [in *The Potter's Freedom*, pp. 211-212]. So does Piper [in *The Justification of God*, pp. 155-181]. In building his lengthy argument concerning the hardening of Pharaoh's heart, he relies heavily upon 4:21. Piper's many pages of erudite citations of the original Hebrew and Greek, with accompanying complicated arguments, lose their luster in view of his disregard of 3:19, which, had he noted it, would have changed the whole picture. Unfortunately, Piper flooded *The Justification of God* with Greek and Hebrew words in those alphabets without the English equivalents that authors usually supply. Thus, readers who are not Greek and Hebrew scholars must take his word for what he says....[117]

In their book titled, *God's Strategy in Human History*, page 75, Forster and Marston write:

> ...God did not give Pharaoh the wicked desire to rebel against him. What God did was to give him the stubborn courage to carry out that desire. Thus God's action merely made the difference between a wicked act and the suppression of an evil desire through fear....[118]

On page 169 of that same work (a quote referenced earlier), Forster and Marston comment:

> The Bible does not teach that God made Pharaoh unrepentant. The main word used for the hardening of Pharaoh's heart is *chazaq*, and it seems to mean that God emboldened or encouraged Pharaoh's heart so that he had the stubborn courage to stand even in the face of very frightening miracles.[119]

God raised up Pharaoh for a special purpose. He did not raise him up to judge him as an end in itself, nor to harden his heart because he was part of the non-elect (the Reformed view). Neither did God raise him up to remove his will, for throughout the entire process of the plagues Pharaoh chose as he pleased. Romans 9:17, a quote from Exodus 9:16, reveals God's *"purpose"*:

> *For the Scripture says to Pharaoh, "FOR THIS VERY PURPOSE I RAISED YOU UP, TO DEMONSTRATE MY POWER IN YOU, AND THAT MY NAME MIGHT BE PROCLAIMED THROUGHOUT THE WHOLE EARTH."* (Romans 9:17)

God's *"purpose"* prevailed (that of demonstrating His *"power"* and having his *"name...proclaimed throughout the whole earth"*), confirmed by Rahab's response in Joshua 2:9:

> *..."I know that the Lord has given you the land, and that the terror of you has fallen on us, and that all the inhabitants of the land have melted away before you.* (Joshua 2:9)

The inhabitants of Canaan were frightened of Israel due to God's protection of the Jews during their exodus from Egypt! This account has served throughout the centuries as a reminder of God's power and unwavering commitment to the Hebrew people. To Him be the glory!

Conclusion: *"Hardens"* (Romans 9:18) points to God providing Pharaoh the strength to stand (while Pharaoh exercised his own free will) as He (God) brought destruction upon Egypt. It does not point to God giving Pharaoh over to his sin (extreme Calvinism's view), nor to God creating fresh evil in Pharaoh's heart (hyper-Calvinism's view). Through their erroneous beliefs, both extreme and hyper-Calvinism negate their definition of total depravity—as confirmed by the following input.

Reformed Theology (extreme and hyper-Calvinism) defines total depravity as the total inability of the depraved to make a willing choice according to God's will. In fact, based on their view, the depraved are spiritual corpses. If so, why would God be required to harden Pharaoh's heart in any way at all, even to the slightest degree? If extreme and hyper-Calvinism's definition of total depravity is accurate, Pharaoh should have resisted naturally, without any additional assistance from anyone or anything. Therefore, the proponents of this error-laden system contradict their definition of total depravity by misinterpreting *"hardens"* in Romans 9:18.

Consider the ease with which Paul's words of Romans 9:18 can be interpreted when viewed from the side of free will:

> *So then He has mercy on whom He desires, and He hardens whom He desires.* (Romans 9:18)

(1) God had *"mercy"* upon the nation of Israel when Moses unwisely requested that He (God) dwell in the midst of the people. God displayed great *"mercy"* in resisting, for had He entered the camp in the manner that

Moses desired the nation would have been consumed (Exodus 33:5). Instead, God's glory entered the camp on Moses' face and the nation was preserved.

(2) God *"hardens whom He desires,"* which in this context points to God granting strength to Pharaoh to pursue what Pharaoh had previously chosen by his own will.

Are you seeing how a proper view of sovereignty and free will makes a highly debated section of Scripture easily understood?

God, in his sovereignty, establishes all authority. He places both evil and righteous men in positions of leadership (Romans 13:1) without removing their freedom of choice. He does, however, due to His foreknowledge, know what choices they will make in advance of their making them. God, in His sovereignty, accomplishes His purposes by strengthening certain leaders as they carry out their choices. Hence, even with Moses and Pharaoh, God raised them up to bring about His desired end with each retaining a free will.

Our proper view of *"hardens"* (Romans 9:18) provides critical insight as we continue. In fact, our gleanings from verses such as Exodus 14:17, Joshua 11:19-20, and Judges 3:12 will take on a delightful freshness. In each case, God hardened (strengthened, or encouraged) men's hearts as they pursued their previously willed course of action.

Before examining Romans 9:19-24, additional input pertaining to Romans 9:17-18 will be helpful, especially since Romans 9:17-18 and Romans 9:19-24 are so closely associated. Note John Piper's words from *The Justification of God*, page 178:

> In 9:14-18 Paul is answering an objector who says that if God acts this way he is unrighteous. The thread of Paul's thoughts, therefore, requires that 9:14-18 concern itself with the divine action described in 9:6-13, namely with God's choosing to save some within Israel while rejecting others, or as 9:13 puts it, with his loving some and hating others.... Must we not conclude, therefore, that the hardening in Romans 9:18 has reference, just as the hardening in 11:7, to the action of God whereby a person is left in a condition outside salvation and thus "prepared for destruction" (9:22)?[120]

Piper, in linking Romans 9:18 to Romans 9:22, fails to mention Pharaoh in his quote pertaining to Romans 9:18. Based on his comments before and after the preceding quote, Piper doesn't view *"hardens"* in Romans 9:18 as referring to Pharaoh's particular hardening in the book of Exodus, but rather to God's hardening of the non-elect within Israel in particular, and all the non-elect in general—a conclusion that frees him (based on his view of *"hardens"*) to incorrectly assume that Paul is teaching the Reformed view of predestination and election. To make my point, I will first present Piper's words from pages 179 and 180 of *The Justification of God*:

> The one task remaining in this chapter is to complete our exposition of *how* Paul intends for Romans 9:15-18 to defend the claim that God is not unrighteous in unconditionally predestining some Israelites to salvation and some to condemnation....
> ...in Rom 9:15 and 17, Paul employs Old Testament texts in which *the exercise of God's sovereign freedom, in mercy and in hardening, is the means by which he declares the glory of his name!* This is the heart of Paul's defense: in choosing unconditionally those on whom he will have mercy (love) and those whom he will harden (hate) God is not unrighteous, for in this "electing purpose" he is acting out of a full allegiance to his name and esteem for his glory.[121]

Piper doesn't perceive *"hardens"* in Romans 9:18 as pointing particularly to the hardening of Pharaoh's heart in Exodus 4-14, even though Pharaoh is mentioned in the preceding verse (Romans 9:17). Rather, he perceives *"hardens"* (Romans 9:18) as addressing the non-elect within Israel in particular, along with all the non-elect of mankind in general, whom God has hardened (given over to their sin) and thus, doomed to destruction—according to his view. He also perceives those who receive *"mercy"* in Romans 9:18 as the elect within Israel in particular, as well as all of the elect of mankind in general. He makes these assumptions in an attempt to prove Calvinism's unconditional election (the "U" of the TULIP), an idea he must attach to Romans 9:20-23 as well. We discovered earlier, however, that the context of Romans 9:10-18 will not allow such an interpretation. After all, if God hardened Pharaoh's heart (as Piper defines *"hardened"*) in all instances in the book of Exodus, then, according to Exodus 9:34, God caused Pharaoh to sin:

> *But when Pharaoh saw that the rain and the hail and the thunder had ceased, he sinned again and hardened his heart, he and his servants.* (Exodus 9:34)

The Scriptures clearly teach that God does not tempt nor cause anyone to sin:

> *...for God cannot be tempted by evil, and He Himself does not tempt anyone.* (James 1:13)

Should the sovereign God we serve cause evil, Satan would be His ally—a total impossibility.

A quote from Dave Hunt's work, *What Love is This?,* page 187, serves as an excellent transition into Romans 9:19-24. Be aware that when Hunt employs the term "Calvinism" he is making reference to those individuals who perceive God as the cause of all things, even causing the elect to believe and the non-elect to reject the gospel—yet judging the non-elect for failing to believe. We have determined previously that should such an arrangement be valid, God would be totally unjust. (Note: You may need to read this paragraph, along with Hunt's ensuing quote, more than once for proper understanding):

> Many of today's Calvinists deny that Calvinism teaches that God *causes* evil. Yet that is clearly what Calvin himself insisted upon: "That men do nothing save at the secret instigation of God, and do not discuss and deliberate on anything, but what he has previously decreed with himself, and brings to pass by his secret direction, is proved by numberless clear passages of Scripture." In fact, there is no such Scripture–and Calvin's examples apply only to some men, not to all.
>
> Could not the sinner blame for his sin and eternal suffering in the Lake of Fire a God who allows him to choose only evil and not good? Who, by eternal decree, sovereignly originated his evil thoughts and caused his evil deeds and then in punishment for that evil predestined him to eternal torment? But wait! Doesn't Romans 9:19-22 declare that no man has the right to complain against God? Paul asks: "Shall the thing formed say to him that formed it, Why hast thou made me thus? Hath not the potter power over the clay, of the same lump to make one vessel unto honour, and the other unto dishonour?"...[122]

A study of Romans 9:19-24 will test: (1) The validity of Calvin's statements (2) The soundness of the theology of those who believe similarly. It should be exciting as well as encouraging as we continue, especially with the contextual backdrop of Romans 9:10-18 at our fingertips. The goal is a correct understanding of God's heart, so prepare to be blessed.

Romans 9:19 *You will say to me then, "Why does He still find fault? For who resists His will?"*

We have proven that Paul is not teaching unconditional election to salvation in Romans 9:6-18, although Reformed theologians (extreme and hyper-Calvinist) believe he is. If Paul were teaching unconditional election (the "U" of the TULIP) in Romans 9:6-18, it would naturally follow that he would teach unconditional election in Romans 9:19-23. Remember that information regarding the TULIP and Calvinism (Reformed Theology being a branch of Calvinism) is provided in the Reference Section of this study.

Reformed theologians generally perceive the critic of Romans 9:19 as questioning Paul because: (1) They view Paul as teaching Reformed Theology's unconditional election to salvation (2) They view the critic as believing in free will, a free will that grants the depraved the ability to repent and believe—the opposite of the Reformed view of depravity. Think hard as Reformed Theology's error is exposed by means of the contextual view of this passage.

A Jewish critic, after hearing Paul's teaching of Romans 9:1-18, asked in Romans 9:19, *"Why does He still find fault? For who resists His will?"* Did the critic properly view Paul's instruction, or did he misrepresent the context of Paul's words altogether? How we answer greatly affects our interpretation of Paul's response in verses 20-23.

Paul uses phrases such as *"vessel for honorable use," "*[vessel] *for common use," "vessels of wrath,"* and *"vessels of mercy"* (verses 21-23) in his reply. Much debate exists as to how these *"vessels"* are to be perceived. Uncovering Paul's perception of each, especially with Romans 9:10-18 fresh on our minds, will be exceptionally stimulating.

We must not lose sight of the fact that we are pursuing a proper view of God's Heart. To correctly perceive His sovereignty, must we view Him as having elected certain individuals to salvation from eternity past by means of an eternal decree? Is His sovereignty such that He had to: (1) give the non-elect over to their sin with no hope of choosing Christ (extreme Calvinism) or (2) sentence the non-elect to damnation in eternity past (hyper-Calvinism)? We will seek correct and appropriate answers to these paramount questions, but quotes from leading Calvinists will first be examined. After all, a willingness to hear every argument against what we believe, regardless of the source, is vital. If what we deem to be acceptable, proper, and right can be refuted in any way by a person or system of thought, we have not yet discovered the truth of the matter.

John Piper's work, *The Justification of God,* has been quoted often in our study of Romans 9:10-18 because of its favor within the Reformed community. In some circles, in fact, *The Justification of God* is perceived as the final word on Romans 9:1-23. Note quotes from the back cover of that resource:

> "I find *The Justification of God* the most compelling and forceful exposition of Romans 9:1-23 that I have ever seen," says Richard Muller of Calvin Theological Seminary. Now newly typeset, *The Justification of God* brings together the best scholarship on the exegesis of Romans 9.

> Undergirded by the author's belief that the sovereignty of God is too precious a part of our faith to dismiss or approach weak-kneed, this book explores the Greek text and Paul's argument with singular deftness.[123]

G. K. Beale, of Gordon-Conwell Theological Seminary, writes:

> "Written in an irenic spirit with a keen awareness and interaction with all significant scholarly studies on Romans 9. Theology aside, it is a work of scholarship in its own right and the best on Romans 9."[124]

Need I say more as to why this work is key to knowing and understanding the Reformed mind?

We have proven that Paul is not teaching Reformed Theology's unconditional election to salvation in Romans 9:6-18, yet Piper believes so. Piper, therefore, discussing Paul's objector of Romans 9:19, writes on pages 185-186 of *The Justification of God*:

> In 9:19, Paul anticipates the next objection to what he has just said in 9:15-18. The objector reasons like this: If, as you say, a person's hardness is owing ultimately to God's will and not to a man's "willing or running," then it is unrighteous of God to condemn a man for that very hardness. In your view, Paul, nobody has ever successfully resisted the divine will, because even when they *are* resisting God's commands (as Pharaoh did), they are still fulfilling God's secret purposes. So God is wrong to find fault with men, since without the freedom of self-determination men cannot justly be condemned for their choices.[125]

On pages 189 and 192 of *The Justification of God*, Piper records:

> ...Paul agrees with the objection that no one can resist God's will and that nevertheless God still finds fault (as God did with Pharaoh, Ex 7:16, 10:3; etc). What Paul rejects is the presumptuous objection which the opponent registers to this divine action....
>
> Therefore, what the objector correctly sees is that God, not man, holds final sway even in the lives of unbelievers. But his premise is that, unless man has the power of self-determination

> over against God, his evil acts cannot justly be faulted, i.e., he cannot be judged as a sinner (cf Rom 3:7). From this premise he opposes Paul's description of how God acted with Pharaoh and by implication the way he acts with all people in all times....[126]

Piper perceives Paul as teaching Reformed Theology's unconditional election in Romans 9:6-18, a view which supposes that God predestined and elected to salvation (from eternity past) whomever He desired—and in the process, withheld from the non-elect an opportunity to choose (will) to be saved. As a result, Piper views Paul's critic as disagreeing with the apostle (Paul in Piper's mind teaching Reformed Theology's unconditional election) due to the critic believing that the depraved can exercise repentance and faith—thus possessing a free will. Is Piper's view of Romans 9:19 correct? A contextual answer to this question is included in the upcoming rebuttal.

Rebuttal:

> *You will say to me then, "Why does He still find fault? For who resists His will?"* (Romans 9:19)

Warning: This rebuttal may need to be read more than once (maybe several times) to comprehend its bottom line. The value of properly interpreting this section of Scripture is beyond description, so think deeply as we progress.

A contextual, non-contradictory interpretation of Romans 9:19 is essential if the entire chapter is to be correctly assessed. To arrive at such an interpretation, we must remember that God's purpose, not man's free will, has been the crucial factor in shaping antiquity. His purpose will shape the future as well, for it (God's purpose) is never thwarted by man's freedom of choice. In fact, free will validates the scope and splendor of God's sovereignty while a will-less mankind diminishes it. A God Who must cause all things to accomplish His goal (through removing man's free will) is inferior to a God Who fulfills His purpose while granting man the freedom of choice.

We have determined that the first eighteen verses of Romans 9 address God's strategy in fulfilling His purpose regarding Abraham: that through Abraham's loins (through Isaac and Jacob) and through Jacob's descendants (Israel), the promised *"seed"* of Genesis 3:15, Jesus, would be born (Galatians 3:16). God, in choosing Abraham as the father of the Jewish nation, in no way chose him to salvation. He was saved by God as a result of choosing (while depraved) to believe God's promises (Genesis 15:6), including the promise regarding the *"seed"* of Genesis 3:15. Isaac and Jacob were saved in the same manner. Even in the case of God's choice of Jacob (Israel) over Esau (the Edomites) referenced in Romans 9:13, Israel was chosen (elected) as the nation to bear the Messiah—not chosen (elected) to be saved. No one within physical Israel or the Edomite nation was chosen/elected by God from eternity past to receive eternal life, nor was anyone within physical Israel or the Edomite nation damned by God from eternity past with no hope of believing. God also desired that Pharaoh repent and believe (1Timothy 2:4; 2Peter 3:9), but Luke 7:30 confirms that His purpose for an individual is resistible:

> *But the Pharisees and the lawyers rejected God's purpose for themselves, not having been baptized by John.* (Luke 7:30)

Thus, Pharaoh was free to reject God's purpose for himself and carry out his own. The evil leader's choices, however, were used of God to fulfill His ultimate purpose in that situation—that of freeing Israel to return to her land. In a different application, God rejected Moses' will for Israel so He could (by means of His own will) preserve the Hebrew people. Hence, God's strategy was fulfilled in each of these scenarios with man retaining his freedom of choice. We can conclude, therefore, that God's ultimate purpose for the world cannot be altered by the free will of man. Yet, God's *"purpose"* for man can be *"rejected"* by man (Luke 7:30). Losing sight of this truth makes Romans 9 extremely contradictory, reducing God's sovereignty in the process.

Paul's Jewish critic misrepresented Paul's teaching because it refuted the critic's belief that God elected Israel to salvation—that Jews are saved due to a choice God made prior to their being born. However, the theme of Romans 9 is that Israel was not chosen to be saved but was chosen to bear the Messiah and take the good news of His coming to the Gentiles—a calling she has only partially fulfilled.

On pages 190-191 of *The Justification of God*, Piper criticizes Forster and Marston, authors of *God's Strategy in Human History*. Piper must be critical, for Forster and Marston's analysis of Romans 9:19 disproves Piper's theory that Paul addresses Reformed Theology's unconditional election in Romans 9:6-18. Consider Forster and Marston's words from page 80 of *God's Strategy in Human History*, words that agree with my previous assessment of Romans 9:19:

> Paul's critic...makes out in Romans 9 that Paul is saying that God's will for an individual is irresistible. Paul has pictured God as moving in history: **He has mercy on whom he will, and whom he will he hardens.** Yet Paul does not say here (nor anywhere else) that God's plan or will for an individual is irresistible—and Luke in his inspired text plainly says they are not [Luke 7:30]. We have seen that the Exodus story to which Paul alludes is far from implying any "irresistible will." It is

> true that God will ultimately achieve his plan for the world in spite of those who resist it, but the individual still has his own moral choice of whether or not to reject God's plan for him. The question of Paul's critic in Romans 9:19—"Why does he still find fault? For who can resist his will?" (RSV) is based on a flagrant misrepresentation of Paul's teaching....[127]

Just as Paul's critic distorted his doctrine in Romans 3:8 and 9:14, he continues in Romans 9:19 by saying, *"Why does He still find fault? For who resists His will?"* The critic didn't distort Paul's doctrine due to his perceiving Paul as teaching Reformed Theology's unconditional election to salvation, as Reformed theologians normally erroneously assume. Paul was addressing God's ability to select certain individuals to fulfill His purpose for the world without removing their freedom of choice—a truth the critic could never accept because of his viewing all Jews as having been chosen to salvation prior to physical birth. According to Paul's teaching, the individuals selected to fulfill His purpose can certainly resist His will (proven by the Jews of Luke 7:30), for God in no way predetermines the eternal abode of those selected to fulfill His plan (as will become progressively obvious when Isaiah 44:28—45:5 is considered later). Each person determines his eternal abode by choosing (while depraved) to accept or reject God's salvation offered through His Son. Remember, Paul taught that Jews and Gentiles alike are required to exercise personal repentance and faith while depraved should they desire to become part of God's family.

Although the unbelieving Jews viewed God as having chosen them to salvation prior to physical birth, they perceived the Gentiles as needing to convert to Judaism (by means of their free will) before God would grant salvation. Thus, Paul's Jewish critic did not perceive God as the cause of all things—nor that man was incapable of resisting His will. After all, should the Gentiles (according to the Jewish mindset that rejected Jesus' Messiahship) be required to choose Judaism over Christianity to "get right with God," the Gentiles were free to resist God's will—proven by so few Gentiles willing to take the leap!

The Jewish critic twisted Paul's words of Romans 9:16 because Paul had annihilated his argument. I can just hear the accuser saying, "If a Gentile's will (as in the case with Pharaoh) has nothing to do with where he spends eternity, how then can God find fault (Romans 9:19)? God would be totally unjust should He condemn a Gentile to hell who was incapable of willing to believe." Such questions would have flowed from a heart that had deliberately misrepresented Paul's teaching. Paul had taught that God, in selecting certain individuals (including Gentiles such as Pharaoh) to play key roles in His strategy, had done so without removing their responsibility of choosing (for themselves, and by their own free will) where they would spend eternity. By rejecting Paul's teaching, as a result of incorrect thinking learned from misguided Jewish Rabbis (such as the Jewish people having been chosen to salvation prior to physical birth), Paul's Jewish critic incorrectly accused him of teaching a theology that disallowed Gentiles such as Pharaoh the freedom of choice.

The book of Habakkuk ties in well with these passages. Habakkuk, a prophet, questioned God's dealings with the Hebrew people until he realized that God could use an evil Gentile nation like Babylon to chasten disobedient Israel. Habakkuk began to understand God's sovereignty only after understanding God's strategy. In fact, Jeremiah 50-51 confirms that the Babylonian Empire, selected to fulfill a special role in God's strategy, was later condemned by God due to excessively punishing the Jews. This example validates, once again, that God's selection of a person or people to fulfill a certain function in His overall purpose does not mean that those selected cannot resist His will. They have the right to choose how they respond, even though selected. This principle applies to the Jews as well, again confirmed by Luke 7:30:

> *But the Pharisees and the lawyers rejected God's purpose for themselves, not having been baptized by John.* (Luke 7:30)

Paul's Jewish critic had falsely accused him of teaching that God's sovereignty prevented man from resisting His will (Romans 9:19). Thus, the critic accused Paul of advocating that man lacks the freedom of choice. The critic, therefore, misrepresented Paul's words of Romans 9:6-18, the context of which validates the free will of man. Hence, Romans 9:18 supports free will by stating that God *"has mercy on whom He desires"* (God had *"mercy"* on Israel, and Moses as well, when Moses desired, based on his own free will, what would have destroyed the nation), *"and He hardens* (strengthens) *whom He desires"* (as was the case with Pharaoh, a Gentile who possessed a free will but consistently rebelled against God when he could have chosen otherwise—God having strengthened him to carry out what he had previously chosen).

Romans 9:20 *On the contrary, who are you, O man, who answers back to God? The thing molded will not say to the molder, "Why did you make me like this," will it?*

John Piper, a proponent of Reformed Theology, records his perception of this verse in *The Justification of God*, page186:

> ...Paul's emphatic *"O man"* at the beginning of 9:20a and his emphatic *"to God"* at the end of 9:20a assign to the objector his proper place: "As a mere man you have no right to accuse God of unrighteousness." Paul has no objection when a person

> seeks to understand as much of God's dealings as possible, but he objects strenuously when a person criticizes and rejects the truth which he discovers.
>
> The rhetorical question of 9:20b gives the reason why a person like Pharaoh (or his advocate in 9:19) should not question God's ways: man is creature; God is creator. For man to advise God about how he ought to act is as out of place as for a statue to advise a sculptor how to chisel. The presumption that a man's sense of values is ultimate and can prevail against God's sense of values is as ludicrous to Paul as a ranting figurine.[128]

In regard to Romans 9:20, on page 193 of that same work, Piper states:

> Paul's response to the objection raised in Rom 9:19 seems to ascribe to God the same absolute control over the destinies of individual men that we have seen in 9:11-13 and 9:16, 18.... [129]

On page 199 Piper writes:

> ...I appeal to the preceding eight chapters of this book that "the whole purpose of St. Paul's argument" in Rom 9:1-18 does *not* exclude, but definitely includes God's eternal dealings with individuals, and that, if anything, the context of 9:19-23 encourages us to interpret this unit with reference to individuals and their eternal destinies.[130]

Without a doubt, Piper views Romans 9:20 as pointing to Reformed Theology's unconditional election to salvation from eternity past—which is defined as God's ability (due to His sovereignty) to have elected only some individuals to salvation while bypassing all the rest.

Rebuttal:

> *On the contrary, who are you, O man, who answers back to God? The thing molded will not say to the molder, "Why did you make me like this," will it?* (Romans 9:20)

In answering *"back to God"* (in a negative sense—or replying against God), Paul's Jewish critic was resisting God's will. His answering back, therefore, proved that God's will can be resisted by man—be he Jew or Gentile. This example supports what we learned in Luke 7:30—that even though the Jews are God's chosen people (having been chosen to office—not destiny), certain individuals within the Jewish nation have preferred to reject (or resist) His will.

Remember that God selects particular nations and individuals within some of those nations (including Jews such as Abraham and Gentiles such as Pharaoh) to play key roles in His strategy without removing their responsibility of choosing (for themselves and by their own free will) where they will spend eternity. Thus, Israel's chosenness to carry out a special function in God's overall strategy does not mean that the individuals within the nation cannot resist His will by rejecting His offer of salvation through Christ. God is *"not willing that any should perish"* (2Peter 3:9 KJV), the *"any"* pointing to all Jews and Gentiles. However, both Jews and Gentiles are free to choose that option (and *"perish"*) should they desire. Paul's Jewish critic could never accept such a view in regard to the Israelite people because he was unwilling to admit that the nation was chosen to office rather than to destiny.

Paul was bursting his critic's proverbial bubble. He taught that God was greatly using the Jewish nation to accomplish His strategy without predetermining the salvation of a single person who made up the nation. God even used a heathen king named Cyrus, a Persian (Gentile), to assist His overall plan for Israel (Isaiah 44:28—45:13). The following historical input explains how God's choice of Cyrus relates to Paul's teachings in Romans 9.

The Babylonians destroyed Jerusalem and King Solomon's temple in 586 BC and carried the Jews into exile (in Babylon). However, the Persians (led by Cyrus) defeated Babylon and allowed the Jews to return to Jerusalem to rebuild the temple and city. With this backdrop in mind, statements concerning Cyrus in Isaiah 44 and 45 should come alive. God raised him up as Israel's *"shepherd"* (Isaiah 44:28) to *"subdue nations"* (Isaiah 45:1—the *"nations"* here included the Babylonians) and to permit Israel to return to Jerusalem for the purpose of rebuilding the temple and city (Isaiah 44:28; 45:13)—which Cyrus sanctioned according to Ezra 1:1-4. Yet, Cyrus was a heathen:

> *"...I will gird you, though you have not known Me;* (Isaiah 45:5)

God selected Cyrus to help fulfill His strategy among the nations—not for the purpose of giving him spiritual life. In other words, Cyrus was chosen to fulfill a special function within God's overall plan for man, a chosenness which did not eliminate his free will nor grant him passage to heaven. Nevertheless, Cyrus' choices and resulting success (he defeated the Babylonian Empire in astonishing fashion due to God's enablement) verified that no God exists besides Jehovah—as confirmed by Isaiah 45:6, the verse following Isaiah 45:5:

> *That men may know from the rising to the setting of the sun that there is no one besides Me. I am the LORD, and there is no other,* (Isaiah 45:6)

Through Cyrus' freedom to choose as he pleased, along with God's empowerment of the leader, God demonstrated to the world that no God exists besides Himself—validating His sovereignty more so than had He ordained Cyrus' every move!

Based on Isaiah 45:9, certain Jews disagreed with God's use of Cyrus to shape Israel's history:

> *"Woe to the one who quarrels with his Maker—An earthenware vessel among the vessels of earth! Will the clay say to the potter, 'What are you doing?' Or the thing you are making say, 'He has no hands'?* (Isaiah 45:9)

As *"the potter"* (Isaiah 45:9) decides which pot will have *"hands"* (handles), God decides which nations will have special privileges as He maps out His strategy for man (as was the case with Cyrus and the Persians). Yet, His strategy never removes man's free will.

Can *"The thing molded"* (Romans 9:20) ask the molder: *"Why did you make me like this?"* Of course not! Paul addresses this issue in the last phrase of Romans 9:20 (evidently with Isaiah 45:9 in mind) for a specific purpose. His Jewish critic would have probably been familiar with Jeremiah 18:1-12, where Jeremiah speaks of the potter who was fashioning a vessel of clay only to have it spoil in his hand. The potter then proceeded to take the same clay and make it into a different vessel. This reshaping of the vessel (Israel) by the potter can be interpreted: God fashioned *"calamity"* (Jeremiah 18:11) against the Israelites who had rejected God's plan for their lives without changing His overall plan for the nation—and without removing the free will of the individuals who brought on the calamity. Forster and Marston, on page 80 of *God's Strategy in Human History*, write:

> ...It is true that God will ultimately achieve his plan for the world in spite of those who resist it, but the individual still has his own moral choice of whether or not to reject God's plan for him....[131]

God's overall plan for Israel was etched in stone—she would bring forth the Savior as well as be a blessing to the Gentile nations. Based on Jeremiah 17, along with much of the book of Jeremiah, the disobedience of the Jews was horrendous. For this reason, Paul refers to the *"vessel for honorable use"* and the vessel *"for common use"* (Romans 9:21). Some translations, such as the ASV, render *"honorable use"* as *"honor"* and *"common use"* as *"dishonor."* Ellison's translation (as verified by Forster and Marston) uses *"honor"* and *"no honor."* Be aware, therefore, that the *"vessel for honor"* brings honor to God, not to the vessel. Also realize that the *"vessel for no honor"* brings no honor to God. Let's watch as Paul continues to build his argument.

Before transitioning into Romans 9:21-23, we need to "digest" Diagram 13 in the Reference Section. God, according to Jeremiah 18:1-6 and Romans 9:20-21, reshaped the nation of Israel (a *"vessel"* according to Jeremiah 18:4; a *"lump"* according to Romans 9:21) into two vessels:

(1) A *"vessel for honorable use,"* or *"honor"* (Romans 9:21)

(2) A vessel *"for common use," "no honor"* or *"dishonor"* (Romans 9:21)

The *"vessel for honorable use,"* or *"honor"* (v.21), one of the two vessels that make up the physical nation of Israel, consists of Jews (*"vessels"*—v.23) who receive God's *"mercy"* (v.23) due to their choice of faith. These Jews are called *"vessels of mercy"* (v.23)—they bring *"honor"* to God.

The *"vessel for common use," "no honor,"* or *"dishonor"* (v.21), the other *"vessel"* that makes up the physical nation of Israel, consists of Jews (*"vessels"*—v.22) who receive God's *"wrath"* (v.22) due to their choice of unbelief. These Jews are called *"vessels of wrath"* (v.22)—they bring no honor to God.

Diagrams 13 and 14 will be extremely beneficial while studying verses 21-23, so keep them readily accessible:

Romans 9:21 *Or does not the potter have a right over the clay, to make from the same lump one vessel for honorable use and another for common use?*

Romans 9:22 *What if God, although willing to demonstrate His wrath and to make His power known, endured with much patience vessels of wrath prepared for destruction?*

Romans 9:23 *And He did so to make known the riches of His glory upon vessels of mercy, which He prepared beforehand for glory,*

This portion of our study presents the bottom line of John Piper's, *The Justification of God*, for he will draw his final conclusions regarding Paul's words of Romans 9:1-23. His analysis greatly concerns me. In fact, it saddens me. God's heart is being addressed here. Because Who God is in His essence must be guarded at all costs, Piper's words will be examined for contextual correctness by means of Scripture alone.

The volume of quotes included in this section demands frequent rebuttals. A final rebuttal is recorded for the purpose of summarizing the entire section. Be sure to consult Diagrams 13 and 14 (in the Reference Section) as we proceed.

Piper, in *The Justification of God*, page 186, commenting on Paul's words in Romans 9:21-23, states:

> The rhetorical question of 9:21 ("Or does the potter not have authority over the clay...?") expects a positive answer and thus aims to introduce something obvious enough to render the point of 9:20b even more certain. The obvious thing is that in a relationship between potter and vessel, that is, between creator and creature, the sole authority for determining what sorts of vessels it is right to make belongs to the potter-creator. It is the right, perhaps even the duty, of a great and gifted craftsman and artist to display the full range of his powers in the various sorts of vessels he makes and the purposes for which he designs them. He has the right to take a single lump of clay, which in itself is no more suitable for one purpose than another, and by his own free choice make vessels for honorable use and vessels for dishonorable use. Because the creator has this unassailable right (9:21), no creature has the right to oppose the sovereign choices of God (9:20b), and, therefore, the objector of 9:19 has no grounds for disputing God's righteousness in "hardening whom he wills." [132]

Piper, using Romans 9:21 in an attempt to tie God's sovereignty to his view of unconditional election to salvation, makes the mistake of using the plural, "vessels," when in actuality the singular, *"vessel,"* is implemented. We will understand why he makes this contradictory substitution as we continue to address his quotes from *The Justification of God.* Piper also stresses that Paul's objector, according to his (Piper's) opinion, "has no grounds for disputing God's righteousness in 'hardening whom he wills.'" Thus, Piper holds to the false assumption that Paul believed in Reformed Theology's view of unconditional election to salvation, as well as Reformed Theology's view of "hardening," and taught it in Romans 9:21.

Piper, in mentioning arguments against his interpretation, writes on page 200 of *The Justification of God*:

> The third argument for the national/temporal view of Rom 9:20f is that the metaphor will not allow the view of individual reprobation, since no potter makes a vessel just to destroy it....
> In order to make this argument stand, Lagrange, Munck and Cranfield must maintain that the pair "vessel unto honor" and "vessel unto dishonor" in 9:21 does *not* have its substantial parallel in the pair "vessel of mercy which God prepared before for glory" and "vessels of wrath prepared for destruction" in 9:22f.... But, against Cranfield, can we really imagine that Paul did not intend his reader to see a substantial parallel between the pair of vessels in 9:21 and the pair in 9:22f?....
> Meyer...is surely much closer to the mark than Cranfield when he says that the two kinds of vessels in 9:22f "are necessarily the same as those meant in verse 21...." As far as I can see there is no reason (except theological aversion) to deny that the image of two sorts of vessels in 9:21 is continued in 9:22f....[133]

(Be sure to use Diagrams 13 and 14 in the Reference Section as we continue.)

Observe that Piper must make the pair of vessels of verse 21 parallel with the many vessels of verses 22-23. For his theology to remain intact, the *"vessel"* (singular) unto *"honor"* and the *"vessel"* (singular) unto *"no honor"* of verse 21 must be individuals, many individuals (Jews as well as Gentiles) according to Piper's previous quote, and not two portions of the singular nation of Israel made from the one *"lump."* (Caution: Before continuing, read the previous sentence until it is fully understood.)

On page 201, Piper writes:

> Therefore, it is highly probable that the vessel made for dishonor in 9:21 is the same as the vessels prepared for destruction in 9:22....
> Therefore, contrary to Cranfield, Lagrange and Munck, it is very probable that when Paul says in 9:21 that God has the right to make a vessel "unto of dishonor," it means he has the right to fit vessels for destruction (9:22)....[134]

Piper's words confirm my previous statements, that Reformed Theology must make the one *"vessel"* (singular) for *"no honor"* in verse 21 equal to the *"vessels"* (plural) *"of wrath"* in verse 22. We have learned, however, that the *"vessel"* (singular) for *"no honor"* in verse 21 is the portion of the nation of Israel (in this case) that dishonors God (reference Diagram 13). Therefore, for their theory to stand, Reformed theologians must incorrectly assume that individuals (Jews and

Gentles), instead of a nation (the nation of Israel divided into two parts), are being addressed in verse 21. Thus, Piper writes on page 202:

> ...I conclude, therefore, that the argument against interpreting Rom 9:21 as a reference to the predestining of individuals to their respective eternal destinies are not compelling. The evidence points the other way.[135]

I disagree, and my previous statements explain why. The notes associated with Romans 9:20 also assist in exposing Piper's erroneous reasoning. Piper is forced to this conclusion regarding Romans 9:21-22 due to his incorrectly viewing Paul as teaching Reformed Theology's unconditional election to salvation in earlier passages in Romans 9. The following quote (from page 203 of *The Justification of God*) helps expose the foundational error in Piper's analysis. Note how he views the words, *"from the same lump one vessel for honorable use, and another for common use"* (Romans 9:21):

> ...The various types of vessels which the potter chooses to make are not at all determined by what the clay itself is, apart from the potter's shaping. Had the vessel for honor and the vessel for dishonor been made from different lumps of clay one might argue that it was some distinctive quality in the different lumps which caused the potter to appoint one vessel for dishonorable use and another for honorable use. But Paul rules that out with the phrase "from the same lump."[136]

Piper's goal is to force Romans 9:21 to agree with his view of unconditional election—note his words, "caused the potter to appoint one vessel for dishonorable use and another for honorable use." We will discover in Piper's subsequent quote that he not only attempts to link the words, *"from the same lump one vessel for honorable use, and another for common use"* (Romans 9:21), to the eternal destinies of Jacob and Esau (the individuals), but to all individuals in general. Yet, the phrases, *"from the same lump one vessel for honorable use, and another for common use"* (v.21), are not referencing individuals. They point to the nation of Israel divided into two parts! Thus, the one *"lump"* of verse 21, which was divided into two lumps (v.21), is the nation of Israel. Hence, verse 21 is not addressing the eternal destinies of individuals (such as Jacob and Esau of verse 13). After all, Genesis 25:23 confirms that the names Jacob and Esau in Romans 9:13 point to nations, Israel and Edom respectively, rather than individuals—a point addressed in depth earlier in our study. Nor can Romans 9:21 point to God's plan for the nation of Israel (Jacob) as compared to His plan for the nation of Edom (Esau). Again, the passage speaks of God dividing the nation of Israel into two lumps. Now back to Piper's words from pages 203 and 204:

> With this phrase [from the same lump] Paul recalls the example of Rebecca and her two sons in 9:10-13. In distinction from the Sarah-Isaac example in 9:9, the stress in 9:10-13 falls on the fact that Rebecca conceived her two sons "by *one man*, Isaac...." In the case of Isaac and Ishmael the parents were not the same: Isaac was born to Sarah and Ishmael was born to Hagar the Egyptian. So it was not perfectly clear in this case that the distinction God made between these two was due only to his "purpose according to election." So Paul gives the better example of Jacob and Esau who had exactly the same parents, occupied the same womb at the same time and were appointed for their respective destinies before they were born. In other words from *"the same lump"* God made one vessel for honor and another for dishonor.
>
> It is clear therefore that in 9:21 Paul still has in mind the issue of unconditional election raised in 9:6-13. For those who remain unconvinced that Paul was concerned with the predestination of individuals to salvation and perdition in 9:6-13, this observation will not strengthen the case for seeing predestination of individuals in 9:21. But if our argument in Chapter Three was sound [where Piper attempted to prove that 9:6-13 points to Reformed Theology's unconditional election of individuals to salvation], then the link between 9:21 and 9:10 is another argument in favor of construing 9:21 as a reference to the eternal destiny of individuals.[137]

Piper attempts to prove that Paul is referring to individuals (Jews and Gentiles) rather than a nation in Romans 9:21. Why must he be so aggressive in his effort? If Paul is addressing a nation, in this case Israel, Reformed Theology cannot stand. Therefore, Piper must, at all costs, perceive Romans 9:21 as referring to the election and predestination of individuals (Jews and Gentiles) to their respective destinies. Hence, if Piper's argument can be refuted, the entire TULIP self-destructs.

Is it not amazing how Piper's improper view of these passages has affected his theology? Reformed theologians are committed to such a mindset due to their overemphasis of God's sovereignty. Yes, God is sovereign, but His sovereignty does not require "the elect" to have been elected and predestined to salvation from eternity past (prior to physical birth)—removing free will altogether as it relates to the depraved choosing Christ as Savior.

On page 207 of *The Justification of God,* Piper makes yet another attempt to insert unconditional election (to salvation) into Romans 9 by expressing his views regarding verses 17 and 22:

> ...God's raising up Pharaoh and enduring him through a tenfold recalcitrance was not *in spite of* his desire to show his power but *because of* his desire to show it.... Therefore, since Rom 9:22 uses the same language as 9:17, it is more probable that God's desire to show his wrath and make known his power is the *cause* of his sustaining and tolerating vessels of wrath than that this sustaining and tolerating are *in spite of* that desire.[138]

On pages 207-209, Piper states:

> The strongest argument against saying that God sustains and tolerates vessels of wrath *in order to* show his wrath and power is that this seems to contradict the fact that God is sustaining and tolerating these vessels "in much long-suffering" [Rom 9:22].... This argument gains force also from Romans 2:4, 5: "Or do you despise the wealth of his kindness and forbearance and long-suffering..., not knowing that the kindness of God is leading you to repentance? But according to your hardness and unrepentant heart you are storing up for yourself wrath on the day of wrath and the revelation of the righteous judgment of God." From this text it appears that God's long-suffering is an expression of his kindness and has the purpose of leading men to repentance.
>
> The problem encountered here is the same as the one we encountered in connection with the hardening of Pharaoh.... God addresses Pharaoh through Moses: "Let my people go." This corresponds to the kindness and long-suffering of pointing the way to repentance (Rom 2:4). Nevertheless, God has already told Moses that he is going to harden Pharaoh's heart so that he will not let the people go. This corresponds to the intention of God expressed in 9:22 to show his wrath precisely by means of enduring in much long-suffering vessels of wrath. If God's command to Pharaoh can be thwarted by God's own decree to harden Pharaoh's heart, then in the same way God's command to men to repent and the time he gives them to obey

> (Rom 2:4) can also be thwarted in the case of the vessels of wrath by God's decree to harden whom he wills and thus show his wrath on the day of judgment.

Are you picking up on the numerous contradictions presented here? Piper teaches that God endures the vessels of wrath, vessels whom He has decreed can never believe. Thus, their disobedience would be caused by God's choice—not theirs. Should God be the cause of all things, as Piper and his Reformed associates believe, why would He decree what He must endure (the non-elect) when the Reformed view agrees that He could have elected all? Did He create the non-elect to inflict pain upon Himself? Reformed Theologians would answer: "God created the non-elect as objects on which He can display His wrath so the elect can appreciate His grace." Hence, the Reformed God condemns individuals whom He causes to disobey—having determined from eternity past that they can never believe. Yet, Romans 10:21 states:

> *But as for Israel He says, "ALL THE DAY LONG I HAVE STRETCHED OUT MY HANDS TO A DISOBEDIENT AND OBSTINATE PEOPLE."* (Romans 10:21)

Would a sovereign, all-wise God stretch out His hands (offer salvation) to individuals whom He had decreed could never exercise repentance and faith (as Reformed Theology supposes)? Such a God would be irrational—proving Him incapable of sovereignly ruling!

Piper's subsequent quotes validate my assessment of his theology:

> ...No man will ever be able to say that God did not provide an opportunity for him to repent, nor that God did not give evidence that should have led him to do so. That God should then act, as he did with Pharaoh, so that some are hardened and do not come to repentance and are yet held to be blameworthy is not an idea forced onto Paul by Calvinistic exegetes. Rather, it is precisely what the spokesman [the critic] in Rom 9:19 saw in Paul's theology and so strongly objected to. Therefore, the summons to repentance in Rom 2:4 (even more pointedly expressed in 10:21) must not be used to silence the absoluteness of God's sovereignty expressed in Rom 9:21-23. Such a procedure...is based on a philosophical conception of the prerequisites of human accountability which Paul evidently did not share. In its haste to preserve the free will of the creature, it fails to perceive the complexity (and far deeper unity) of the will of the creator.

> But we have yet to answer the question why Paul says the vessels of wrath are endured "in much patience" if he does not mean that they are being given time for repentance (which the context seems to rule out), but that they are only storing up wrath for themselves (as 2:5 says) in order that God's "desire to show his wrath" (9:22) might be fulfilled in them. Is there any evidence that [*"patience"* 9:22, NASB] could mean patiently holding back judgment with a view to a greater display of wrath and power?[139]

After citing quotes from three non-biblical texts in an attempt to prove that God does not extend His patience (longsuffering KJV) and kindness toward the *"vessels of wrath"* for the purpose of leading them to repentance, Piper writes on page 210:

> Since the language of Rom 9:22 is so clearly reminiscent of 9:17, where God's dealings with Pharaoh are in view, there is good reason, therefore, to infer that the divine action of 9:22 is indeed the action of a mighty commander who wills to display his power and wrath in defeating his enemies (the "vessels of wrath") for the sake of his people, the "vessels of mercy."...[140]

Piper attempts to prove that God does not display His kindness and patience (Romans 2:4) toward the *"vessels of wrath"* so they might repent, but rather tolerates the non-elect (*"vessels of wrath"*) so He might "display his power and wrath" against them for the good of the *"vessels of mercy."* Wow! Can you, at this stage, understand why he is obligated to make these interpretational leaps? Do you see the gross contradiction associated with his ideology? According to Reformed Theology, the "non-elect," the *"vessels of wrath"* as Reformed theologians perceive them, cannot repent and believe. Yet, Piper states in a previous quote, "No man will ever be able to say that God did not provide an opportunity for him to repent, nor that God did not give evidence that should have led him to do so." Therefore, for God to sincerely offer the non-elect "an opportunity" to choose Christ when the non-elect, according to the Reformed view, are incapable of choosing Him (due to God's choice, not theirs), would make God out to be absurd, foolish, and ridiculous—that is, unless you classify such contradiction as "mystery." Thus, by inserting "mystery" into the equation, Piper and his fellow Reformed theologians can view God as enduring the *"vessels of wrath"* (who according to their perception have no opportunity to repent and believe—that is, when their theology is taken to the bottom line) so He might later pour His "wrath" upon them for the good (benefit, encouragement) of the "elect." Should this ideology be correct, the non-elect could rightly say, *"our unrighteousness demonstrates the righteousness of God"* (Romans 3:5)—an idea

Paul vehemently resisted in Romans 3:6 (*"May it never be!"*). The non-elect could also proclaim with accuracy and authority, *"Let us do evil that good may come"* (Romans 3:8)—error that Paul likewise condemned in Romans 3:8 (*"Their condemnation is just."*).

Let's once again read Piper's earlier quote and sum up Reformed Theology's gross error:

> ...No man will ever be able to say that God did not provide an opportunity for him to repent, nor that God did not give evidence that should have led him to do so....[141]

Piper can't be serious! How can he suggest that God provides an opportunity for the non-elect to repent (and believe) when he (Piper) adheres to the idea that the non-elect cannot believe (or be saved) due to having never been elected? Piper also perceives God as having rejected the non-elect from eternity past (through giving them over to the consequence of their sin) so He might have something on which to display His wrath so the elect can appreciate His grace. Such is the fruit when one disregards the full counsel of God's Word.

This stockpile of information may be overwhelming, but the rewards (a proper view of the subject matter) will greatly outweigh the challenge of the journey. We have a magnificent adventure awaiting us as we pursue simple answers to these highly debated theological matters.

Piper's handling of the phrase, *"prepared for destruction"* (NASB), or *"fitted for destruction"* (KJV) in Romans 9:22, is another example of improper context. Let's again read the verse:

> *What if God, although willing to demonstrate His wrath and to make His power known, endured with much patience vessels of wrath prepared for destruction?* (Romans 9:22)

Consider Piper's thoughts from page 211 of *The Justification of God* regarding this passage:

> There are at least four views: 1) *God* is the one who fits (or creates) the vessels of wrath for destruction; 2) the voice is middle not passive and thus means that the vessels of wrath have fitted themselves for destruction...; 3) the participle is to be construed adjectivally as "fit for destruction" with no implication intended about who did the fitting...; 4) the passive is intended to express a mystery no human can break through.[142]

Realizing that Piper perceives Romans 9:6-23 as teaching that God has unconditionally elected the elect to salvation (from eternity past) and rejected the rest, which view do you think he would most oppose? He would most oppose the second, which has the *"vessels of wrath"* (v.22) preparing (fitting) themselves *"for destruction"* (the middle voice pointing to the subject acting upon itself rather than being acted upon by an outside source). With this in mind, let's dig deeper.

All persons are born *"children of wrath"* according to Ephesians 2:3, but they are not required to remain in that state. The context of Romans 9:22, therefore, relates to the Jews who fit themselves *"for destruction"* due to rejecting Jesus' Messiahship (a fact confirmed to a greater degree shortly). Hence, just as God makes *"children of wrath"* (Ephesians 2:3) into *"vessels of mercy"* (Romans 9:23) once they choose (while depraved) to repent and believe, *"children of wrath"* (Ephesians 2:3) fit themselves *"for destruction"* (Romans 9:22) by refusing to repent and believe while depraved. Let's consider the dilemma this truth creates for Piper's view of the Scriptures—thus, Reformed Theology.

Piper can't begin to accept the middle voice, for Reformed Theology's definition of sovereignty is obliterated should the choices of the non-elect fit them *"for destruction"* (Romans 9:22). Why? Reformed Theology's sovereignty portrays God as the cause of all things, even the damnation of the non-elect—when taken to the bottom line. Consequently, should man's choices, not God's choices, fit (prepare) the lost *"for destruction,"* God would no longer remain sovereign within Reformed Theology (extreme and hyper Calvinism). Yet, the Scriptures uphold the middle voice. This input magnifies Piper's error on page 211 of *The Justification of God*:

> The least likely of these is the second, according to which ["prepared" or "fitted"] is construed as "having fitted themselves." In a context where the sovereignty of God as a potter over clay has been stressed, Paul would have had to use a clearer grammatical construction to signify all of a sudden that man's destiny is *self*-determined....[143]

After rejecting the third and fourth views, Piper attempts to justify his choice of the first view on page 212 of *The Justification of God*:

> It seems to me that, after the clear and powerful statements of double predestination in Rom 9, it is grasping at a straw to argue that the passive voice [Piper views *"prepared"* or *"fitted"* in verse 22 as being in the passive voice rather than middle] proves that Paul denied divine agency in fitting men for destruction. "Jacob I loved and Esau I hated" (9:13). "He has

> mercy on whom he wills and he hardens whom he wills" (9:18). "He makes from the same lump a vessel for honor and a vessel for dishonor" (9:21). Is it really plausible after such assertions to argue that the differences between "vessels of wrath fitted for destruction" and "vessels of mercy which he prepared before for glory" are such that Paul is now denying or even trying to conceal the divine agency in the former? Paul has just stated unabashedly that God makes from *the same lump* vessels for dishonor (9:21). I cannot escape the implication that anti-Calvinistic apologetic is in control when in the next verse we are forbidden to suggest that the divine Potter is at work in the phrase "vessels of wrath fitted for destruction." Moreover, in view of the parallels between Rom 9:22 and 9:17..., a most natural suggestion is that Pharaoh serves as an example of a "vessel of wrath fitted for destruction." And since Paul's inference from the Pharaoh story is that "God hardens whom he wills" (9:18), the most natural suggestion from the context is that "fitted for destruction" (9:22) refers precisely to this divine hardening.[144]

Is Piper correct in his assumptions? On page 213, he also writes:

> We can only guess why Paul used the passive verb in reference to vessels of wrath and an active verb...in reference to vessels of mercy. Since the grammar of Rom 9:22, 23 is awkward, it is not unreasonable to suggest that a shift occurred in Paul's thought as he was writing the sentence....[145]

Piper admits that "the grammar" in Romans 9:22-23 "is awkward," but he leaves no room for the action in the phrase, *"prepared for destruction,"* or *"fitted for destruction"* (Romans 9:22), to be in the middle voice (with the subject performing the action rather than being acted upon). He states, therefore: "We can only guess why Paul used the passive verb" in 9:22 while using the "active verb" in 9:23—*"which he prepared beforehand for glory"* (9:23). Again we see that Piper cannot, under any circumstance, allow *"prepared"* (verse 22) to be in the middle voice. Should the voice be middle, Paul would be teaching that the non-elect (the unsaved who die without accepting Christ) fit themselves *"for destruction"* rather than the sovereign action of God. Yet, this is exactly what Paul is communicating.

Warren Wiersbe, in his book, *Be Right,* agrees. He states that *"prepared"* (*"fitted"*) in Romans 9:22 does not suggest that God fits a person for destruction. He writes:

> The verb is in...the middle voice, making it a reflexive action verb. So, it should read: *"fitted himself* for destruction." ...sinners prepare themselves for judgment.[146]

Pharaoh's own choices, therefore, *"fitted"* him for destruction. Don't misunderstand. All people are born *"children of wrath"* (Ephesians 2:3) due to the sin nature inherited from Adam, but man's continued disobedience (to use Paul's terminology) fits him *"for destruction."*

Conclusion: God allowed Pharaoh to choose his own eternal destiny and in no way elected or predestined him to it. This, in fact, is how God deals with all mankind without diminishing His sovereignty in the least.

Romans 2:5 ties in well here, not once violating the middle voice of Romans 9:22 (where the subject is acting upon himself):

> *But because of your stubbornness and unrepentant heart you are storing up wrath for yourself in the day of wrath and revelation of the righteous judgment of God,* (Romans 2:5)

Note that Paul does not say in regard to the lost: "Because of God's action upon your heart you are storing up wrath for yourself...." Rather, the lost store up wrath for themselves because of action initiated from within themselves.

The following quote from Piper (pages 218-220 of *The Justification of God*) summarizes how he perceives Romans 9:6-23. Note that his interpretation of Romans 9:21-23 rests upon his assumptions associated with Romans 9:6-13. As a result, if his assessment of Romans 9:6-13 is faulty, his assessment of Romans 9:14-23 lacks credibility. In first addressing Jacob and Esau (Romans 9:10-13), and continuing by considering the subject matter of Romans 9:14-23, Piper writes:

> ...Within the context of Rom 9 this means that God maintains his sovereign "purpose of election" by determining, before they are born, who will belong to the "saved" among Israel [making reference to Jacob and Esau in Romans 9:10-13]....
>
> Paul denied in Rom 9:14 that God is unrighteous...
>
> ...It can scarcely be overemphasized, for the sake of Paul's justification of God, that in Rom 9:15 and 17 Paul employs Old Testament texts in which the exercise of God's sovereign freedom, in mercy (Ex 33:19) and in hardening (Ex 9:16), is the means by which he declares the glory of his name! This is the

> heart of Paul's defense: in choosing unconditionally those on whom he will have mercy and those whom he will harden God is not unrighteous, for in this "electing purpose" he is acting out of a full allegiance to his name and esteem for his glory.
>
> Paul's justification of God does not end at Rom 9:18, because someone registers another objection in 9:19: "Why does God still find fault since no one can successfully resist his sovereign will?" That is, if God is in absolute control of whether men are hardened or not, then he has no right to condemn them for their hardness. How Paul responds to this final objection is ...the climax of our study. God is our creator and as such has as much right to make of us what he wills as a potter has over his clay to make from the same lump a vessel for honor and a vessel for dishonor (9:21). We have no right to dispute with God our maker....
>
> The final statement of this justification of God's ways is given in Rom 9:22, 23. God's desire is "to show wrath and make known his power." But even more he desires "to make known the wealth of his glory on his people, the vessels of mercy." The ultimate aim of God is to show mercy. But to do this he must place it against a backdrop of wrath....[147]

Piper then quotes Daniel Fuller, from his book, *Unity of the Bible*, pages 446-447:

> ...how could God's mercy appear fully as his great mercy unless it was extended to people who were under his wrath and therefore could only ask for mercy? It would be impossible for them to share with God the delight he has in his mercy unless they saw clearly the awfulness of the almighty wrath from which his mercy delivers them. Thus to show the full range of his glory [and thus be righteous] God prepares beforehand not only vessels of mercy but also vessels of wrath, in order that the riches of his glory in connection with the vessels of mercy might thereby become more clearly manifest.[148]

Do you understand Piper's purpose in including Fuller's quote? First, he attempts to prove that God prepared beforehand (from eternity past) certain individuals (the non-elect) as *"vessels of wrath."* Second, he builds on this error by teaching that God wields His rage against the *"vessels of wrath"* so the elect might better appreciate His choice of them as *"vessels of mercy."* Again, we see that

Reformed Theology's "Sovereign" takes great pleasure in exhibiting His wrath upon those whom He never gives opportunity to believe. Is this the God we serve?

Piper vigorously attempts to defend his position because, as we have seen on a variety of occasions, Calvinists must yield to mystery when addressing the fundamental inconsistency within their system of thought—that God, Who is capable of saving all, yet chooses only to save some, can somehow remain a just and loving God by condemning individuals who were never given opportunity to believe. Once again Piper is forced to yield to mystery when addressing, even in Romans 9:22-23, this contradictory issue within Calvinism in regard to the *"vessels of wrath"* and *"vessels of mercy."* Note his words from pages 188 and 189 of *The Justification of God*:

> Now in 9:23 Paul takes one last step into the divine mystery [note the word "mystery"]. There is another, final purpose which God aims at in patiently tolerating vessels of wrath made for destruction. By this he aims "to make known the wealth of his glory on vessels of mercy which he prepared beforehand for glory...."
>
> ...The acts of God come forth not in continuous reaction to autonomous external stimuli but from a unified, sovereign purpose. They cohere to achieve one great end–the magnification of God's great glory for the eternal enjoyment of his chosen people. The fact that this purpose "requires"...the demonstration of wrath upon vessels of wrath will no doubt be disputed by men to the end of the age. But for Paul it was beyond dispute....[149]

Piper perceives Paul as agreeing with the fundamental inconsistency within Calvinism— that God, Who is capable of saving all, yet chooses only to save some, can somehow remain a just and loving God by condemning those He never granted opportunity to believe. Piper concludes his discourse by choosing to convert an assumption into an absolute. How so? He originally assumed that the phrase, *"Jacob I loved, but Esau I hated"* (Romans 9:13), points to the election of Jacob (the individual) to salvation and the outright damnation of Esau (the individual) to destruction. His argument is discredited by his failing to properly interpret passages such as Genesis 25:23, which confirm that Romans 9:13 points to nations rather than individuals (a topic addressed earlier in our study). In fact, Genesis 25:23 states unequivocally that God viewed Rebecca as carrying two nations in her womb:

> *And the LORD said to her, "Two nations are in your womb; And two peoples shall be separated from your body; And one people*

> *shall be stronger than the other; And the older shall serve the younger.*" (Genesis 25:23)

Once again, the Calvinists are required to neglect key passages which prove their fundamental beliefs to be false.

Strange doctrines have emerged from Calvinism's rationale, much like that addressed by R.C. Sproul Jr. in *Almighty over All*, pages 52-53. Sproul, in this instance, presents one of the best examples of how God's character is assaulted through Calvinism. Observe how he ties Eve's disobedience into Paul's words of Romans 9:22-24:

> ...What reason would God have for wanting Eve to fall into sin? Imagine God before the creation of the world. The members of the Trinity are enjoying the fellowship of which we spoke earlier. They are noting their excellencies, praising each other, if you will. God considers his strength and finds it wonderful. He considers his mercy and finds it delightful. He then considers his wrath. Many of us have difficulty imagining God finding any glory in his wrath, but he does. He is pleased with his wrath. If his wrath exists, and we know from his Word that it does, then we know he is pleased with it. We cannot imagine God looking at his wrath like unwanted pounds he wants to lose, if only he had the power. No, God is as delighted with his wrath as he is with all of his attributes. Suppose he says, "What I'll do is create something worthy of my wrath, something on which I can exhibit the glory of my wrath. And on top of that I'll manifest my mercy by showering grace on some of these creatures deserving my wrath."
>
> Can you imagine God thinking such a thought? I can, and I'm not alone in this. The apostle Paul not only speculates that such a line of reasoning is possible with God but that in fact God did reason this way. "What if God, wanting to show His wrath and to make His power known, endured with much longsuffering the vessels of wrath prepared for destruction, and that He might make known the riches of His glory on the vessels of mercy, which He had prepared beforehand for glory, even us whom He called, not of the Jews only, but also of the Gentiles?" (Romans 9:22-24).
>
> These are perhaps some of the hardest words to swallow in all of Scripture. We could be sure, however, even without this passage that God would have a motive for Eve's fall into sin.

> We know that, because it came to pass. Every Bible-believing Christian must conclude at least that God in some sense desired that man would fall into sin. The only other option is to say that this event became reality against God's wishes, that God sat upon his throne wringing his hands in frustration as Eve took a bite. Such a notion is repugnant, for it means that someone or something is more powerful than God himself.[150]

Appallingly, Sproul concludes that, in order to display the glory of His wrath to the elect, God elected the non-elect to damnation. Being a Reformed theologian, Sproul would also view the recipients of God's wrath (the non-elect) as never having opportunity to exercise faith (if he is straightforward regarding his beliefs). This mindset is absolutely unjustifiable if you base your theology on all the verses in God's Word rather than a select few interpreted out of context!

Do you believe that God said, as Sproul assumes, "What I'll do is create something worthy of my wrath, something on which I can exhibit the glory of my wrath. And on top of that I'll manifest my mercy by showering grace on some of these creatures deserving my wrath." Sproul then asks, "Can you imagine God thinking such a thought?" My answer is, "No, and neither could Paul."

In an attempt to justify their extreme view of sovereignty, Calvinism's contradictions tamper with God's character—that is, Who He is in His essence. For this reason I have addressed Calvinism's theology in this present study. Our goal has been, and will continue to be, a proper view of God's heart. Absolutely nothing is more important to the wellbeing of the soul.

One of the purposes of the previous quotes from Reformed theologians is to confirm that their God, being the cause of all things, must be the author of evil (the Reformed theologian R.C. Sproul Jr., in *Almighty Over All* [pp. 52-54], teaches that God "created sin"). Interestingly, atheists normally reject (and mock) the Christian God due to their viewing Him ("should He exist," they say) as the author of evil. They conclude that in causing all things, even evil, He would cause all sickness, heartache, sin, even the death of an innocent child at the hands of an evil tyrant. They then ask, "How could such a God be worthy of man's worship?"—and walk off into the sunset, rejecting Him to the grave due to their exposure to a system of thought that defames His character. Yes, should Reformed Theology's God be the sovereign of the universe, the atheist could rightly question His right to rule and, in turn, His very existence!

Based on our findings, the next few paragraphs will be worth your time.

The Full Counsel View of Romans 9:21-23

A majority of the full counsel view has already been stated, so I will be as brief as possible. In fact, Diagrams 13 and 14 (included in the Reference Section) present this view in graphic form and should be accessed before continuing.

Romans 9:21-23 is rendered as follows in the NASB:

> *21 Or does not the potter have a right over the clay, to make from the same lump one vessel for honorable use, and another for common use? 22 What if God, although willing to demonstrate His wrath and to make His power known, endured with much patience vessels of wrath prepared for destruction? 23 And He did so in order that He might make known the riches of His glory upon vessels of mercy, which He prepared beforehand for glory,*
> (Romans 9:21-23 NASB)

Some translations render *"honorable use"* (v.21—NASB) as *"honor."* These same translations also render *"common use"* (v.21—NASB) as *"dishonor"* (ASV) or *"no honor"* (Ellison's translation). These renderings are taken into consideration strictly for clarity.

The one *"lump"* (Romans 9:21), or *"vessel"* (Jeremiah 18:4), the nation of Israel, was divided into two vessels (parts) due to sin:

(1) The *"vessel for honorable use,"* or *"honor"*—one part of the physical nation of Israel (Romans 9:21)

(2) The *"vessel…for common use," dishonor*, or *"no honor"*—the other part of the physical nation of Israel (Romans 9:21)

According to Romans 9:21-23, the two single vessels (two parts of physical Israel) into which the original *"lump"* (physical Israel) was divided (v.21)—the *"vessel"* (singular) *"for honorable use,"* or *"honor,"* and the *"vessel"* (singular) *"for common use," "dishonor,"* or *"no honor"*—are made up of two types of Jews. The believers within physical Israel are *"vessels"* (plural) *"of mercy"* (v.23), Jews who make up the *"vessel"* (singular) of the nation which brings *"honor"* to God (v.21). On the other hand, the unbelievers within physical Israel are *"vessels"* (plural) *"of wrath"* (v.22), Jews who make up the *"vessel"* (singular) of the nation which brings *"no* honor*"* (*"dishonor"*) to God (v.21). Don't overlook the fact that the *"vessel for honor"* (v.21) within physical Israel brings honor to God (not to itself), while the vessel for *"no honor"* (or *"common use"*—v.21) within physical Israel brings no honor to God. In fact, the unredeemed portion of the nation of Israel (the *"vessel for no honor"*—Romans 9:21) causes God's *"name"* to be *"blasphemed among the Gentiles"* (Romans 2:24).

Like Romans 9:10-19, Romans 9:20-23 teaches the free will of man. All Jews within physical Israel are granted the freedom to choose their destiny while depraved. If a Jew chooses (while depraved) to repent and believe, God makes him a vessel *"of mercy."* If a Jew chooses blatant rebellion, he remains one of the *"vessels of wrath."* In no way has God predetermined a single Jew's destiny from eternity past. Yet, the *"vessels of wrath"* within physical Israel (each possessing a free will) are used of God to bring about His desired end as they prepare themselves *"for destruction"* (v.22). Note: The phrase, *"prepared for destruction"* (v.22), is in the middle voice (considering its context) rather than the passive, confirming that these vessels prepare themselves for destruction while remaining committed to a lifestyle of sin. Theologians such as Warren Wiersbe, Arnold Fruchtenbaum, Adam Clarke, Matthew Henry, and Dave Hunt (for starters) are in agreement with this conclusion. Reformed Theology naturally views the passive voice as applicable (with God preparing the vessels of wrath for destruction), a view previously proven unacceptable.

All persons are born *"children of wrath"* (Ephesians 2:3), but any Jew who spends eternity separated from God will do so as a result of a choice he has made, not a choice that God made. The same truth applies to Gentiles.

Let's consider an additional critical matter regarding Romans 9:23:

> *And He did so to make known the riches of His glory upon vessels of mercy, which He prepared beforehand for glory,* (Romans 9:23)

Moderate Calvinists and Reformed theologians (extreme and hyper-Calvinists) perceive the phrase, *"which He prepared beforehand for glory,"* as supporting their view of unconditional election to salvation from eternity past. Certainly, *"prepared"* is past tense action (aorist indicative for you Greek students). However, should all of the "elect" of all time have been elected and predestined to salvation from eternity past, the elect not yet saved would already be *"called," "justified,"* and *"glorified"*—since *"predestined," "called," "justified,"* and *"glorified"* in Romans 8:30 are each in the past tense (aorist, indicative). Note the passage:

> *and whom He predestined, these He also called; and whom He called, these He also justified; and whom He justified, these He also glorified.* (Romans 8:30)

If you can comprehend the following paragraph, you have gleaned a significant truth from this portion of the study:

Should any form of Calvinism (including Reformed Theology) be a viable system of thought (teaching that all of the elect were elected and predestined to salvation from eternity past), the elect of today who are not yet believers would have also been *"called," "justified,"* and *"glorified"* in eternity past—that is, should the past tense *"predestined," "called," "justified,"* and *"glorified"* of

Romans 8:30 be taken into account. Stated differently, should all of the elect of all time have been elected and *"predestined"* to salvation from eternity past, the elect who are alive today yet still unbelievers would already be *"called," "justified,"* and *"glorified."* This same scenario would apply to the elect who are not yet born, for not only would they already be elected and *"predestined,"* but *"called," "justified,"* and *"glorified."* This arrangement is impossible according to Ephesians 2:3—which states that every person is born "*a child of wrath*."

Do you see how the full counsel view of the Scriptures totally refutes all forms of Arminianism and Calvinism, including Reformed Theology (review Diagram 11 in the Reference Section)? Our *Romans 1-8* study covers Romans 8:30 in much greater depth, so you might reference that resource should it be included in your library.

Let's take our examination of Romans 9:23 to an even deeper level. Because the phrase, *"which He prepared beforehand for glory"* (Romans 9:23), is in the active voice (with God acting upon the subject), Calvinists (including Reformed theologians) incorrectly conclude that God *"prepared"* the elect for salvation from eternity past through predestination and election (an idea proven invalid from our previous findings regarding Romans 8:30). Unsurprisingly, Romans 9:23 exacerbates the error within Calvinism. Follow closely.

Paul, a Jewish believer, is writing to Gentile believers in Rome—not to unbelievers. This fact is vital for proper understanding. We should also take into consideration that in the following verse, verse 24, Paul teaches that even Gentiles become vessels of mercy (yet, not part of physical Israel, of course) once they repent and believe while depraved:

> *even us, whom He also called, not from among Jews only, but also from among Gentiles.* (Romans 9:24)

The next two paragraphs are crucial for proper understanding, so think hard!

Scripture teaches that God justifies (Romans 5:1) and forgives New Testament believers (Ephesians 4:32; Colossians 2:13; 1John 2:12) once they repent and believe while depraved. In fact, God makes them *"holy"* (Ephesians 1:4), *"complete"* (Colossians 2:10), *"sanctified"* (Hebrews 10:10), perfect (Hebrews 10:14), *"saints"* of God (1Corinthians 1:2)—even *"the righteousness of"* Himself (2Corinthians 5:21). Thus, He glorifies New Testament believers (Romans 8:30) in soul and spirit when they are made new—in view of that day when they will receive their glorified bodies at the Rapture of the church (1Corinthians 15:50-54; 1Thessalonians 4:16-17), that to which they were predestined the instant they repented and believed while depraved (Ephesians 1:5; Romans 8:23). Hence, God *"prepared"* Paul and his readers *"for glory"* when they submitted to Christ—an event that transpired before this epistle was written (placing the action in the past tense as Paul penned this letter, as is required by the Greek text). This interpretation allows *"even us"* of Romans 9:24 to fit the context free of inconsistency, for Paul (a Jew) and his readers (Gentile believers at Rome) were *"prepared...for glory"* the moment they repented and believed while depraved—hence, prior to the writing of this epistle and, therefore, in the past tense (*"beforehand"*). In fact, all *"vessels of mercy"* during the church age (an age which began in Acts 2) are *"prepared...for glory"* in conjunction with their becoming *"vessels of mercy"*—when they exercise personal repentance and faith while depraved.

Conclusion: The unsaved fit themselves for destruction, but God prepares New Testament believers (both Jews and Gentiles) for glory once they repent and believe while depraved. Their behavior will not be perfected until physical death, although it progressively improves during their stay on the earth. Thus, Paul and his Gentile readers were prepared for glory the moment they repented and believed while depraved and, thus, prior to the writing of this epistle—a past tense action on God's part as required by the passage. Had *"vessels of mercy"* (Romans 9:23) within the nation of Israel been predestined and elected to salvation from eternity past as *"vessels of mercy,"* none of the elect within physical Israel could have been born *"vessels of wrath."* Yet, the Scriptures teach that a Jew is a *"vessel of wrath"* so long as he is an unbeliever.

We will now transition into *God's Heart as it Relates to Depravity*, the third book of this *God's Heart* series. Holding Calvinism's view of the "T" of the TULIP, Total Depravity, accountable to the full counsel of God's Word will be exceptionally interesting. In doing so, additional verses will be addressed, further validating that God's sovereignty and mans' free will can be reconciled void of contradiction. These passages will not only encourage us, but greatly enhance our ability to defend what we believe concerning these intriguing theological matters.

Having you join us has been delightful. I look forward to spending additional time with you examining God's perception of man's depravity. Prepare to be blessed!

Sovereignty
Free Will
Scripture Index

Scripture — page number

Diagram 1

Eternity
No Beginning And No End

∞ ∞

Diagram 2

Why God's Foreknowledge Cannot Precede His Eternal Decrees

Calvinism and Arminianism adhere to the idea that the elect are elected (chosen) and predestined to salvation from eternity past by means of an eternal decree. This arrangement is impossible, and the following explains why.

Scripture teaches that God's decrees are eternal (Jeremiah 5:22), having always existed in His heart.

> *'Do you not fear Me?' declares the LORD. 'Do you not tremble in My presence? For I have placed the sand as a boundary for the sea, An eternal decree, so it cannot cross over it. Though the waves toss, yet they cannot prevail; Though they roar, yet they cannot cross over it.* (Jeremiah 5:22)

Scripture also requires God's foreknowledge (which means to know beforehand) to precede the predestination and election (choosing) of a New Testament believer.

> *For those whom He foreknew, He also predestined to become conformed to the image of His Son, so that He would be the firstborn among many brethren;* (Romans 8:29)

> *Peter, an apostle of Jesus Christ, To those who reside as aliens, scattered throughout Pontus, Galatia, Cappadocia, Asia, and Bithynia, who are chosen according to the foreknowledge of God the Father, by the sanctifying work of the Spirit, to obey Jesus Christ and be sprinkled with His blood: May grace and peace be yours in the fullest measure.* (1Peter 1:1-2)

Should God's foreknowledge, meaning "to know beforehand," precede His eternal decrees, eternity would have a beginning (a starting point)—a total impossibility.

Because God's decrees are eternal (Jeremiah 5:22), and foreknowledge is required to precede the predestination and election (choosing) of the New Testament believer (Romans 8:29; 1Peter 1:1-2), it is impossible for Him to have predestined or elected (chosen) New Testament believers to salvation from eternity past by means of an eternal decree.

Thus, the Scriptures teach that New Testament believers are elected and predestined to blessings (rather than to salvation) subsequent to exercising personal repentance and faith while depraved, which allows God's foreknowledge to precede such an arrangement. This is displayed graphically below.

FOREKNOWLEDGE	Predestination of New Testament Believers Election/Chosenness of New Testament Believers

∞

Diagram 3

God, The Eternal I AM

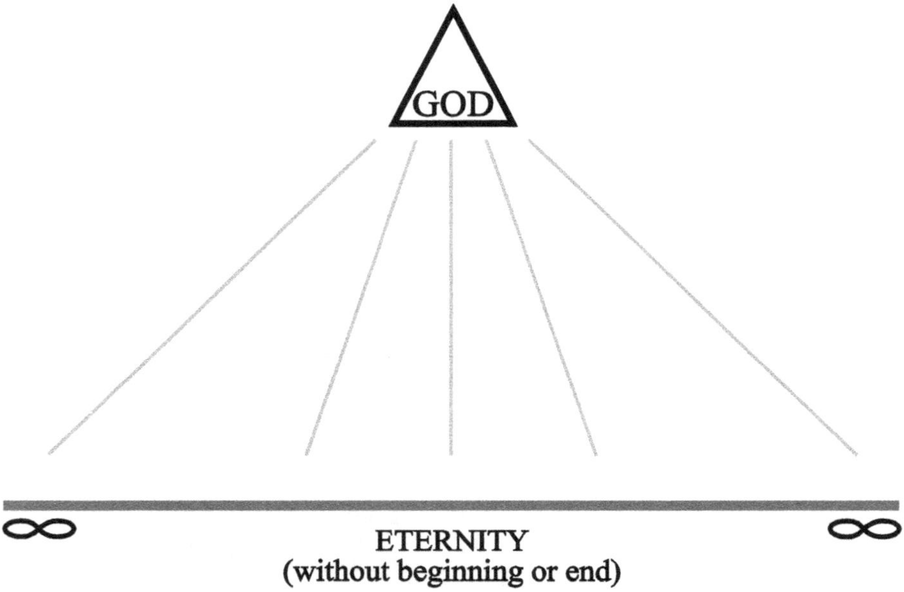

God sees all events, from eternity past through eternity future throughout His eternal existence. In other words, He possesses the ability to see all things at once. He therefore, is never caught off guard since He possesses foreknowledge of all past, present, and future events. God is not required to cause these events to foreknow them.

Diagram 4

Arminius' Beliefs

Election
Predestination

| FOREKNOWLEDGE |

∞

Arminius' belief regarding foreknowledge affected his view of salvation. He believed that God looked into the future and, by means of His eternal foreknowledge, saw who would choose to repent and believe while depraved. God then, based on Arminius' theology, elected (chose) and predestined them to salvation from eternity past by means of an eternal decree.

Diagram 5

What Arminius' Belief System Actually Communicated

Election
Predestination
God's Foreknowledge

∞ ∞

Arminius believed that God's decrees, as well as His foreknowledge, are eternal. He also believed that individuals are elected (chosen) and predestined to salvation by means of an eternal decree. This order, however, leaves no room for God's foreknowledge to precede the New Testament believer's election and predestination. Arminius' theological chronology actually stacked election, predestination, and God's foreknowledge on top of each other, when Romans 8:29 and 1Peter 1:1-2 require God's foreknowledge to precede the election and predestination of a New Testament believer. Arminius arrived at this contradiction due to equating the blessings associated with salvation with salvation itself.

Diagram 6

Calvin's Beliefs

Election
Predestination
(God's Foreknowledge = Foreordination or Predestination)

∞ ∞

Calvin believed that God, from eternity past and by means of an eternal decree, elected (chose) and predestined the elect to salvation. This view contradicts Romans 8:29 and 1Peter 1:1-2, both of which require God's foreknowledge to precede the election (chosenness) and predestination of a New Testament believer. Thus, according to Calvin's theology, room does not exist for foreknowledge to precede the election (chosenness) and predestination of a New Testament believer. Therefore, Calvin deemed foreknowledge as synonymous with foreordination or predestination. In other words Calvin redefined foreknowledge as foreordination or predestination, which required the writing of volumes of materials in an effort to remedy such contradiction. Calvin arrived at the contradiction due to equating the blessings associated with salvation with salvation itself. D

Diagram 7

The Remedy to Calvin's and Arminius' Error

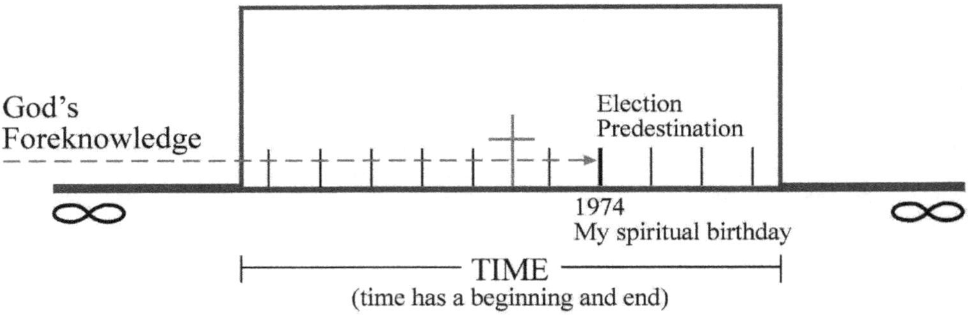

The remedy to Calvin's and Arminius' error is found in allowing God's foreknowledge in this case to point to His foreknowledge of the thoughts, actions, and decisions of those who choose to repent and believe during the church age. Once they exercise repentance and faith while depraved, they are placed in Christ. God then predestines them to one day receive a glorified body (Romans 8:23; Ephesians 1:5). He also elects (chooses) them in Christ (Ephesians 1:4), after they repent and believe while depraved, bestowing upon them the office (gifting--1Peter 4:10) to which he elects them.

New Testament believers are placed in Christ, subsequent to repenting and believing while depraved, and only then are elected (chosen) and predestined. At that point they receive eternal life, life with no beginning and no end, and are viewed by the Father as having always been in Christ (Ephesians 1:4).

Diagram 8

Scriptural Election/Chosenness and Predestination

The Father sees all New Testament believers, subsequent to their exercising personal repentance and faith while depraved and being made new, as having always been in Christ. This is due to the type of life they receive at the point of salvation - eternal life.

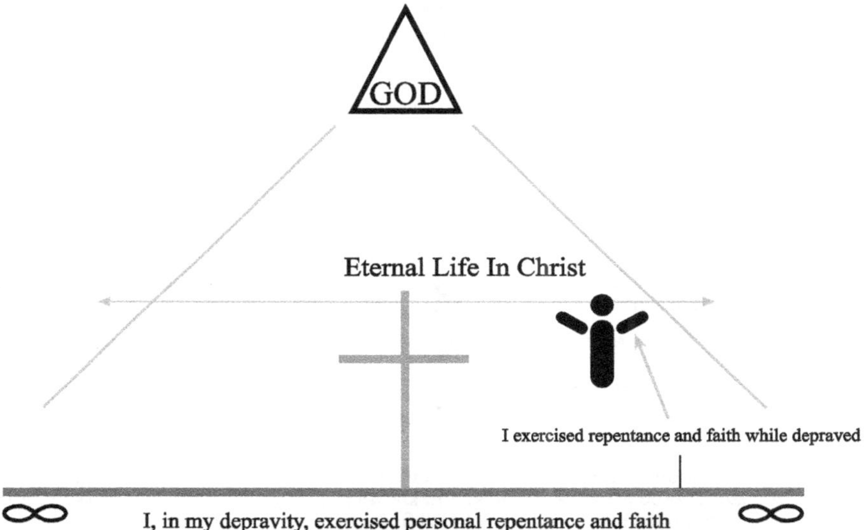

I, in my depravity, exercised personal repentance and faith and was placed in Christ. At that moment I received eternal life.

The Holy Spirit places those seeking salvation into Christ when they repent and exercise faith while depraved (1Corinthians 12:13). Once this occurs, God makes them new (2Corinthians 5:17). He also predestines them (at that time) to receive a glorified body at the Rapture of the church (Ephesians 1:5; Romans 8:23; 1Corinthians 15:35-58; 1Thessalonians 4:13-18). They are also elected/chosen (at that time) to office due to having been placed into Christ, the Father's elect/chosen one (Luke 9:35; Isaiah 42:1), Who was elected/chosen to the office of Messiah. The office to which New Testament believers are elected/chosen is the special office or position (gift) they receive (1Peter 4:10) once they are placed in Christ and made new. Therefore, we were not predestined and elected/chosen to salvation from eternity past by means of an eternal decree. We were predestined the moment we were made new in Christ subsequent to repenting and believing while depraved; predestined to receive a new body (Ephesians 1:5; Romans 8:23) at the Rapture of the church. We were also elected/chosen to office when we were placed in Christ, subsequent to repenting and believing while depraved, Who was elected/chosen to office, the office of Messiah. Ephesians 1:4 states:

> *just as He chose us in Him before the foundation of the world, that we should be holy and blameless before Him. (Ephesians 1:4)*

Once we were placed in Christ, we received His kind of life, eternal life (Romans 6:23; Colossians 3:4), life with no beginning and no end. As a result, the Father sees us as having always been in Christ, even "*before the foundation of the world*" (Ephesians 1:4). Consequently, our point of entry into Christ was when we repented and believed while depraved, but once we were placed in Him through the power of the Holy Spirit, the Father saw us as having always been in His holy Son. He will continue to view us in this manner throughout eternity.

Diagram 9

The Predestination of Jesus' Death and the Hidden Wisdom

Acts 4:27-28; 1Corinthians 2:7

For trully in this city there were gathered together against Your holy servant Jesus, whom You annointed, both Herod and Pontius Pilate, along with the Gentiles and the peoples of Israel, to do whatever Your hand and Your purpose predestined to occur. (Acts 4:27-28)

but we speak God's wisdom in a mystery, the hidden wisdom which God predestined before the ages to our glory; (1Corinthians 2:7)

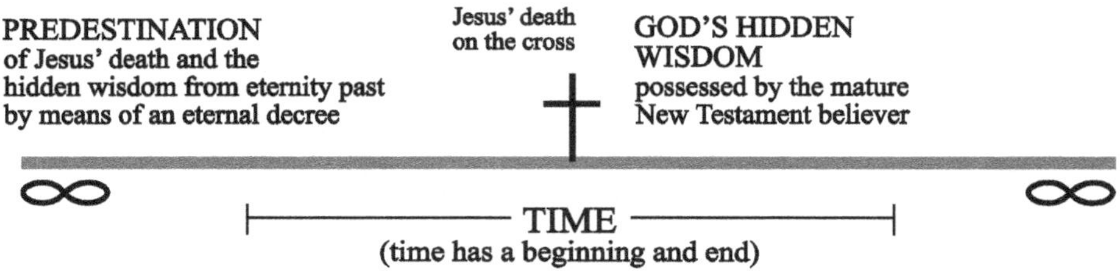

The Scriptures do not require that the predestination of the cross (Acts 4:27-28) and the hidden wisdom of God (1Corinthians 2:7) be preceded by God's foreknowledge. This difference leaves room for God to predestine the cross and the hidden wisdom of God from eternity past by means of an eternal decree. Such an arrangement is unlike the predestination of the New Testament believer, which occurs in time, and requires that God's foreknowledge precede it.

Diagram 10

Reformed Theology (Extreme and Hyper-Calvinism)

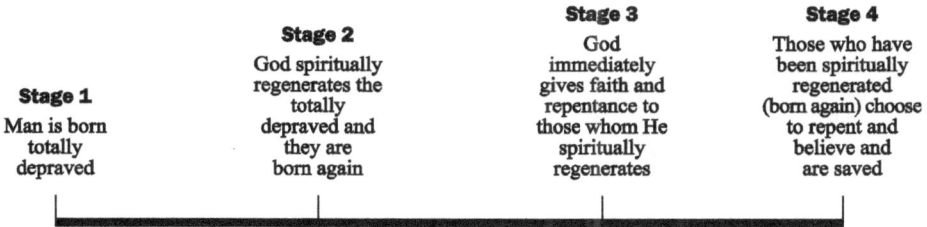

Stage 1
Man is born totally depraved

Stage 2
God spiritually regenerates the totally depraved and they are born again

Stage 3
God immediately gives faith and repentance to those whom He spiritually regenerates

Stage 4
Those who have been spiritually regenerated (born again) choose to repent and believe and are saved

This view is contradictory because Scripture equates spiritual regeneration and being born again with salvation. With Reformed theology's configuration, believers would be saved twice - a total impossibility.

The Scriptual View

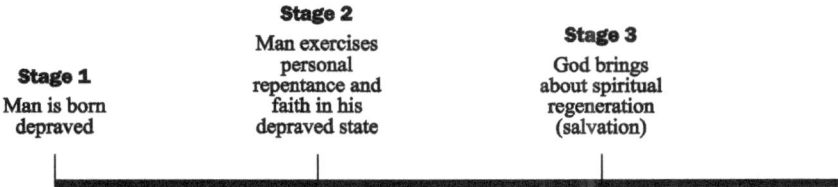

Stage 1
Man is born depraved

Stage 2
Man exercises personal repentance and faith in his depraved state

Stage 3
God brings about spiritual regeneration (salvation)

Be aware that man is brought out of his state of depravity and into the kingdom in a flash, in fact, less than a flash. Therefore, the brevity of time between man's choice to repent and believe while depraved and God's act of spiritual regeneration (salvation) is impossible to imagine.

Diagram 11

Hyper-Calvinism (One Brand of Reformed Theology)

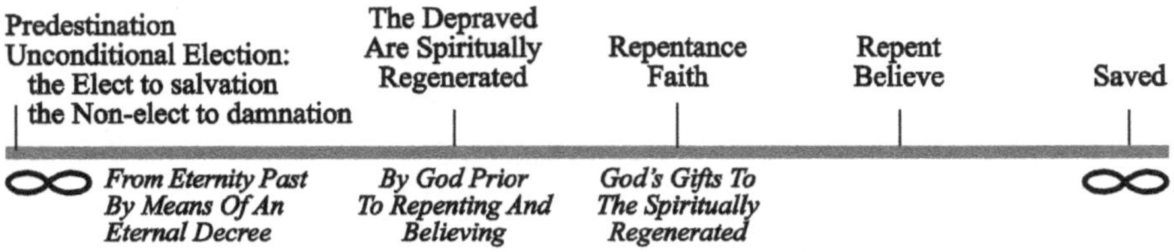

Strong (Extreme) Calvinism (A Second Brand of Reformed Theology)

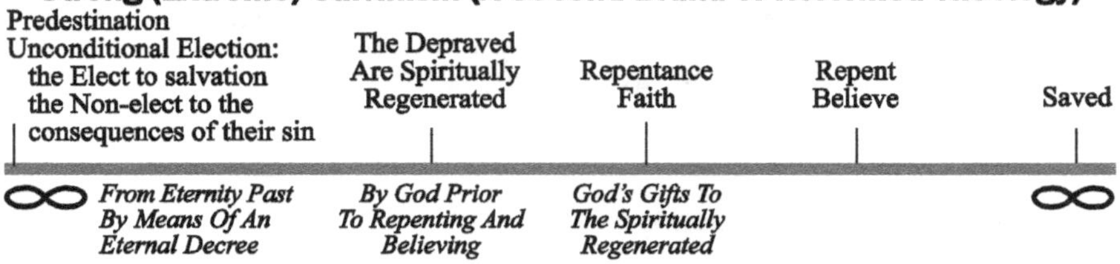

Moderate Calvinism

Arminianism

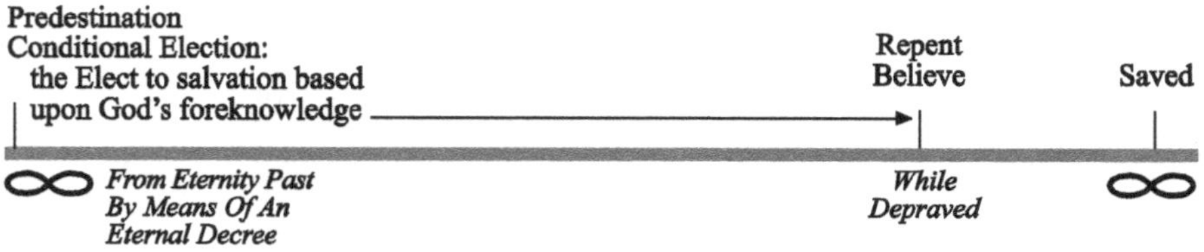

Diagram 12

Hyper Supralapsarianism	Strong (Extreme) Infralapsarianism	Moderate Sublapsarianism	Arminian Wesleyanism
(1) Decree to elect some and reprobate others	(1) Decree to create all	(1) Decree to create all	(1) Decree to create all
(2) Decree to create both the elect and the non-elect	(2) Decree to permit the Fall	(2) Decree to permit the Fall	(2) Decree to permit the Fall
(3) Decree to permit the Fall	(3) Decree to elect some and pass others by	(3) Decree to provide salvation for all	(3) Decree to provide salvation for all
(4) Decree to provide salvation only for the elect	(4) Decree to provide salvation only for the elect	(4) Decree to elect those who believe and pass by those who do not	(4) Decree to elect based on the foreseen faith of believers
(5) Decree to apply salvation only to the elect	(5) Decree to apply salvation only to the elect	(5) Decree to apply salvation only to believers (who cannot lose it)	(5) Decree to apply salvation only to believers (who can lose it)

Diagram 13

Jeremiah 18:1-6; Romans 9:20-23

Jeremiah 18:1-6 *1 The word which came to Jeremiah from the LORD saying, 2 "Arise and go down to the potter's house, and there I shall announce My words to you." 3 Then I went down to the potter's house, and there he was, making something on the wheel. 4 But the vessel that he was making of clay was spoiled in the hand of the potter; so he remade it into another vessel, as it pleased the potter to make. 5 Then the word of the LORD came to me saying, 6 "Can I not, O house of Israel, deal with you as this potter does?" declares the LORD. "Behold, like the clay in the potter's hand, so are you in My hand, O house of Israel.*

Romans 9:20-23 *20 On the contrary, who are you, O man, who answers back to God? The thing molded will not say to the molder, "Why did you make me like this," will it? 21 Or does not the potter have a right over the clay, to make from the same lump one vessel for honorable use, and another for common use? 22 What if God, although willing to demonstrate His wrath and to make His power known, endured with much patience vessels of wrath prepared for destruction? 23 And He did so to make known the riches of His glory upon vessels of mercy, which He prepared beforehand for glory,*

The Potter (God) originally made the nation of Israel into one clay vessel.

The Potter (God), due to Israel's unbelief and resulting disobedience, made Israel, originally one clay vessel, into two clay vessels: (1) One vessel, a *"vessel for honorable use"* (for honor—v.21) (2) Another vessel, a vessel *"for common use"* (no honor—v.21).

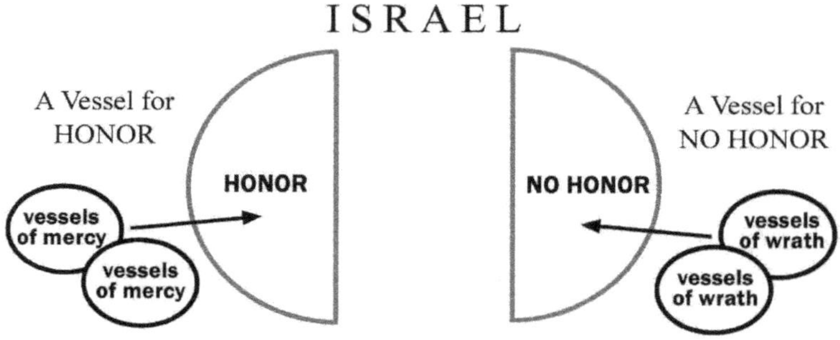

The *"vessel for honorable use,"* or *"honor"* (v.21), one of the two vessels that make up the physical nation of Israel, consists of Jews (*"vessels"*—v.23) who receive God's *"mercy"* (v.23) due to their choice of faith. These Jews are called *"vessels of mercy"* (v.23)—they bring honor (v.21) to God.

The *"vessel for common use," "no honor,"* or *"dishonor"* (v.21), the other *"vessel"* that makes up the physical nation of Israel, consists of Jews (*"vessels"*—v.22) who receive God's *"wrath"* (v.22) due to their choice of unbelief. These Jews are called *"vessels of wrath"* (v.22)—they bring no honor (v.21) to God.

Many Calvinists, especially extreme and hyper (Reformed theologans), argue that all the vessels addressed in Romans 9:21-23 point to both Jews as well as Gentiles in an attempt to credit Paul with teaching their view of unconditional election. These verses teach otherwise, for the vessel for honor and the vessel for no honor point to the division of the nation of Israel into two vessels. The vessels of mercy (believing Jews) and the vessels of wrath (unbelieving Jews) are Jews who are part of either the vessel for honor or the vessel for no honor.

This scenario can apply to any nation, for the basic lump from which a nation is formed will either be strengthened or divided depending on the moral response of the people who make up the nation. Romans 9:20-23, however, applies only to physical Israel.

Diagram 14

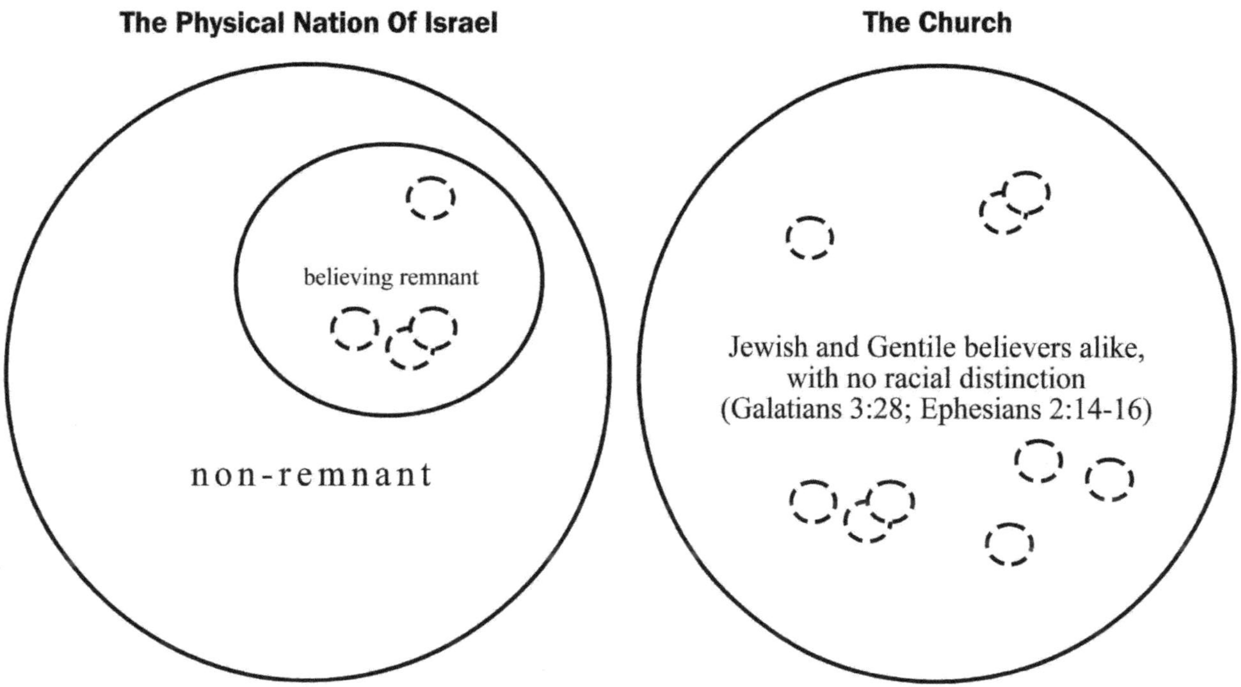

The believing remnant of the physical nation of Israel is not only part of the physical Jewish nation that God entered into covenant with in the Old Testament, but also part of the church, which is not a nation (Romans 10:19; Galatians 3:28; Ephesians 2:14-16). The fact that the believing remnant of the physical nation of Israel is part of the church does not mean that God is no longer committed to fulfilling the unconditional covenants previously granted to the physical Jewish nation. Therefore, the church has not replaced the physical nation of Israel as God's chosen people.

Bibliography/End Notes

[1] *Why I am not a Calvinist,* Jerry L. Walls & Joseph R. Dongell, InterVarsity Press, www.ivpress.com, permissions@ivpress.com, © 2004, page 47.
[2] Ibid., page 44.
[3] Ibid., page 50.
[4] Taken from *Chosen by God,* by R.C. Sproul, pages 23-24, © 1986 by Tyndale House Publishers, Used by permission of Tyndale House Publishers, Inc. All rights reserved.
[5] Ibid., page 27.
[6] Reprinted by permission. *The Love of God: He Will Do Whatever It Takes to Make Us Holy,* John MacArthur Jr., © 1998, page 17, Thomas Nelson Inc., Nashville, Tennessee. All rights reserved.
[7] From *Debating Calvinism: Five Points, Two Views,* by Dave Hunt and James White, copyright © 2004 by Dave Hunt and James White, page 14. Used by permission of WaterBook Multnomah, an imprint of Crown Publishing Group, a division of Random House, Inc.
[8] Ibid., page 36.
[9] Sola scriptura from Wikipedia, the free encyclopedia, 2012, http://en.wikipedia.org/wiki/Sola_scriptura.
[10] Edwin H. Palmer, *The Five Points of Calvinism,* Baker Academic, a division of Baker Publishing Group, copyright © 1999, from the Forward pages. Used by permission.
[11] From *Debating Calvinism: Five Points, Two Views,* by Dave Hunt and James White, copyright © 2004 by Dave Hunt and James White, pages 14-15. Used by permission of WaterBook Multnomah, an imprint of Crown Publishing Group, a division of Random House, Inc.
[12] Taken from *Chosen by God,* by R.C. Sproul, pages 45-46, © 1986 by Tyndale House Publishers, Used by permission of Tyndale House Publishers, Inc. All rights reserved.
[13] R.C. Sproul Jr., *Almighty over All: Understanding the Sovereignty of God,* page 132, Published by Baker Books, a division of Baker Publishing Group, Copyright 1999, Used by permission.
[14] Ibid., page 52.
[15] Ibid., page 46.
[16] Ibid., pages 47.
[17] Ibid., pages 53-54.
[18] Ibid., pages 54-55.
[19] Ibid., page 57.
[20] Taken from *Chosen by God,* by R.C. Sproul, page 37, © 1986 by Tyndale House Publishers, Used by permission of Tyndale House Publishers, Inc. All rights reserved.
[21] R.C. Sproul Jr., *Almighty over All: Understanding the Sovereignty of God,* Baker Academic, a division of baker Publishing Group, copyright © 1999, page 52. Used by permission.
[22] Taken from *Chosen by God,* by R.C. Sproul, pages 72-73, © 1986 by Tyndale House Publishers, Used by permission of Tyndale House Publishers, Inc. All rights reserved.
[23] Dave Hunt, *What Love Is This?*, Third Edition, Published by The Berean Call, 2006, page 188, Used by permission.

[24] Taken from *Chosen by God,* by R.C. Sproul, page 58, © 1986 by Tyndale House Publishers, Used by permission of Tyndale House Publishers, Inc. All rights reserved.
[25] Ibid.
[26] Ibid.
[27] Ibid.
[28] *The Sovereignty of God*, Arthur W. Pink, page 104, © 2008 Wilder Publications.
[29] Ibid., page 104.
[30] Dave Hunt, *What Love Is This?*, Third Edition, Published by The Berean Call, 2006, page 159, Used by permission.
[31] From *Debating Calvinism: Five Points, Two Views,* by Dave Hunt and James White, copyright © 2004 by Dave Hunt and James White, page 40. Used by permission of WaterBook Multnomah, an imprint of Crown Publishing Group, a division of Random House, Inc.
[32] John Calvin, *Institutes of the Christian Religion,* Book 3; Chapter 23; Section 6.
[33] Ibid.
[34] John Calvin, *Institutes of the Christian Religion,* Book 1; Chapter 16; Section 8.
[35] Ibid.
[36] Edwin H. Palmer, *The Five Points of Calvinism,* Baker Academic, a division of Baker Publishing Group, copyright © 1999, pages 98-99. Used by permission.
[37] Reprinted by permission. *The Love of God: He Will Do Whatever It Takes to Make Us Holy,* John MacArthur Jr., © 1998, page 16, Thomas Nelson Inc., Nashville, Tennessee. All rights reserved.
[38] Ibid., page 17.
[39] Dave Hunt, *What Love Is This?*, Third Edition, Published by The Berean Call, 2006, page 192, Used by permission.
[40]From *The Pleasures of God* by John Piper, copyright © 2000 by Desiring God Foundation, pages 338-339. Used by permission of WaterBrook Multnomah, an imprint of the Crown Publishing Group, a division of Random House, Inc.
[41] Ibid., page 315
[42] Reprinted by permission. *The Love of God: He Will Do Whatever It Takes to Make Us Holy,* John MacArthur Jr., © 1998, page 120, Thomas Nelson Inc., Nashville, Tennessee. All rights reserved.
[43] Ibid., page 13.
[44] Ibid., page 14.
[45] From *The Pleasures of God* by John Piper, copyright © 2000 by Desiring God Foundation, page 315. Used by permission of WaterBrook Multnomah, an imprint of the Crown Publishing Group, a division of Random House, Inc.
[46] Ibid., page 339.
[47] Ibid., page 316.
[48] Ibid., page 314.
[49] Reprinted by permission. *The MacArthur Study Bible*, John MacArthur, © 1997, Thomas Nelson Inc. Nashville, Tennessee. All rights reserved. Commentary on 1 Timothy 2:4, page 1862, NKJV.

[50] From *The Pleasures of God* by John Piper, copyright © 2000 by Desiring God Foundation, page 313. Used by permission of WaterBrook Multnomah, an imprint of the Crown Publishing Group, a division of Random House, Inc.
[51] Ibid., page 328.
[52] Ibid.
[53] *The Sovereignty of God,* Arthur W. Pink, page 40, © 2008 Wilder Publications.
[54] Ibid., page 41.
[55] Dave Hunt, *What Love Is This?*, Third Edition, Published by The Berean Call, 2006, page 126, Used by permission.
[56] Ibid., page 158.
[57] Ibid., page 254.
[58] Ibid.
[59] Edwin H. Palmer, *The Five Points of Calvinism,* Baker Academic, a division of Baker Publishing Group, copyright © 1999, page 97. Used by permission.
[60] Ibid., page 97.
[61] Ibid., page 116.
[62] *Jamieson, Fausset, and Brown Commentary*, Biblesoft, PC Study Bible, V3.3A for Windows, Copyright © 1988-2002, www.biblesoft.com.
[63] From *The Pleasures of God* by John Piper, copyright © 2000 by Desiring God Foundation, page 327. Used by permission of WaterBrook Multnomah, an imprint of the Crown Publishing Group, a division of Random House, Inc.
[64] Ibid., pages 329-330.
[65] Ibid., page 330.
[66] Ibid.
[67] Ibid.
[68] RC Sproul Jr., *Tabletalk*, Ligonier Ministries, Inc., © Spring 1992, page 2.
[69] John Piper, *TULIP: The Pursuit of God's Glory in Salvation,* Disk 1, Title 5, Chapter 1, © 2009 by Desiring God, DVD.
[70] From *The Pleasures of God* by John Piper, copyright © 2000 by Desiring God Foundation, page 136. Used by permission of WaterBrook Multnomah, an imprint of the Crown Publishing Group, a division of Random House, Inc.
[71] Ibid., footnote.
[72] Reprinted by permission. *The Love of God: He Will Do Whatever It Takes to Make Us Holy,* John MacArthur Jr,, © 1998, page 161, Thomas Nelson Inc., Nashville, Tennessee. All rights reserved.
[73] John Calvin, *Institutes of the Christian Religion,* Book 2; Chapter 17; Section 2.
[74] Reprinted by permission. *The Love of God: He Will Do Whatever It Takes to Make Us Holy,* John MacArthur Jr,, © 1998, page 161, Thomas Nelson Inc., Nashville, Tennessee. All rights reserved.
[75] *Why I am not a Calvinist,* Jerry L. Walls & Joseph R. Dongell, InterVarsity Press, www.ivpress.com, permissions@ivpress.com, © 2004, page 76.
[76] From *The Pleasures of God* by John Piper, copyright © 2000 by Desiring God Foundation, page 136, footnote. Used by permission of WaterBrook Multnomah, an imprint of the Crown Publishing Group, a division of Random House, Inc.

[77] John Piper, *TULIP: The Pursuit of God's Glory in Salvation,* Disk 2, Title 5, Chapter 1, © 2009 Desiring God, DVD.
[78] Ibid.
[79] Dave Hunt, *What Love Is This?*, Third Edition, Published by The Berean Call, 2006, page 237, Used by permission.
[80] *The Attributes of God*, Arthur W. Pink, page 39, © 2008 Wilder Publications.
[81] Reprinted from *Berkouwer's Doctrine of Election: Balance or Imbalance,* by Alvin L. Baker, Page 174, © P & R Publishing, Phillipsburg, NJ. Used by permission.
[82] Reprinted by permission. *The Love of God: He Will Do Whatever It Takes to Make Us Holy,* John MacArthur Jr,, © 1998, page 109, Thomas Nelson Inc., Nashville, Tennessee. All rights reserved.
[83] Ibid., page 165.
[84] Sir Winston Leonard Spencer-Churchill of England, born, November 30, 1874, deceased, January 24, 1965.
[85] John Piper, *The Justification of God*, Second Edition, Baker Academics, a division of Baker Publishing group, copyright © 1993, page 62. Used by permission.
[86] Ibid., page 73.
[87] Ibid., page 175.
[88] Ibid., pages 203-204.
[89] John Calvin, *Institutes of the Christian Religion,* Book 3; Chapter 22; Section 4.
[90] John Piper, *The Justification of God*, Second Edition, page 49, Published by Baker Books, a division of Baker Publishing Group, Copyright 1993, Used by permission.
[91] Reprinted by permission. *The MacArthur Study Bible*, John MacArthur, © 2006, Thomas Nelson Inc. Nashville, Tennessee. All rights reserved. Commentary on Romans 9:11, page 1710.
[92] Wayne Grudem, *Bible Doctrine, Essential Teachings of the Christian Faith,* Published by Zondervan, 1999, page 287, Used by permission.
[93] John Piper, *The Justification of God*, Second Edition, Baker Academics, a division of Baker Publishing group, copyright © 1993, page 175. Used by permission.
[94] Ibid.
[95] Ibid.. page 93
[96] Ibid., page 104.
[97] Ibid., page 157.
[98] Taken from *Chosen by God,* by R.C. Sproul, page 151, © 1986 by Tyndale House Publishers, Used by permission of Tyndale House Publishers, Inc. All rights reserved.
[99] Ibid., pages 154-155.
[100] From *The Pleasures of God* by John Piper, copyright © 2000 by Desiring God Foundation. page 321. Used by permission of WaterBrook Multnomah, an imprint of the Crown Publishing Group, a division of Random House, Inc.
[101] Taken from *Chosen by God,* by R.C. Sproul, pages 74-75, © 1986 by Tyndale House Publishers, Used by permission of Tyndale House Publishers, Inc. All rights reserved.
[102] John Piper, *The Justification of God*, Second Edition, Baker Academics, a division of Baker Publishing group, copyright © 1993, pages 158-159. Used by permission.
[103] Ibid., pages 179.
[104] Ibid., page 160.

[105] Ibid., pages 161-162.
[106] Ibid.
[107] Ibid., page 163.
[108] Ibid., page 178.
[109] Taken from *Chosen by God,* by R.C. Sproul, pages 144, 147, © 1986 by Tyndale House Publishers, Used by permission of Tyndale House Publishers, Inc. All rights reserved.
[110] John Calvin, *Institutes of the Christian Religion,* Book 1; Chapter 18; Section 2.
[111] John Calvin, *Institutes of the Christian Religion,* Book 3; Chapter 23; Section 1.
[112] *The Sovereignty of God,* Arthur W. Pink, page 91, © 2008 Wilder Publications.
[113] Taken from *Chosen by God,* by R.C. Sproul, pages 143, © 1986 by Tyndale House Publishers, Used by permission of Tyndale House Publishers, Inc. All rights reserved.
[114] Dave Hunt, *What Love Is This?*, Third Edition, Published by The Berean Call, 2006, pages 334-335, Used by permission.
[115] Roger T. Forster and V. Paul Marston, *GOD'S Strategy in Human History*, Published by Send The Light Trust, 1973, page 169-170, Used by permission.
[116] John Piper, *The Justification of God*, Second Edition, Baker Academics, a division of Baker Publishing group, copyright © 1993, page 168. Used by permission.
[117] Dave Hunt, *What Love Is This?*, Third Edition, Published by The Berean Call, 2006, pages 333, Used by permission.
[118] Roger T. Forster and V. Paul Marston, *GOD'S Strategy in Human History*, Published by Send The Light Trust, 1973, page 75, Used by permission.
[119] Ibid.. page 169
[120] John Piper, *The Justification of God*, Second Edition, Baker Academics, a division of Baker Publishing group, copyright © 1993, page 178. Used by permission.
[121] Ibid., pages 179-180.
[122] Dave Hunt, *What Love Is This?*, Third Edition, Published by The Berean Call, 2006, pages 187, Used by permission.
[123] John Piper, *The Justification of God*, Second Edition, Baker Academics, a division of Baker Publishing group, copyright © 1993, back cover. Used by permission.
[124] Ibid.
[125] John Piper, *The Justification of God*, Second Edition, Baker Academics, a division of Baker Publishing group, copyright © 1993, pages 185-186. Used by permission.
[126] Ibid.. pages 189, 192.
[127] Roger T. Forster and V. Paul Marston, *GOD'S Strategy in Human History*, Published by Send The Light Trust, 1973, page 80, Used by permission.
[128] John Piper, *The Justification of God*, Second Edition, Baker Academics, a division of Baker Publishing group, copyright © 1993, page 186. Used by permission.
[129] Ibid.. page 193.
[130] Ibid.. page 199.
[131] Roger T. Forster and V. Paul Marston, *GOD'S Strategy in Human History*, Published by Send The Light Trust, 1973, page 80, Used by permission.
[132] John Piper, *The Justification of God*, Second Edition, Baker Academics, a division of Baker Publishing group, copyright © 1993, page 186. Used by permission.
[133] Ibid., page 200.
[134] Ibid., page 201.

[135] Ibid., page 202.
[136] Ibid., page 203.
[137] Ibid.
[138] Ibid., page 207.
[139] Ibid., pages 207-209.
[140] Ibid., page 210.
[141] Ibid., page 208.
[142] John Piper, *The Justification of God*, Second Edition, Baker Academics, a division of Baker Publishing group, copyright © 1993, page 211. Used by permission.
[143] Ibid.
[144] Ibid., page 212.
[145] Ibid., page 213.
[146] Copyright 2008, Warren W. Wiersbe, *Be Right*, page 117, published by David C. Cook. Publisher permission required to reproduce. All rights reserved.
[147] John Piper, *The Justification of God*, Second Edition, Baker Academics, a division of Baker Publishing group, copyright © 1993, pages 218-220. Used by permission.
[148] Ibid., page 220.
[149] Ibid., pages 188-189.
[150] R.C. Sproul Jr., *Almighty over All: Understanding the Sovereignty of God,* page 52-53, Published by Baker Books, a division of Baker Publishing Group, Copyright 1999, Used by permission.

www.ingramcontent.com/pod-product-compliance
Lightning Source LLC
Chambersburg PA
CBHW021401090426
42742CB00009B/949
* 9 7 8 1 6 2 7 2 7 0 3 0 4 *